Marco De La Cruz, MD

BALANCING
ACT

A Mind, Body,
Spirit Approach to
Optimal Health

REDFeather

MIND | BODY | SPIRIT

1880 Lower Valley Road, Atglen, PA 19310

Designed by Brenda McCallum
Cover design by Brenda McCallum

Type set in Archer/Century Gothic

ISBN: 978-0-7643-6282-8

Printed in India

Published by REDFeather Mind, Body, Spirit
An imprint of Schiffer Publishing, Ltd.
4880 Lower Valley Road
Atglen, PA 19310
Phone: (610) 593-1777; Fax: (610) 593-2002
E-mail: Info@schifferbooks.com
Web: www.redfeathermbs.com

For our complete selection of fine books on this and related subjects, please visit our website at www.schifferbooks.com.
You may also write for a free catalog.

Schiffer Publishing's titles are available at special discounts for bulk purchases for sales promotions or premiums. Special editions, including personalized covers, corporate imprints, and excerpts, can be created in large quantities for special needs. For more information, contact the publisher.

We are always looking for people to write books on new and related subjects. If you have an idea for a book, please contact us at proposals@schifferbooks.com.

Acknowledgments

There are many people to thank for their help in the making of this book. Thanks to my wife, Ann, for her patience, help, and support. Many thanks to B.W. Donner, Lisa Stuart, and Kristen Wienandt Marzejon, who worked closely with me on the first publication of the book.

Several selfless individuals assisted me with the manuscript, including Richard Forrest, Sasha Kloss, Margo De Ley, Diane Richmond, Marie Jordan, Jennifer Mann, Joaquin Castillo, and others who helped and encouraged me through the process.

Contents

Introduction

Balancing Act is a program for self-awareness, growth, and improvement of health. It is accomplished through the development of new knowledge, new attitudes, and new abilities that can provide increased consciousness, participation, and effectiveness in the creation and maintenance of better health.

Some of you will be working within an actual Balancing Act workshop or seminar; others will be working on your own, proceeding only with this book. In either case, some space for activities and exercises, and for working out your thoughts and ideas, and for notes and planning, is provided in this volume.

In this program, you will be given access to a new paradigm of health, based on certain key actions, and on your own development in key areas:

1. Observing and becoming aware of your personal energy as a measure of your health

2. Using the measurement of your personal energy as a tool for planning, choosing, and applying positive actions to increase your personal energy and improve your health

3. Recognizing that you live in a series of ongoing continuums and are always connected to calm, health, and well-being

4. Combining this awareness with a perspective of self based on understanding and appreciation of the fundamental mind-body-spirit domains of human beings

5. Learning the use of conscious breathing, and additional positive mental,

physical, and spiritual (mind-body-spirit) activities that you can apply to move yourself continually away from poor health and onward toward better health

6. Creating a Personal Energy Plan (your PEP) to help you maintain ongoing development and growth toward increased personal energy and personal health

Balancing Act is divided into five parts:

Part I Presents the main concepts behind Balancing Act in two chapters: chapter 1 develops the central point that personal energy level is a reliable measure of overall health. Chapter 2 presents a fresh perspective on stress and demonstrates how mind, body, and spirit dimensions impact personal energy.

Part II Covers the mind dimension and how perceptions create your response to everyday life events.

Part III Reviews the body dimension through chapters on nutrition, exercise, and sleep.

Part IV Discusses spirituality and the use of the spirit dimension to influence personal energy positively and negatively.

Part V Summarizes the main points of the first four parts and describes how to "put it all together" to create your personal energy program.

The lessons presented here renew hope in the goodness and wisdom of life and reveal that a better life is not only available, but also attainable. Life is set up to help you.

How to Use This Book

This book is about *life management* and, perhaps its single most important challenge, *managing stress and change*. Certainly this has always been a challenge, but in recent years it has become increasingly important as we struggle to deal withour increasingly stressful world

Change and Stress. Each person has a different set of stresses in daily life, and a unique set of aptitudes, talents, and skills with which to meet them, yet we all have in common the need to *manage stress and change* so that it is a *dynamic part of our lives* rather than a draining or defeating part.

The medical community has long recognized that some stress is absolutely essential to our well-being. Stress stimulates: it makes rabbits run, makes birds defend their nests, and makes tigers hunt. In humans, it sparkes motivations of all kinds: it urges us to compete and urges us to cooperate; it awakens us and makes the adrenaline flow.

But when there is too much stress—when we feel overwhelmed—how are we to handle that? How are we to deal with overload?

The Balancing Act Program. This book presents a logical and self-supporting program of awareness, measurement, and action—that I have named Balancing Act. This program will help you meet the stress of change in your life and manage it, with increased energy, understanding, and focus.

Some of you will be using this book while you attend workshops, and others will be using it independently. The material presented here is designed to provide ample options for your use in either case, including regular activities and suggestions to help you understand, visualize, internalize, and apply the concepts and activities of the program.

Using Interactive Materials. The material presented here has grown out of the interactive stress management programs that I have developed and taught to my patients since 1988. Teaching these workshops has convinced me that the material is more effective when it is presented in an interactive manner, along with anecdotal examples and specific suggestions for practical applications.

When a student interacts with the materials, learning is easier. This book asks many of the same questions asked in my live class sessions. Take the time to answer these questions. They are designed to guide and encourage your thinking and help you develop your skills of perception. The questions are usually open-ended, having no single "right" answer. Most answers will derive from your personal and individual experiences, observations, and thoughts. Answering the questions also aids you in developing the Self-Health concepts presented in *Balancing Act*. Descriptive answers reflecting the author's perspective are also provided in small print with the questions/ activities, as an additional aid to extending your understanding of the concepts being presented. The text following these questions/activities also reinforces your understanding by expanding on these concepts.

Features. Some sections of the text are presented in italics and contain anecdotes and discussions to further your understanding of the material. The side margins contain "take-home ideas" that include key concepts and relevant quotations for quick review and emphasis of the material presented.

Repetition and Learning. Repetition facilitates learning. First-time participants in this course report immediate benefits; repeat participants are even more likely to receive and report long-term benefits. Reviewing parts or the entire course will give you a practical, working knowledge of Self-Health principles and techniques. *What you practice is what you do better.* Some of the more important concepts are repeated to enhance learning. Some of the more important concepts are repeated to enhance learning. Reiewing the course materials accelerates learning. It is more important to develop the "habit" of learning, through practicing the materials presented here, than to finish the book in a short period of time. Each time you review this material you will gain more insights and facilitate the practice of desired attitudes and behaviors. Note that *repetition increases efficiency*, and this is true for desirable as well as undesirable attitudes and behaviors.

Benefits of Pracice and Habit. Human beings are creatures of habit. Take a momemnt to reflect on some of your own personal patterns you repeat on a daily basis. How often do you repeat the same attitudes and behaviors? You eat the same foods, take the same route to work and back, watch the same TV programs. Daily life is about habits. Habits can reduce stress. In fact, stress often goes up when daily routines are distrupted. However, there may be some habits that you want to change. You may want to exercise more, quit smoking, drink less alcohol, or eat less junk food. Developing positive and health-enhancing habits will mean *practicing and repeating* the positive behaviors while *decreasing* negative behaviors. *Succeess in changing is enhanced by practice.* It is encouraging to remember that *every time you practice the desired attitude or behavior, you cannot be practicing the undesired one.*

PART

ONE

LESSONS FROM STRESS

Health and Your Personal Energy

Your health correlates with your personal energy level. The quest for health is really a quest for optimal personal energy. We want to be healthy because we want to be fully alive. Optimal personal energy is the difference between energy gained and energy drained in everyday life.

Actions in your interrelated mind, body, and spirit domains can be used for increased energy. Body energy is influenced by lifestyle activities such as nutrition, exercise, and sleep. Mind energy is influenced by mental attitudes and perceptions. Spirit energy is influenced by spiritual beliefs and activities. The energy flow between body, mind, and spirit is reciprocal but not necessarily equal between any of these at any time. Envisioning health as personal energy with a body, mind, and spirit perspective creates a useful and practical model of health that makes self-care easier.

Life is a mystery. All that the centuries of human religion, art, and science have revealed about life is but a tiny glimpse. If life could be filmed and condensed into a single movie, all that we actually know about life would still be but a few frames of a movie reel. Nevertheless, although life remains a mystery, we can learn how life works by thoughtfully observing and by reflecting upon what we observe.

If you know how a motor works, you have a better chance of caring for it, fixing it, and making it run better. Likewise, if you know how life works, you increase your chances of caring for yourself and for maintaining a better, smoother-running life. There are different ways to describe how life works. One way is to say that life reveals how it works with observable patterns, such as the relationship between personal energy and health.

Life is energy. When you see that this is true, this simple concept will change the way you live. This is because it is also true that *how you see life influences what you do in your own life.* Consider these simple but quite different descriptions of life views and the ways that each one influences how a life is lived:

1. If life is a challenge—you can meet it head on.

2. If life is an opportunity—you can go for it.

3. If life is a pain—you can try to avoid it.

An essential technique that can change the way you look at life and ensure your success in this program is the practice of Breath Awareness.

Breath Awareness for Awareness and Energy

Near the start of each workshop, the important technique called Breath Awareness is introduced. Breath awareness is a natural, simple-to-use technique for reducing stress and increasing energy. It works because during the moments that you are practicing it, you stop moving toward stress.

Before you start practicing Breath Awareness, pause a moment to notice your surroundings. Look around at the objects in your room or in the space outside your window. Do not judge. Take notice of what is around you without judging, or labeling. Now, follow the directions in the next paragraph for practicing Breath Awareness.

Begin the practice of Breath Awareness by drawing your attention to your breathing. Become aware of the rhythm of your breathing. Notice how your abdomen moves out and in with each breath. Bring your attention to the sound the air makes as it moves in and out through your nostrils. Keep your attention on the soft, gentle rhythm of your breathing. Do not change your breathing; just take note of your breathing while you look around at your surroundings. Continue observing your breathing while you continue to take in the sights and sounds around you. As you look around, with Breath Awareness, notice how it is different from the first time you looked around without Breath Awareness.

When you look at your surroundings while practicing Breath Awareness, you should notice a subtle sense of alert calmness that you did not have before. That is one of the immediate benefits of Breath Awareness: a subtle sense of calmness. Another benefit of practicing Breath Awareness is that you focus your attention on the immediate present. Worries are about the future. Guilt and "should haves" are about the past. One effective way to stop agitating yourself with negative thoughts that create so much tension is to take a shortcut to the present. *Breath awareness is a shortcut to the present.* During the few seconds you are with your breath, you release the thoughts that agitate you. When you stop experiencing agitating thoughts,

When you change the way you look at life, your experience of life changes.

Breath awareness is a natural, simple-to-use technique for reducing stress and increasing energy.

you naturally move toward calm. However, because you are so used to being in the future or the past, the agitating thoughts are likely to return. Generally, within a matter of seconds you are up and running again away from the present into the future or back to the past. The sense of calm is brief at first. With practice you are able to stay in the present moment longer and longer. With practice, Breath Awareness becomes a toggle switch allowing you to flip between stress and calm.

The short-term result is a calmer you in your everyday activities. Long-term results also include more personal energy and peace of mind. More-advanced variations of Breath Awareness are described in appendix VI.

Practicing Breath Awareness

Practice Breath Awareness whenever possible. Just check in with your breathing anytime you think of it; like now! It is well suited for practice when you are walking, driving, and listening. Waiting periods during the day at a traffic light, the ATM machine, or elevators are other ample times for practicing Breath Awareness. Uncomfortable elevator rides become opportunities to practice being in the moment. Using this technique whenever someone is speaking to you has a calming effect that makes it easier to listen. When practicing Breath Awareness you are not as quick to react to what others are saying. People will think you are a good listener too. Since you are not draining your energy by internally reacting to everything you are hearing, you will be able to listen more comfortably. The best part is that while you are listening with your breath, you are actually recharging your personal energy.

The Breath Awareness exercise is one of the most important things you will learn in this program. If you learn only one thing from me, learn to practice Breath Awareness as presented here. *Practicing it will change your life forever.* It will help you see more and remember better the wisdom you already have. Breath awareness is so important to your success in this program that, throughout the rest of this book, I will keep reminding you periodically to "bring your attention to your breathing." Throughout the book, the Chinese symbol ☯, which represents balance, will be used to remind you to be aware of your breathing.

Health and Personal Energy

The statement *"Life is energy"* means that *you can use your personal energy level as a marker for health and well-being.* Your personal energy level is the overall energy that you are experiencing right now, and from moment to moment during each day of your life.

Much of the information presented in this course has come, paradoxically, from the study of stress, which is, of course, a major energy drainer. Like most people, you are already familiar with the dark side of stress: the energy-

Breath awareness is a short-cut to the present.

Practicing Breath Awareness will change your life forever.

You can use your personal energy level as a marker for health and well-being.

draining uneasiness, the escalating tension, the uncomfortable "on edge" feelings. Yet, within the manifestations of what is referred to as "the Stress Response" are valuable insights into how life works—insights that dramatically reveal that *health* is about *energy*. This view of health is radically different from the many more traditional conceptions about personal health that are commonly understood in our society.

What Is Health?

....

....

....

....

Health is having enough energy to feel good and do the things that are important to you.

Functional capacity has long been recognized as a marker for health.

Dorland's Medical Dictionary defines health as "a state of physical, mental, and social well-being." Another definition of health still used by some is that health is "the absence of disease."

A more useful definition of health takes into account the importance of *being able to function* as well as *being able to feel good.* Self-report studies with people with cancer or serious chronic illnesses support this view. In spite of having a serious disease, the people who are still able to perform the activities of daily living that are important to them are more likely to report feeling in *good health.*

Having a purpose and meaning in life is a powerful positive influence on personal energy.

The approach to defining health that I use with my patients combines three variables:

1. personal energy level

2. well-being

3. functional ability

Again, health is having enough energy to feel good and to do the things that are important to you.

In physics, energy is defined as the capacity for doing work. For our purposes, energy is the capacity for doing—for functioning in our daily activities. *This functional capacity has long been recognized as a marker for health.* When you perform tasks that are important to you, and do them well, you are likely to experience an increased sense of well-being, often accompanied by increased energy.

Similarly, *having a purpose and meaning in life is a powerful positive influence on personal energy.* When your personal energy level is high, you are more inclined to be active. This inclination toward activity is useful for choosing more-healthful habits, which in turn give you even more energy. More energy means more possibilities too. This program will help you become *a master of your own life. A master of life is one who is able to see and perform several solutions to the problems of life.*

The amount of energy needed for the important tasks of daily living is different for different people, and the amount necessary also varies with age. *Accepting health as a function of energy* facilitates developing short-term and long-term strategies for improving functional capacity and health, by working on improving personal energy levels. In the popular press there are many books presenting different programs to improve health by following guidelines for eating more healthfully, or exercising, or taking supplements, or practicing relaxation exercises, and the like.

A more comprehensive and realistic approach to health is to use your personal energy as the measure of your health and of your success in improving your health.

The use of your personal energy as a measure of your health is further supported by learning to reflect upon stress, not as an occasional or separate occurrence but as part of a continuum.

Continuums and the Other Side of Stress

Let us reflect on the topic of stress for more insights into how life works. Picture a plastic bottle of carbonated soda in your hand. If you shake the bottle vigorously, pressure begins to build up inside. Allow this pressure in the bottle to represent the buildup of pressure you experience when you feel stressed out. If you wanted to decrease the pressure in the bottle you could open the bottle . . . very slowly.

Now consider, is there another way that you could get that built-up pressure to go down? Of course there is. If you just place the bottle on a flat surface and leave it alone, it will return to a state of calm, every time. The question is why?

Why does the increased pressure in the bottle return to calm?

....

....

....

The pressure in the bottle returns to calm because that is its natural state.

Calm is your natural state.

The pressure in the bottle returns to calm because calm is the natural state of the liquid in the bottle. And so it is with you. *Calm is your natural state.*

This may sound surprising because, in so much of daily life so far, it is stress, and not calm, that feels like your natural state.

You know that if you stop agitating the soda-pop bottle, the liquid in it will return to calm. Similarly, if you stop agitating your mind with thoughts, worries, and preoccupations, you too will move away from stress toward calm. This suggests that stress and calm are connected and that connection can be illustrated as follows.

Stress ←--→ Calm

This diagram depicts a relationship called a *continuum*, which provides a very helpful concept for managing stress. The *Oxford Dictionary* defines "continuum" as a "continuous thing or substance."

You are always somewhere on the continuum between stress and calm.

You are always somewhere on a continuum between stress and calm. Therefore, no matter where you may be along that line, you are always connected to calm. This concept is very useful in creating a self-care or, more specifically, a self-health program.

Continuums remind us that change is possible. There is hope and comfort in remembering that calm is your natural state, and that *as you are on a stress-calm continuum, there is always something you can do that will move you toward calm.* It may be a walk, a hot shower, a nap, a prayer, or laughter, but there is always something you can do that will move you *away* from the stress and *toward* calm. This concept of the continuum that connects what seems like two opposites can also be applied to related pairs of variables, such as health–illness and low energy–high energy.

Reflecting further on continuums, consider your health as part of a continuum between illness and health.

Illness ←--→ Health

Your state of health is somewhere along this line, though it may seem difficult to say where it is right now, or if you are exactly a certain degree healthier now than you were yesterday. Your point on this continuum is always moving one way or the other, under the influence of numerous variables, such as when and what you ate, how much activity you had, and how you slept. Some believe that variables such as pain, worries, laughter, and hopelessness may influence your health too.

Attitudes and activities that make up your daily life may also be influencing your position between illness and health, so it is difficult to pinpoint a position. In helping patients work on improving health, especially *before*

You are always somewhere on the continuum between stress and calm.

Continuums remind us that change is possible.

As you are on a stress-calm continuum, there is always something you can do that will move you toward calm.

they get sick, it would be useful to have an easier way to tell where you are on that line between illness and health.

Personal Energy Continuum

When you compare the stress-calm and illness-health continuums you see that they can be lined up so that *stress* is to *illness* as *calm* is to *health*. Reflecting on this relationship, it becomes apparent that energy is a common denominator in these continuums; more specifically it is *your personal energy level* that is the common denominator.

There is an inverse relationship between how much stress you experience and your personal energy level. When your personal energy is low, as in illness, poor sleep, or grieving a personal loss, you are more vulnerable to stress. Conversely, when your energy is high, such as after a revitalizing vacation, a good night's sleep, or falling in love, you are less susceptible to stress. This relationship between stress and personal energy can be described as follows:

Stress / Low Energy ←----------------- ------------→ Calm / High Energy

If stress and illness are associated with low personal energy, while calm and health are associated with high personal energy, it becomes apparent that your personal energy level is on a continuum between low and high personal energy. *Combining a personal energy continuum with the health-illness continuum leads to a model of health that correlates personal energy with health and illness.* This creates a functional model of health where attitudes and behaviors that increase personal energy level also improve health.

Stress ←------- ---→ Calm

Illness ←- --------------------------- ----------------------------→ Health

Low Personal Energy ←----------------------→ High Personal Energy

Though the three continuums above may be used interchangeably, you'll find that using the personal energy continuum will make it easier to recognize where you are along the continuum. You may not be able to judge precisely if you are healthier today than you were last night, but you can recognize if your overall energy level is higher today than yesterday.

> *The continuum concept grew out of workshops on stress management. When talking about stress management, the key word is management. We need a certain amount of stress in our lives. Programs like Balancing Act are intended to help anyone in managing stress more effectively, not eliminating it entirely.*

> *The original continuum described people as always being on a line between stress and calm. You already practice attitudes and behaviors*

Combining a personal energy continuum with the health-illness continuum leads to a model of health that correlates personal energy with health and illness.

that move you in the direction of increased stress. The good news is that you also already know things that can move you away from stress toward calm: exercise, hot shower, nap, laughter, and prayer. Some of these stress-reducing actions are guaranteed to move you toward calm, even if only a small amount and even if briefly. Any movement toward calm helps because calm—like stress—is cumulative; it builds up over time. A twenty-minute walk is guaranteed to move you toward calm, and soaking in a hot bath does the same. Regular exercise, inspirational reading, or prayer will gradually build upon itself, helping to move you toward a higher degree of calm on the continuum.

In our workshops, after working with the stress-calm continuum for some time, the idea of a health-illness continuum evolved. The correlation between health and high energy made it easy to imagine a high–low personal energy continuum.

When these three continuums are superimposed, their interrelatedness becomes apparent. Stress, illness, and low-energy states go together, as do calm, health, and high energy.

Managing
stress now
becomes more
about practicing
attitudes and
actions that
move you
toward calm
and higher
energy.

Managing stress now becomes more about practicing attitudes and actions that move you toward calm and higher energy. Because various situations that appear to move you toward stress will continue to be present, it is important to practice the actions that move you toward calm. The more you practice calm-enhancing actions, the more personal energy you'll have as well.

Monitoring Your Personal Energy

For most people a hectic schedule leaves little time for awareness of how healthy they are—where they are on the continuum between health and disease. However, you can sense if your personal energy is increasing or decreasing in the course of daily activities. *Do you have more energy today than yesterday? Is your energy higher or lower than two hours ago? Monitoring your energy level facilitates the management of your personal energy.* Monitoring your energy level facilitates energy management just as monitoring your expenses or what you eat facilitates managing your finances and your weight, respectively. Generally, if you write down all your expenses, you start to spend less. Likewise, as you write down everything you eat, you are more likely to start eating better.

Personal energy level refers to the energy that you subjectively experience at a given point in time. When you say, "I feel great," you probably have a lot of energy. When you feel "down in the dumps," your energy is probably low too. Your personal energy level fluctuates in the course of everyday life— influenced by numerous variables: food, sleep, exercise, attitude, optimism, humor, music, mediation, and prayer.

It is very easy to monitor your personal energy level. Simply check in with yourself and take notice of your overall personal energy level. Take a few seconds right now to check your overall energy. Your personal energy level is the overall energy you feel at a given moment. Rate your energy level on a scale of 1 to 10 (10 being the best). If you had a good night's rest, your energy should be around 8 or higher in the morning once you get going. After lunch your energy might be in the middle range, around 5 to 7. You can trust your subjective rating of your personal energy. To better manage your energy, you need to take note of your personal energy level several times a day. Rate your energy at least three times a day—morning, afternoon, and evening—and write it down in the table below. **In the appendix** *you will find a full-page monitor card similar to the one shown below for you to copy and use. Each day has three boxes: the AM box is for your overall energy between waking up and noon, the second box is for your overall energy between noon and 6:00 p.m., and the third box is for your overall energy between 6:00 p.m. and bedtime.*

WEEK 1

Date							

	S	M	T	W	T	F	S
AM							
12 N							
6 PM							

With a little practice you can quickly assess your energy level at the moment. Soon it becomes apparent that your energy is affected by difficult situations or negative interactions. Rating your energy after any energy-gaining activities like a positive interaction reinforces the energy benefits of positive activities. As you become aware of your personal energy level, you will naturally want to respond in ways that maintain higher energy levels. *Practicing Breath Awareness makes it easier to be aware of your personal energy-level fluctuations during the day, as well as block or reduce loss of energy. Breath awareness is your first response to decreasing energy,* by allowing you to mentally detach from an energy-draining experience. Your second response to low energy levels is to practice energy-restoring activities. When your energy moves below an acceptable range, you may opt to practice an energy gainer or avoid an energy drainer. Use any of your mind, body, and spirit activities as discussed below to maintain your energy in a comfortable range, like 7 to 10. *The personal energy continuum facilitates managing stress and health by using a variable—your energy—that you can readily assess and modify.*

A practical goal is to keep your personal energy within a desirable range, rather than trying to always have it be at a 10. For example, at work I want my energy between 7 and 9. When my energy is between 7 and 9, not only am I closer to health and calm, but I also have more of the positive thoughts and feelings that come with this side of the continuums. When energy is low, such as below 5, I have more negative thoughts and moods and am less likely to follow what I know. Impulsive eating, for example, occurs more when my energy is lower.

Personally, when I feel my energy at 6 or less, I take measures to increase my personal energy. Running in place for five minutes can move me from a 5 to a 7 or 8. A twenty-minute nap can take me from a 3 to an 8.

In summary, the concept of continuums is useful for monitoring, understanding, and managing stress and health. The Personal Energy Continuum facilitates managing stress and health by providing a measure that you can use readily. Using continuums to describe stress also highlights some important points about life:

1. In life there is always some stress present.
2. You manage stress, not eliminate it.
3. With less stress, you move toward your natural state of calm and health.
4. Daily attitudes and activities move you back and forth along this continuum.

A desirable goal is to have this back-and-forth activity in a range closer to calm.

To clarify working with continuums, picture a football field. Your goal is the Calm side. At the opposite end of the field is the Stress side. If you are not moving the ball toward Calm, the other team will be moving the ball toward Stress. As the game is played back and forth between the opposing goals, you want to choose and use plays that keep the ball on the side of the field that is closer to your goal. This increases your chance of reaching the goal. The closer you are to the goal, the better you feel, and the better your chances of scoring.

The concept of a continuum illustrates and supports the relationship between stress, health, and personal energy and shows that change for the better is possible by moving along the continuums toward the desired end. Thus, a practical approach to reduce stress or enhance health is to practice attitudes and actions that lead to overall increased personal energy. Such an approach is sure to work, as long as you persist in your efforts.

More on Personal Energy as a Marker of Health

In the philosophy of Eastern—or traditional Asian—medicine, it is thought that blockage or interruptions of the normal flow of the life energy could lead to changes in the corresponding physical form, leading to disease. For example, if the energy flow in the energy center or *chakra* in the area of the central chest were to be interrupted, this could lead to disease in the heart or lungs. There are innumerable material and nonmaterial things that influence the flow of this life energy. In my understanding of this health paradigm, mental suffering—as in prolonged grieving or holding a grudge, for example—could hamper the normal flow of life energy and make one sick. Conversely, the healing power of love, laughter, and spiritual optimism works by increasing the proper flow of one's life energy, thus enhancing health.

One lesson from Eastern medicine is the realization that your personal energy level may be used as a marker of health. All of the alternative therapies that I as a doctor have reviewed, such as acupuncture, massage, homeopathy, and prayer, seem to have a positive influence on the body's energy level. It has become apparent to me that whatever the remedy, the move toward health was generally associated with an overall increase in the energy of the mind-body system. Thus, health can be described as proportional to overall personal energy level, and *mind-body health correlates with your personal energy level.* Embracing the concept of personal energy level as an indicator of health has made helping patients easier and more fulfilling.

> *Discovering the correlation between health and energy changed the way I work with patients. Earlier, in trying to motivate a patient to take an active interest in their health, I might have said, "Let's work on improving your health." This sounded good, but it was too vague and did not provide a simple, clear course to take. Having accepted energy as a marker of health, patients could begin to check in with themselves during the day to become aware of their personal energy level. Then we could review simple strategies they could use to keep their personal energy level in a desirable range.*

Generally speaking, a physician cannot give energy to patients. What he or she can do is to help patients get access to the energy they are genetically meant to have. Now, an important part of my role as a physician is helping patients to optimally manage their energy. My patients are taught to monitor their energy, and to practice behaviors and attitudes that increase personal energy and health. This may mean practicing activities that increase energy or removing obstacles that are limiting their energy. Each person has a potential *optimal energy balance* that will support her or his optimal health. Especially in chronic and recurrent illnesses, a mind-body-spirit approach for improving personal energy is essential. Striving for your optimal personal energy is of primary importance.

The concept of a continuum illustrates and supports the relationship between stress, health, and personal energy and shows that change for the better is possible by moving along the continuums toward the desired end.

Mind-body health correlates with your personal energy level.

Personal
energy is
influenced by
numerous factors
such as age,
time of day,
state of health,
mood, and
personal
stressors.

Optimal Energy Balance

"Optimal" means "the most favorable" or "best." It is important to recognize that your optimal personal energy level is not static, or permanent. Your energy level fluctuates over time and even from moment to moment. *Personal energy is influenced by numerous factors such as age, time of day, state of health, mood, and present stressors.* Knowledge of which variables influence your personal energy allows you to better manage your personal energy.

Think about your everyday life, over the past week or the past month, or the past year. What are some general factors that usually influence your personal energy level? List all that you can think of, including those that seem major and those that seem minor.

....

....

....

....

....

....

....

Of course, your overall energy level is influenced by *hundreds* of factors. What you eat, how much you exercise, worrying, the quality of your sleep, how much fun you are having, and many other mental and physical variables influence energy levels.

All of these factors can be divided into two groups:

1. those that increase your energy (*energy gain*)
2. those that decrease your energy (*energy drain*)

Factors that increase your energy include many of the things you've been told are good for you, such as healthful eating, exercise, and good sleep. Factors that decrease your energy include things like high-sugar diet, insomnia, and worrying. In order to foster optimal energy, just increasing energy-gaining activities is not enough. You must also be aware of energy-draining activities, since they can be very effective in wasting your energy.

I have worked with patients who were doing all the right energy gain actions but were experiencing less than optimal energy. The reason was that they were experiencing significant energy drain through insomnia, worrying, or other energy-draining factors. To keep us aware of the interaction between energy gain and drain, we do well to think in terms of *optimal energy balance*. *Optimal energy balance is the key to optimal health.* In the Balancing Act program the goal is optimal energy balance. At any given time you are in a state of balance, but *optimal energy balance* is the most favorable balance possible for you. My energy level as I write this is the balance between the factors that increase my energy and those that decrease it. If I had gone to bed earlier, I probably would feel more energetic than I am now. If I ride my bicycle for thirty minutes, I will feel more energy. If I meditate for twenty minutes, my energy will go up as well. So, what I have at any given time is an energy balance. What is more desirable is the optimal energy balance. Optimal energy balance is an attainable goal, if you understand and work with the variables that influence your energy.

> *Psychologists have described different forms of energy that influence your capacity to get things done, such as acquiring or maintaining money, love, social support, and religion. A review of the basics of money management will illustrate the dynamics of optimal energy balancing. If you have more money, you have the equivalent of more energy—you can do more. You can fly instead of walk; you can have things delivered to you; you don't have to wait in line; you can save your physical energy. If you have more money coming in than going out (positive balance), you are said to be financially healthy. Even if you have millions, but there is more money (energy) going out than coming in (negative balance), you are at risk for a financial breakdown (bankruptcy.) With low reserves, bankruptcy can be sudden. However, if you have a large amount of money in savings (energy reserves), this reserve will allow you to weather a strong drain on your money, reducing your immediate risk of bankruptcy. Your financial health, then, is an optimal state of balance between the money you earn/gain, and what you spend/drain.*

> *To improve your financial health, you would be wise to both increase your income and decrease your expenses. The same can be said for optimal energy balance: you want to increase energy gain and decrease energy drain.*

Optimal energy balance is the difference between the energy gained and the energy drained in everyday life. To improve this balance, you may increase the activities that increase your energy (energy gainer), or decrease the activities that decrease your energy (energy drainer). How much energy you have at a given point in time is the balance between the energy you gain and the energy you drain in your mind, body, and spirit domains.

Optimal Energy Balance = Energy Gained − Energy Drained

Once you start monitoring your personal energy, you can start your personal self-health program: by practicing activities that increase your personal

Optimal energy balance is the key to optimal health.

Your financial health is a balance between the money you earn/gain, and what you spend/drain.

Optimal energy
balance is the
difference
between the
energy gained
and the energy
drained in
everyday life.

energy and avoiding activities that decrease you personal energy. Let's briefly preview some general factors that influence personal energy and health.

During my late twenties, while I was doing a three-year residency in family medicine, I had as a spiritual director a wonderful, wise priest and writer named Mark Link. One day I went to visit him. It was during the beginning of the season of Lent, the period of religious observance in Catholicism that extends over the forty days leading to Easter. Traditionally, for Catholics, it is also a time to make some personal sacrifice, to "give up something" for Lent.

Father Link asked me what I was going to give up for Lent. I said, "I don't know, Mark. I don't want to give up going out. I don't want to give up having fun." His response was full of wisdom and has stayed with me since that time.

If you can't stop
doing bad things,
just do more
good things.

—Father
Mark Link

Father Link said, "If you can't stop doing bad things, just do more good things." That phrase has helped me a lot during times when I was trying to change. What he was saying to me was that in trying to improve your life, there were two ways to increase your positive balance (grow in spirit and awareness). You can increase positive actions or decrease negative actions, and—either way—you will grow.

Applied here, it means that to keep the momentum moving toward positive energy balance, you can increase energy-gain behaviors or decrease energy-drain behaviors, and either way, you will grow in energy and health. And, of course, if you can do both, you will grow even more and more quickly.

Take a few minutes to consider some of the actions that drain your energy level. Note some of them in the space below.

....

....

You can
increase positive
actions or
decrease
negative actions,
and—either
way—you will
grow.

....

....

....

Now, consider some of the positive actions that gain energy for you, or positive actions that you would like to take that will gain energy for you. List them in the space below.

....

....

Each day you
make countless
decisions in which
you choose
behaviors and
attitudes that
make up your
everyday life.

Mind-Body-Spirit Domains and Your Personal Energy

Each day you make countless decisions in which you choose behaviors and attitudes that make up your everyday life. You decide whether to eat or not, what to eat, whether to walk or drive, whether to forgive or hold a grudge. The choices you make all influence your personal energy balance. If health and energy are important to you, you will want to work with the numerous attitudes and activities available to you for positively influencing your energy level.

One way to make more choices readily available is to acknowledge the mind, body, and spirit domains of your life experience. Years of practicing traditional medicine and mind-body medicine have taught me that beyond physical activities, *mental attitudes and spiritual beliefs have a powerful and undeniable influence on energy and health.* Thus, an approach to health that acknowledges the mind, body, and spirit domains of human experience is not New Age talk—it is just common sense and is supported by the scientific evidence for a mind-body connection, as described in the next chapter. For the sake of discussion, it is useful to separate life experience into the three interrelated domains of mind, body, and spirit. Within each domain, there are various activities that you can use to influence your personal energy.

Mental attitudes
and spiritual beliefs
have a powerful
and undeniable
influence on
energy and health.

- *Mind energy is influenced by mental attitudes, feelings, and perceptions,* such as optimism, pessimism, worrying, blaming, or feeling victimized. In practice, conventional medicine generally considers these mental variables as having little, if any, relevance to health. Psychologically or holistically oriented practitioners view thoughts and emotions as very relevant to health. It is interesting to note that individuals experiencing a major or terminal illness often see the relevancy of attitudes and feelings to their healing more than the general population.

- *Body energy is readily influenced by lifestyle activities* related to the mechanical functions of the body such as nutrition, sleep, exercise, smoking, and alcohol use. Vitamins, supplements, and herbs would also be included under body energy, since their primary effect, like nutrition, is on the body. Lifestyle factors known to be harmful, such as smoking, alcohol, and illegal-drug use, are referred to as *risk factors for disease.* These would be considered energy drainers. There are also lifestyle behavioral factors favorable to energy and health, such as good sleep and good nutrition. Up to now, the practice of conventional medicine has

Mind energy
is influenced
by mental
attitudes,
feelings, and
perceptions.

Body energy
is readily
influenced by
lifestyle
activities.

traditionally emphasized the link between negative lifestyle behaviors and disease more than the link between positive lifestyle behaviors and health.

- *Spirit energy is influenced by spiritual beliefs and activities.* Spiritual beliefs place importance on a nonmaterial world view that perceives a connection between everyone and everything. A later section on spirituality presents a discussion of spirit-related variables that increase personal energy, such as prayer, love, forgiveness, and gratitude. Variables such as judging, grudge holding, and hopelessness that drain personal energy are discussed as well.

Spirit energy
is influenced
by spiritual beliefs
and activities.

Though we separate life energy into three distinct parts for the sake of discussion, it is important to remember that they are inseparable, interrelated, and interactive. They work as one. What happens in the body affects the mind and spirit, while happenings in the spirit will affect the body and mind. George Solomon, MD, a pioneer researcher in psychoneuroimmunology, once said to me, *"We don't know where the body ends and the mind begins."* His words lead me to reflect on a seamless connection between mind and body, and spirit.

A New Model of Health

Though we
separate life
energy into three
distinct parts, they
are inseparable,
interrelated, and
interactive.

Your belief system about how life works influences how you think and feel about life. This belief system can also be called a *paradigm* or *worldview*. Your paradigm about health is your idea of how health works. A paradigm is a model; it is not life. Still, we can make use of this model of health, even if we don't understand everything about health. Balancing Act *presents a paradigm of health that combines health as energy within the three domains of mind, body, and spirit.* This paradigm makes sense of how numerous factors that influence your personal energy can influence the creation, maintenance, or loss of health.

Though energy is a common denominator in mind-body-spirit health, there is a difference in how you benefit from working with each of these three domains: the cost-to-benefit ratio.

Of the three, the body is the *least* efficient since its needs must be attended to, at the expense of a very significant amount of energy. The body must be provided with air, water, food, and shelter. Energy must be spent providing these basic necessities to the body, before the body can release energy.

We don't know
where the body
ends and the
mind begins.

—George
Solomon, MD

For example, to gain energy from eating, you must expend energy gathering, cooking, and digesting food. To increase mind and spirit energy, less energy needs to be spent up front. In the mind domain, you may experience increased energy by dwelling on a positive thought, without having to spend much energy. In the spirit domain, you may experience a surge of personal energy after briefly contemplating your Higher Power, with minimal energy expense. Generally, the cost/benefit energy ratio is much more expensive for the body than for mind and spirit.

Though I recommend working in all three domains to improve your personal energy, the potential benefits of each domain are different. My understanding of the relative differences between mind, body, and spirit energy may be illustrated by a metaphor using "gumballs."

Years ago, when I used to take my kids to the video store to rent videos, they routinely asked "to buy a gumball." The gumballs that used to be a penny when I was young are now twenty-five cents! In a reflective moment, I saw how to describe the difference in energy benefits between mind, body, and spirit, using gumballs and that quarter.

If you give the body a quarter, or twenty-five cents' worth, of energy, it will give you a gumball. If you give the mind a quarter, it will give you a pack of gumballs. But if you give the spirit a quarter, it will give you a gumball machine.

As you practice monitoring your personal energy levels throughout the day, you will see how these three interacting domains influence your overall personal energy level. *The energy flow between body, mind, and spirit is reciprocal. Increasing energy in one domain can influence the energy of the other areas as well, but not equally.* It is common to find people focusing on body-energy variables for improving energy, and all the while remaining oblivious to mind and spirit imbalances. Likewise, many very intellectual people, high in mind energy, often disregard the health needs of the body.

Several years ago in the New Yorker *magazine, there was a cartoon that poked fun at this common disconnectedness between mind and body. The picture depicted a street scene, with various individuals walking casually along. All the people's heads were disconnected from their bodies and floated and bobbed like balloons, several inches above the tops of their necks.*

In my clinical practice, decreased awareness of the body often presents itself in otherwise very bright, hard-working individuals who exhibit an obvious disregard for the health or hygiene of the body. Their lifestyle habits suggest a wide gap between their care of the mind and their care of the body.

I have often found that individuals who are actively high in spirit energy will often have more positively balanced body and mind energy. Much spiritual literature suggests that *as one grows in spirit, the body and mind are likely to benefit as well.*

In everyday life, people with increased awareness of their spirituality often seem to tend to be more at peace and more health conscious in both the care of the body and the use of the mind, as well. They practice good body

Your belief system about how life works influences how you think and feel about life.

Balancing Act presents a paradigm of health that combines health as energy within the three domains of mind, body, and spirit.

The energy flow between body, mind, and spirit is reciprocal.

health habits of moderation and foster neutral-to-optimistic thinking, being careful to avoid pessimism and cynicism. Conversely, growing in body or mind awareness may not always benefit the spiritual experience and may actually hinder it. It is disconcerting to think about great minds that have chosen suicide as a final path in life.

Development in body and mind domains alone may foster a materialistic and self-centered perspective that contrasts with the nonmaterial, "big-picture, connected-to-others" perspective that is more often associated with spirituality. While health-enhancing energy is common to the development of mind, body, and spirit, the health-enhancing potential of each domain varies somewhat with the individual.

The diagram below may be useful in describing the relative influences of mind-body-spirit interaction.

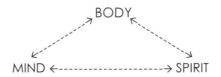

Influencing Mind-Body-Spirit Energy

Whatever the journey, you must begin where you are. To start working on improving your personal energy balance, it is essential that you start monitoring your personal energy level regularly, as discussed earlier. Once you start monitoring your energy level, you see more clearly that certain attitudes and activities can increase your energy, while others drain your energy. Answering the following questions will help you get a picture of how you are currently positively and negatively influencing mind, body, and spirit energy levels.

Influencing Mind Energy Levels

What are some general mind activities you engage in that cause energy gain? Energy drain?

....

....

....

Mind energy gain: meditation, optimism, living in the present.
Mind energy drain: worry, pessimism, blaming.

In the mind domain, various mental activities such as meditation and visualization exercises can be used to increase energy. Optimism and related positive mental attitudes can also be used to increase energy. *Practicing Breath Awareness readily helps decrease energy drain and supports energy gain.* These very easily accessed avenues for increasing energy and overall health are usually quite underused.

Energy-draining activities in the mind domain include worrying, pessimism, and blaming. Participants in the Balancing Act classes often admit early on as they begin the workshop to more frequent use of mind energy drainers, especially the fear-related ones—anxiety and worry—than to using mind energy gainers like optimism. If you are one of these folks, take heart, because there is room for hope, and you'll soon find that you can learn useful techniques to create a more positive, energy-increasing lifestyle.

As you learn of the energy-draining effects of—let's say—constant worrying, for example, such habits may soon appear to you as an expensive liability and a much less desirable option. *Thoughts and perceptions precede most behaviors, making perceptions very influential in effective energy and life management.*

Attention to the dynamics of perception and its effect on personal energy is of pivotal importance for success in this program. How your perceptions influence your energy and your life will be discussed in detail in a later section of this book, "The Life Formula."

The mind conceives of and plans actions that will be carried out in the body and the mind. In your mind, you decided to read this book to help yourself. It is in the mind that you decide to eat junk food or healthful food, to exercise or not, to go to bed early or stay up late. It is also in your mind that you decide to judge, criticize, or hold a grudge. One of the goals of this book is to train you to engage your mind in the practice of the ideas and techniques presented here, in order for you to become more able to access increased energy and well-being. *If the mind is positively engaged, positive attitudes and behaviors are more likely to follow.*

Now that you have considered the ideas contained in this section, what are some additional and specific-to-you mind behaviors and attitudes that cause energy drain, and that you would like to do less?

....

....

....

....

....

....

In the mind domain, various mental activities such as optimism, meditation, and visualization exercises can be used to increase energy.

Practicing Breath Awareness readily helps decrease energy drain and supports energy gain.

What are some additional and specific-to-you mind behaviors and attitudes that cause energy gain, and that you would like to do more?

....

....

....

....

....

....

Part Two, on "The Mind Domain," provides a more in-depth discussion of how your perceptions influence your experiences and personal energy. This knowledge will facilitate your ability to manage stress and negative reactions in favor of more neutral or energizing responses to life events.

Influencing Body Energy Levels

What are some general body activities you use that cause energy gain? Energy drain?

....

....

....

....

....

....

Energy gain: good diet, exercise, and good sleep. Energy drain: poor diet, alcohol, and smoking.

The health benefits of restful sleep, regular physical activity, and eating a diet high in whole grains, fruits, and vegetables are undisputed. These activities help increase energy gain and improve resistance to stress and disease. They should be an integral part of any optimal health plan.

Because the creation of optimal health involves removing any obstacles to health, optimal body energy is facilitated by a reduction of energy drain factors such as a poor diet (high-fat, high-sugar, low-fiber diet), substance abuse (alcohol, illegal drugs, and smoking), physical inactivity, and insomnia.

A common cause of energy drain is insomnia. In my medical practice I find a surprisingly high number of people accept poor sleep as a common—if not normal—fact of life. This is unfortunate because poor sleep can be as much an energy drain as chronic blood loss.

What are some specific-to-you body behaviors and attitudes that cause energy drain?

....

....

....

....

....

....

Now list a few of your healthy body behaviors and attitudes that gain energy.

....

....

....

....

....

....

In Part Three, on "The Body Domain," the body-related variables of nutrition, exercise, and sleep will be discussed at length to support the use of specific behaviors and attitudes for increasing your personal energy level.

Influencing Spirit Energy Levels

Spirit refers to that part of a person that, like the mind, is nonmaterial, but also a part of something higher, deeper, and older. While spirit is something that I believe is a part of everyone, the topic may be difficult for many and is often the source of conflict and misunderstanding.

To me, spirit refers to that identity of a person that is timeless. My spirit is closer to my true identity than the mind-driven personality I experience as self. Descriptions of the characteristics of my spirit make up the basis for my spiritual beliefs.

The health benefits of restful sleep, regular physical activity, and eating a diet high in whole grains, fruits, and vegetables are undisputed.

A common cause of energy drain is insomnia.

Spirit refers to
that part of a
person that,
like the mind,
is nonmaterial, but
also a part of
something higher,
deeper, and
older.

Matters of the spirit are related to one's deepest sense of identity and meaning—who you really are (not just your body), and the purpose of your life. Spirit refers to something more than the domain of the mind, where self is usually the personality acquired during years of living.

Spirit is beyond personality and culture. It is timeless.

In short, *my spirit is my true identity, which persists when my body dies and my mind no longer exists.*

Spiritual beliefs may or may not be tied to organized religion. Often people say, "I am spiritual, but I don't believe in religion." That's okay. Use "spirit" in whatever personal way you understand this term.

For now, let's look at spirit-related activities that influence personal energy.

What are some general spirit-related activities that cause energy gain? Energy drain?

....

....

....

....

....

....

Spirit energy gain: forgiveness, love, prayer, and faith.
Spirit energy drain: judging, worry, grudges, and hopelessness.

My spirit is my
true identity,
which persists
when my body
dies and my
mind no longer
exists.

In the domain of Spirit, energy is gained by acts of unconditional love, forgiveness, prayer, faith in a Higher Power, and inspirational reading. Conversely, energy may be drained by hopelessness, dwelling in fear, holding grudges, judging, and attachment to material things.

What are some specific-to-you spiritual activities that cause energy drain?

....

....

....

....

....

What are some specific-to-you spiritual activities that cause energy gain?

....

....

....

....

....

....

In Part Four, on "The Spirit Domain," a general discussion of what spirituality means will be presented to help you access more concepts of this important topic. The spirit-related variables of prayer, forgiveness, and gratitude will be discussed to further enhance your ability to use these powerful energy gainers.

> *To me, an immediate benefit of this mind-body-spirit energy paradigm of health is an "I can" feeling within. It gives me hope. It is reassuring to know that no matter what the situation, there is always something I can do to move in the direction of higher personal energy and well-being. I may not want to do anything, but, in truth, there is always something I can do to improve personal energy.*

The concepts presented here relating personal energy balance to mind, body, and spirit domains can be summarized in table 1, Personal Energy Program Worksheet, below. The first column lists energy gain activities that are to be encouraged, while the second column lists energy drain activities that are to be limited or avoided altogether. The chapters that follow will go into more detail into how you can take this holistic approach to personal energy management.

☯ **Return to your breathing.**

In the domain of Spirit, energy is gained by acts of unconditional love, forgiveness, prayer, faith in a Higher Power, and inspirational reading

Summary

An immediate benefit of this mind-body-spirit energy paradigm of health is an "I can" feeling within. It gives me hope.

You now have access to a new paradigm of health based on observing and becoming aware of your personal energy as a marker of health combined with a mind, body, and spirit approach to increasing your overall personal energy.

You have been introduced to several key concepts, and each of these will be developed and expanded in the following chapters:

1. *In this paradigm you are always on a continuum between stress and illness at one end and calm and health at the other end.* As such, no matter how stressed you feel, you are still connected to calm; no matter how ill you feel, you are still connected to health.

2. *Health is more accessible if you employ personal energy as a measure of your health.* Using a personal energy continuum quickly reveals the many different ways you can influence your energy level and the quality of your life.

3. *Monitoring and rating your personal energy level on a 1-to-10 scale increases awareness of how you are doing.* On a scale of 1 to 10, where might you rate your energy level right now?

    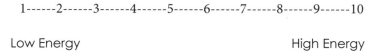

    1------2------3------4------5------6------7------8------9------10

    Low Energy   High Energy

4. *The goal is to have optimal personal energy, which is the result of the energy gained minus the energy drained in everyday life.* You reach this goal by increasing activities that gain energy and decreasing activities that drain energy.

5. *Combining a personal energy continuum with your mind, body, and spirit domains expands the options available to you for improving your personal energy level and your health.*

6. *At any point in time you can choose activities related to one or all of these three domains to increase your energy.*

    a. Mind energy may be positively influenced by practicing optimism and choosing more-positive perceptions.
    b. Body energy may be positively influenced by lifestyle activities such as nutrition, exercise, and sleep.
    c. Spirit energy may be positively influenced by activities such as prayer, forgiveness, and gratitude.

PERSONAL ENERGY PROGRAM WORKSHEET

	Increase Energy GAIN (+)	Decrease Energy DRAIN (-)
BODY	Breath Awareness Natural Diet Sleep/Rest Mind-Body Activities Exercise	Smoking Fast/Processed Food Insomnia Alcohol/Drugs Pessimism ....
MIND	Breath Awareness Go with Flow Inspirational Reading Verify Assessments Meditation	Worry Distorted Perceptions Self-Criticism ....
SPIRIT	Prayer Forgiveness Gratitude	Grudges Hate Hopelessness ....

Stress and the Mind-Body Connection

By observing stress, you can discover strong evidence for an ever-present mind-body connection and also gain an introduction into the power of your own perception. Your Stress Response is the body's reaction to a perception of threat or danger. This response has obvious physical and mental components that confirm the presence of an ongoing mind-body connection in our everyday lives, as well. Medical research confirms that stress can negatively influence the health of the body. In addition, positive experiences have been shown to positively influence health.

The mind-body connection works for positive or negative, and in both directions. The mind influences the body and the body influences the mind. With a heightened awareness of this two-way mind-body connection, you can consciously use physical activities to enhance how you feel mentally, and use mental activities to enhance how you feel physically.

☯ **Bring your attention to your breathing.**

The Stress Response

Picture yourself in the scenario described below, which is an example of a common situation in which the Stress Response is turned on.

It is the evening rush hour, and you are driving home on a busy eight-lane highway. Suddenly, out of the corner of your eye, you notice that the car on your right is drifting into your lane. Immediately you experience a wave of fear, accompanied by pounding heart and sweaty palms. You grip the wheel tighter and begin an avoidance maneuver, then the other car corrects itself and returns to its place in the next lane. The driver hand-signals a "sorry" and you continue on your way home.

Though you are safely out of danger, you notice that your heart is still racing and you still feel nervous. By the time you get home, you feel your usual self, and the incident is forgotten. You experienced your built-in, protective Stress Response.

At times when the mind perceives a potential danger, the body experiences immediate changes that are part of an alarm system meant to help you survive that danger. The Stress Response is the body's reaction to a perception of threat or danger. It is also called the "fight or flight" response because the body responds by preparing itself either to fight an attacker or to run away.

The fight-or-flight response uses up a lot of energy. If you actually have to fight off an attacker or run away, the increased energy expenditure is obvious. However, even if you are not fighting or running away, if you have to maintain a constant state of readiness to respond to a perceived threat that may never come, the resulting tension can be just as energy draining.

The constant state of readiness of our armed forces during the Cold War with the USSR drained a lot of energy. Having ships, planes, and submarines constantly patrolling in a state of readiness, ready to attack if ordered to do so, was emotionally and financially draining.

Chronic stress is a major energy drainer. When patients come to see me with what are called stress-related symptoms, such as insomnia, headaches, and fatigue, they are usually experiencing *chronic stress*. In such cases, their experiences at work or at home are associated with the recurrent turning on of their Stress Response. The cases I find most concerning are those who report increased stress at work and at home. These people get no break from stress if it is present in both places. In the face of chronic stress, it is important to find ways to reduce the amount of time the Stress Response is being elicited. *Any time we can reduce the frequency and intensity of our Stress Response to common, everyday events, we save energy and suffer less.*

Consider the following example:

You are walking down a dark street late at night. Suddenly, you hear the sound of footsteps. Perceiving a threat from an unknown attacker, your body responds by increasing its heart and breathing rates. Your muscles tense. Your pupils dilate to see better in the dark. Inside your body, the surge of stress hormones prompts your liver to pour sugar into your bloodstream for fuel. Your blood flow shifts away from the skin to become available for your muscles. These instantaneous changes are just a small part of the many actions in the Stress Response that your body is turning on to prepare you to run away or successfully defend yourself. You can feel them building up. Suddenly, you hear a familiar voice speak your name, and, as you turn back, your body's intense Stress Response begins to fade away.

The fight-or-flight response uses up a lot of energy.

Chronic stress is a major energy drainer.

Any time we can reduce the frequency and intensity of our Stress Response to common, everyday events, we save energy and suffer less.

During any average day in the average modern, urban environment, your body may experience the Stress Response scores of times, in varying degrees. Most of the time you will be unaware that it has turned on.

Still, this can be very costly immediately in terms of personal energy and, later, in terms of health. Consider what happens when your Stress Response is turned on in response to a perceived threat.

Here are just a few of the immediate changes and their possible impact on health:

- The heart rate increases. This can increase blood pressure and increase the risk of heart attack or stroke. Increased heart rate also makes you feel nervous.

- The breathing rate increases. This is often shallow, rapid breathing that can make you feel as though you can't take a deep breath. If it is actually hyperventilation, it can also make you feel light-headed, nauseated, or weak and, if severe, can cause fainting.

- The liver pours sugar into the bloodstream for fuel. This can elevate your blood sugar to unhealthful levels. Cholesterol is also poured into the bloodstream from the liver, possibly aggravating any already-developed partial blockages in the coronary arteries.

- The blood thickens and coagulates faster. This increased clotting action may be very helpful in a case of hemorrhage, but it can also increase the risk of heart attack or stroke.

- The adrenal glands release stress hormones, including steroids like cortisol, which can, over time, suppress the immune system and increase the risk of infections and cancer.

There are numerous other effects of the Stress Response, such as increased stomach acid, increased muscle spasm, loss of magnesium, and decreased sex drive. This brief review of the multisystem Stress Response reveals that *the Stress Response is a powerful, energy-draining event that can have serious health consequences,* especially in the face of chronic stress. *One can argue that stress is truly one of the major diseases of modern civilization.*

Stress and the Mind-Body Connection

For years researchers sought scientific proof that thoughts and emotions in the mind could influence the health of the body. Researchers looked for a link between certain personality types and specific diseases. In the 1970s, George Solomon, MD, and fellow researchers were describing an "arthritis" personality. Others were writing about a "cancer" personality. The relationship between "type A" personality and heart attacks had been explored since the 1950s. Work in these areas suggested a relationship between the mind and

The Stress Response is a powerful, energy draining event that can have serious health consequences.

One can argue that stress is truly one of the major diseases of modern civilization.

For years researchers sought scientific proof that thoughts and emotions in the mind could influence the health of the body.

the body, but there was not enough hard data to convince most people. In search of hard data, researchers sought a direct and measurable link between stress and illness. By the 1970s, research technology had advanced to the point where it was possible to measure many of the changes in the activity of the immune system in response to stress.

The immune system's active role in defending the body from various internal and external agents of disease is pivotal in health maintenance. *Earlier research on stress had established that chronic stress has an inhibitory effect on immune system activity.* In search of a link between stress and illness, researchers sought to measure the effect of varied life stressors on the activity of the immune system. If researchers could show that stressful life events had a measurable negative impact on the immune system, it would support the idea that the mind could influence illness and, perhaps, also could influence healing of the body. Stress might impact health by weakening the immune system and increasing susceptibility to disease.

Many research studies that examined the stress/illness relationship had a similar design. First, researchers would choose a group of subjects (patients) associated with increased stress, such as students during finals, to be studied. Then a baseline measure of the immune system activity was made. A specific stressor would be introduced, and the immune system activity would be measured again, looking for a change. Finally, the stressor would be removed and the measures taken again, to see if the measured changes went back to the prestress baseline level.

The effect of stress on health has been studied by measuring the effect of final exams on different groups of students. Students in college or medical school had blood tests taken to measure a specific marker of immune system activity before, during, and after final exams. Repeated studies have shown that the immune system activity decreased during final exams and returned to its usual level after finals were over. The same pattern occurred with college, graduate, and medical students. These findings helped explain a common occurrence I noticed during college. It was common for many students to go home after finals with a cold. Perhaps, the stress of finals had weakened their immune systems enough to allow a passing virus to get past the defenses, incubate for a few days, and lead to a cold by the time the students got home for the break after final exams.

Think about the everyday life stressors that occur in your own daily life—both those that occur every day and those that occur occasionally. Consider which ones you think may be having a negative impact on your health. List some of them on the lines below.

....

....

Earlier research on stress had established that chronic stress has an inhibitory effect on immune system activity.

Repeated studies have shown that the immune system activity decreased when a stressor was introduced, like during final exams, and returned to its usual level after finals were over.

....

....

....

....

Besides final exams, other stressors include such things as going through a divorce, public speaking, and being the primary care giver for someone with Alzheimer's disease.

Researchers have examined the effect of various common negative life stressors on the immune system. The husband-wife research team of Ronald Glaser, PhD, and Janice Kiecolt-Glaser, PhD, of the Ohio State University, as well as other researchers, has shown that *common life stressors such as going through a divorce, public speaking, taking care of a spouse with Alzheimer's disease, and taking final exams can all have a measurable negative impact on immune system activity.*

Some of the Life Events Shown to Affect the Immune System Negatively

- Caring for Alzheimer spouse
- Divorce
- Doing long-term care for another
- Experiencing a robbery or attack
- Final exams
- Getting a new job
- Losing a job
- Loss of a spouse
- Marriage
- New baby at home
- Demanding boss
- Public speaking

A very familiar example of the relationship of stress and illness is seen in studies of the common cold. Many adults readily concede that *there may be a connection between stress and their susceptibility to catching a cold.* In 1993, an important study linking stress and the common cold was published in the *New England Journal of Medicine.*

To study the relationship between stress and the common cold, researchers asked more than five hundred healthy adults to fill out questionnaires that measured their overall daily stress. The responses were separated into three levels of stress: low, medium, or high. Participants were asked to use a nasal spray containing viruses that cause colds. After a few days, viral cultures were made of specimens taken from participants' nasal passages to determine how many were infected with the virus. Several days later, participants were interviewed to determine how many developed clinical symptoms of a cold (runny nose, low fever, congestion, etc.)

For both the rate of infection with the virus and of development of the cold symptoms, there was a direct correlation with the stress reported. Those reporting low stress had a low rate of infection and actual colds. Those reporting high stress had a much-higher rate of infection and actual colds. The authors concluded "something about stress could make people more susceptible to the common cold." This study confirms what many have personally suspected about stress and illness in their own lives: stress can lead to greater susceptibility to colds.

Other studies have examined the effect of more-serious life stressors, such as losing a spouse to illness. Researchers concluded that *a powerful stressor such as the loss of a spouse could make the survivor much more susceptible to illness.*

One study looked at the impact of the death of women with advanced terminal breast cancer on their widowed spouses. To establish a base level, researchers measured the activity of the immune system in men whose wives had advanced breast cancer with metastases and a short life expectancy. The husbands' immune system activity was tested again as early as one month after the deaths of their wives. The results revealed significant decrease in immune system activity as early as one month following the death of the wife. The implication is that the widowed husbands' negative experience of mourning the loss of a spouse is a powerful stressor that may weaken the activity of the immune system. The researchers suggested that male widowers may also be at a higher risk for illness and death in the first year after the loss of a spouse. This finding helps us understand that Grandpa is more likely to get sick and perhaps die in the first year after the death of Grandma. The same risk may apply to Grandma after the death of Grandpa.

Stress studies have proliferated in recent years and, there have been, and are, currently, hundreds of studies confirming that *stress, or more specifically, the perceptions that turn on the Stress Response, can have a negative impact on health and personal energy.* Fortunately, it is also true that positive perceptions can have a positive impact on health and personal energy.

The Mind-Body Connection for Health and Energy

Some of the scientific studies that examine the relationship between stress and illness are examples of research in a new scientific field called *psychoneuroimmunology* or **PNI**. PNI is the study of the interaction between the mind (*psych-*), the brain (*-neuro-*), and the immune system (*-immun-*). Most of the early PNI studies looked at the effect of negative mental stress on health and the immune system. It was just a matter of time before researchers asked if positive emotions could influence the immune system and health in a positive way. In the popular literature, there was a well-known example of laughter as a health-enhancing intervention.

In a highly publicized and award-winning book, *Anatomy of an Illness as Perceived by the Patient: Reflections on Healing and Regeneration*, author and *Saturday Review* editor Norman Cousins famously described his use of laughter, through watching films of comedies, to cure himself in 1964 of an otherwise chronic, crippling disease called *ankylosing spondylitis*. Cousins's experience suggested that laughter is therapeutic and may improve the protective activity of the immune system. PNI researchers also found evidence to support the idea that laughter could influence health in a positive way.

> *Several studies found that hearty laughter, in response to a comedian like Richard Pryor on videotape, could improve short-term pain tolerance. Participants were divided into two groups. A baseline level of pain tolerance was taken from all participants. The control group was shown an instructional video, and the experimental group was shown the comedy video. Pain tolerance was measured again after the videos. The experimental group that watched the comedy video was found to have increased pain tolerance when compared to the control group. The implication of this study is that laughter may be a useful natural aid for reducing the suffering of chronic, painful illnesses like arthritis and chronic back pain. It also suggested that the mind-body connection can have a negative or positive influence on health and should be considered as an adjunct to conventional medical interventions. The therapeutic physical effect of laughter may be related to the overall effect that laughter has on the whole person. A good laugh is very relaxing, so relaxing that sometimes it is hard to stand up when you are laughing really hard.*

> *Good laughter is also associated with more positive and less negative thinking.*

> *Laughter is a must in any health enhancement program.*

Other studies have found that soothing touch can be a positive influence on the growth and development of premature infants who were given brief massages three times a day.

> *Premature infants in a nursery were divided into two groups. Both groups were given the usual standard medical care for premature babies. The infants in the experimental group also received a gentle, fifteen-minute massage three times a day. At the end of two weeks, the study group showed a significant improvement in weight gain and developmental markers compared to the control group. Not only were the massaged infants growing faster, but their brains were developing faster as well. Interestingly, the study was terminated early for ethical reasons.*

> *Once it was obvious the massaged infants were getting important benefits, it would have been unethical not to offer the same benefits to all of the infants.*

Hearty laughter could improve short-term pain tolerance.

Laughter is a must in any health enhancement program.

Positive feelings, generated by touch, may have a health-enhancing influence on the body.

The mind-body connection can carry positive as well as negative influences.

The increased rate of growth and development in premature infants receiving a fifteen-minute massage three times a day suggests that *positive feelings, generated by touch, may have a health-enhancing influence on the body.* Mind-body medicine, or PNI research studying the relationship between the mind and the body (*the mind-body connection*), confirms what many people intuitively suspect: that the mind can influence the health of the body toward illness or healing. Hope and hopelessness, joy and worry, can influence health. *The mind-body connection can carry positive as well as negative influences.* The mind-body connection transmits positive or negative messages, compliments, or criticisms. This research in PNI along with my personal observations and experiences convinced me that there is ample evidence to support the use of the mind-body connection for the reduction of illness and the enhancement of health. Interestingly, in my medical practice many of my patients were already unknowingly using the mind-body connection to influence health, but more often for negative than positive influences.

Which is more often transmitted to the body through the mind-body connection: positive or negative influences?

....

....

....

....

....

> Negative influences are transmitted to the body more often than positive ideas, mostly due to habit.

Though the mind-body connection can be used to send a positive message as easily as a negative one, most people admit using this marvelous connection more often on negative messages.

Review some of your recent experiences, and you will find that you are quicker to criticize yourself or replay a worry than you are to praise yourself or to replay a success. The most obvious reason for taking the negative perspective is that *in everyday life we have more practice using negative thoughts and attitudes than positive ones.* In addition, we tend to replay our worries as if it might help to worry. In your own experience, another reason may be that you did not know the negative thoughts and attitudes might be hurting you. People who are interested in healing and self-health will want to become aware that the cause-and-effect relationship between the mind and body impacts your health whether you know it or not. Modern medicine can now offer a message of hope and encouragement: *people can learn to use the mind-body connection for sending positive, health-enhancing*

In everyday life we have more practice using negative thoughts and attitudes than positive ones.

People can learn to use the mind-body connection for sending positive, health-enhancing messages.

messages. You can begin—right now—to use the ever-present mind-body connection to carry more-positive thoughts by using the exercise that follows.

Positive **Mind**-Body Exercise

Practice positive words to yourself by complimenting yourself. Say to yourself positive things such as these:

- I am a good mother, father, sister, brother, spouse, friend, etc.
- I do a pretty good job at home/work.
- I am a good person.

Notice how your body "feels" when you say these things to yourself. Notice any increase in your personal energy level. Try this exercise while looking into your eyes in a mirror. Try saying positive—and sincere—things to someone else—at home, at school, or at work. Observe their responses and see if you can see facial muscles relaxing or shoulders losing some of their tenseness. You'll find more on how this practice works, later in this book, in the section on "affirmations."

The mind-body connection is a two-way line. Another helpful aspect of the mind-body connection is that, like a telephone line, it can transmit messages in both directions. *That is, the mind can influence the body, and the body can influence the mind.* Look for evidence of this connection in your own everyday experiences. You may notice signs that worry, for example, can make you feel tense, nervous, and headachy. Those physical symptoms may make you feel less confident, and so you may worry more. Worrying is a mental experience, and it is usually accompanied by a physical reaction such as insomnia, muscle spasms, or nausea.

A physical activity like a twenty-minute walk, on the other hand, can have a positive effect on both mood and energy level. An optimistic or humorous mental perspective can often revitalize the body with newfound energy. Awareness of these characteristics of the mind-body connection opens up many paths to wellness and many avenues for restoring health and improving personal energy.

Positive **Body**-Mind Exercise

Try any of the following body activities to positively influence your mind:

- Take a hot bath/shower.
- Go for a twenty-minute walk during your lunch break.
- Take a five-minute break to lightly jog in place at work or home.
- Practice slowly stretching your back and leg muscles for five minutes.

The positive influence of positive thoughts and activities on your body's health

The mind-body connection is a two-way line.

The mind can influence the body, and the body can influence the mind.

The positive influence of positive thoughts and activities on your body's health affirms the connection between the mind and the body.

affirms the connection between the mind and the body. The Stress Response helped us understand the negative side of the mind-body connection.

The positive side of the mind-body connection may be explained by the Relaxation Response, a term coined by Herbert Benson, MD.

The Relaxation Response— a Built-In Healing Aid

In the late 1960s, Herbert Benson MD, a researcher on high blood pressure at Harvard, decided to study the effects of a form of meditation on students. To his surprise, he found that by using a simple form of meditation, students could directly impact aspects of their physiology. Heart rate, blood pressure, breathing rate, and muscle tension all decreased with meditation. These were not people who had been practicing meditation for many years, but ordinary students with relatively little experience with it. The physiological changes were the opposite of what occurred with the Stress Response. Benson used the term "Relaxation Response" to describe the group of physiological changes that counterbalanced the fight-or-flight (stress) response.

Body Function Response	In Relaxation Response	In Stress
Heart Rate	Decreases	Increases
Breathing Rate	Decreases	Increases
Muscle Tension	Decreases	Increases
Blood Pressure	Decreases	Increases
Metabolism	Decreases	Increases

The Relaxation Response is an integrated physiological response that reverses the alarm effect of the Stress Response. The Relaxation Response can be elicited by various techniques. Meditation, repetitive prayer, yoga, repetitive exercise, or diaphragmatic breathing can be used to elicit this natural stress reducer. As a result of his study of various methods for eliciting the Relaxation Response, Benson found there are two components common to all techniques for turning on the Relaxation Response. The minimum requirements for turning on this healing response are

1. the repetition of a word, sound, phrase, image, or physical activity
2. a passivity to any outside thoughts that occur

The positive side of the mind-body connection may be explained by the Relaxation Response.

The Relaxation Response is an integrated physiological response that reverses the alarm effect of the Stress Response.

Numerous published research studies point out the beneficial effects of eliciting *the Relaxation Response* as a means of reducing high blood pressure, insomnia, nausea caused by chemotherapy, chronic pain, and certain chronic abnormal heart rhythms. The Benson-Henry Institute for Mind Body Medicine at Harvard runs wellness programs for stress-related disorders that include training to elicit the Relaxation Response. The institute reports positive changes for course participants, including a decrease in stress-related physical symptoms, anxiety, and worry, as well as an increase in self-esteem, concentration, and awareness. *Most, if not all, stress management programs include training in turning on your Relaxation Response.* In this program, you will learn to elicit your Relaxation Response using the Breath Awareness you are already practicing. Note that the Breath Awareness you are practicing whenever you can meets the first criteria for eliciting the Relaxation Response. When you close your eyes and practice letting go of outside thoughts you are doing a relaxation exercise.

Numerous published research studies point out the beneficial effects of eliciting the Relaxation Response.

Steps for Eliciting the Relaxation Response

- The repetition of a word, sound, phrase, image, or physical activity.
- Practice letting go of any outside thoughts that occur.

Relaxation Exercise

Start by finding a quiet place where you won't be disturbed. Sit in a comfortable chair and close your eyes. Bring your attention to your breathing. Stay with your breathing and let go of outside thoughts. When you find yourself distracted by outside thoughts, acknowledge them and let them go, as you bring your attention back to your breathing. Let go of any outside thoughts and return to your Breath Awareness. Stay with your breathing. Let go of all outside thoughts as if they were passing clouds, as though they were like leaves on a stream.
Continue this cycle of staying with your breathing and letting go of outside thoughts for the time allotted for this relaxation exercise. Start with five or ten minutes. Over time, build up to twenty to thirty minutes. A soft timer/alarm can be helpful so you can relax and avoid having to keep checking the clock. After finishing your relaxation exercise, notice the difference in your personal energy level.

Most stress management programs include training in turning on your Relaxation Response.

My class/workshop participants have learned to *use the mind-body connection for the reduction of stress-related symptoms and illness.* Many reported experiencing less pain and using less prescription medication with the help of stress-reducing techniques and concepts. Others reported that they were managing chronic symptoms, such as insomnia, more effectively.

A woman in her late twenties had attended one of my six-week workshops looking for help with controlling her frequent and severe migraines.

Use the mind-
body connection
for the reduction
of stress-related
symptoms and
illness.

Several weeks after completing the program, she wrote me a letter describing how she was managing her migraines more effectively and with less medication by using the relaxation techniques.

A man in his late seventies came to see me very frustrated because he had to use the bathroom to urinate about fifteen to twenty times per day while awake. This had been going on since his surgery for prostate enlargement two years earlier. After going to bed he would wake up only two or three times during the whole night to urinate. With relaxation training he was able to reduce his trips to the bathroom during the day to six to eight times. He was elated with his more manageable urinary frequency.

A woman in her late fifties was referred by another physician to our class for help with her insomnia. Her difficulty sleeping persisted despite the use of various prescription sleep aids. During the fifth session of our weekly classes, she stood up and reported that with the help of the relaxation exercises she was practicing, she was getting natural sleep, without medications, for the first time in years.

Despite the many exciting successes that patients experienced with this approach, it soon became obvious that mind-body medicine was not for everyone. *Some patients resisted the idea that the mind could influence health.* Others did not want to bother with the exercises. They preferred having the doctor provide an "instant fix" for their problem, with a pill or other medication, so they could be on their way.

Some patients
resist the idea that
the mind could
influence health.

A woman in her midforties came to see me for recurrent, severe headaches. I had seen her years earlier for the same problem. Past evaluation with special x-rays and by a neurologist revealed no organic cause, and she had left my practice for a while. In reevaluating her symptoms, it was important to review the history. When asked what made her headaches better, she stated, "When my husband leaves town." As funny as it sounds, it was—sadly enough—quite true. When asked what made her headaches worse, she stated, "When he comes back to town." Her answers strongly suggested that she was having severe muscle-tension headaches related to her relationship with her husband, a long-distance truck driver. She seemed an obvious candidate for stress management and relaxation exercises. I recommended specific relaxation exercises that could help her muscle-spasm headaches. She politely acknowledged that while those exercises might help, she was not interested, and she requested a prescription medication instead.

It was an eye-opening experience for me to realize that some patients might not be interested in a self-health approach to their medical problems. Nevertheless, I continue to find that *most patients are interested in, and willing to learn to use, the mind-body connection, most often to relieve stress symptoms and to avoid prescription medications.* Less often, some patients have been willing to explore the mind-body connection for generally enhancing their health. These fewer numbers may be because the general concept of health may seem somewhat vague and abstract and does not provide the immediate and concrete motivation of trying to deal with a specific and present pain. Providing patients with a paradigm of *health as personal energy* helps them focus their efforts and makes health management more accessible and attractive, because they can more easily visualize and internalize the goals of personal energy management.

Life Lessons from Stress

Studying the Stress Response reveals two important insights into how life works:

1. the power of perception
2. the mind-body connection in action

Stress itself wastes a lot of energy. The numerous energy-draining physical reactions that make up your Stress Response are usually preceded by a perception of danger. This is an example of the ubiquitous mind-body connection. This connection holds true for positive perceptions as well. When you are in love, the mind-body connection influences your body to respond with more energy, pleasure, and sense of well-being. Most people, however, have more experience with negative mind-body connections than with positive ones. Perhaps learning more about how perceptions work could lead to more-positive experiences

In understanding stress, the key point is perception. In the face of most everyday stressors, without the perception of danger there is no Stress Response, even if the threat is real. Yet, if the mind perceives danger, even if there is no real threat, the Stress Response is turned on. When Herbert Benson, MD, probably the most recognized name in modern stress management, was asked during an interview to describe stress in one word, he chose the word "perception." *Stress in one word is perception. Since perception is in the mind, then the mind is important in creating stress.*

That is, *your perception of life events creates much of what you experience as stress.* Once this is understood, it is a short step to realizing that since stress is a subset of life, the mind has an active role in creating your life experience as well. Perceptions as such will have a similar impact on your everyday personal energy. The power of your perceptions to influence your experience of life can be illustrated using the Life Formula. The Life Formula may be written as

$$\text{Event} \rightarrow \text{Assessment/Perception} \rightarrow \text{Response}$$

The Life Formula states that life is a series of events that *turn on* assessments or perceptions, which in turn *create* responses. As discussed in the next chapter, the Life Formula will illustrate your everyday experience of the

Most patients are interested in learning to use the mind-body connection to relieve stress symptoms.

Stress in one word is perception.

As perception is in the mind, then the mind is important in creating stress.

Your perception of life events creates much of what you experience as stress.

53

mind-body connection and the influence of your perceptions on your life and personal energy.

☯ Return to your breathing.

Summary

Excessive stress is energy draining and can often be dangerous. Stress also reveals important insights into how life works. In stress, as perceptions of danger are turned into physical responses, we see that there is a mind-body connection, wherein the mind, through perceptions, influences the body. This mind-body connection is a two-way street wherein the body can influence the mind as well. The mind-body connection can carry negative or positive messages. Research has shown that stress may contribute to illness and that, conversely, positive experiences may enhance health. Stress and illness are both associated with decreased personal energy. Increased health correlates with increased personal energy. Positive perceptions may be positive influences on health and, thus, on personal energy as well. For proactive personal energy management, it may be helpful to practice Breath Awareness and relaxation exercises and to choose more-positive perceptions to create more positive experiences and increase personal energy.

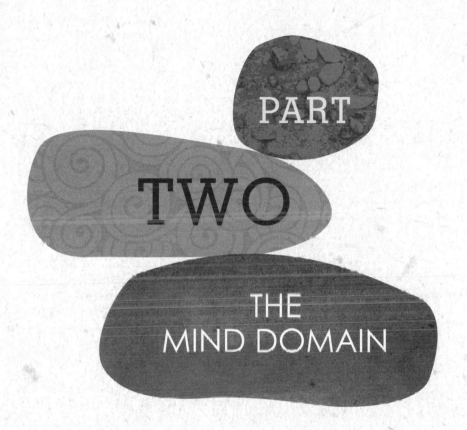

PART

TWO

THE
MIND DOMAIN

Mind Concepts

3

Life is lived mostly in the mind. We spend most of our lives in thoughts and feelings. Yet, as children, we hear very little about how the mind works, and how our perceptions influence what we experience. This chapter will show you how changing your perceptions can change your experience of life's situations and help you reduce suffering and personal energy loss from stress in everyday life. It also discusses the Life Formula, a useful tool for understanding the mind-body connection and how your mind influences how you experience your life. The Life Formula describes our lives as a series of events that turn on assessments or perceptions, which in turn create responses. Our responses to life events are made up of behaviors, emotions, sensations, and thoughts, which we experience in unique and personal patterns. The Life Formula provides a simple and effective method of measuring the effects of your responses to stress in life events, and it helps you to make positive adjustments, without delay.

☯ Bring your attention to your breathing.

As children, we go through life moving from one situation to the next, learning by reacting to the outside environment. During the early years, little if anything is said about how much of what we experience is influenced by the perceptions of our minds. Without this knowledge, it is easy to think that what you are experiencing is really what is going on. Without this awareness, it is easy to misunderstand people and to miss opportunities to learn how life works.

Not recognizing how our perceptions influence our life experiences often leads to adults who feel like victims of life. Yet, we have heard occasional clues. Growing up, you probably heard references to the "power of the mind." "The mind is a terrible thing to waste" suggests there are great possibilities in the power of the mind. The phrase "mind over matter" is often used to imply that the immaterial, amorphous mind can solve problems and overcome difficult situations. "You use only 10 percent of your brain" suggests that there is much untapped potential that could be applied to give you more power to do things. So, we come into the world with a potentially great and powerful mind, which we don't understand. Growing up, few of us are taught to understand how the mind works.

Some of the ways that perceptions in the mind influence personal experience are evident to me in the ways that my patients respond to having blood drawn or to receiving a shot in the medical office. Some children are crying the whole time they are in the office, even if they are not going to have any shots or a blood test; some cry even if the appointment is not for them. Just seeing the doctor come into the exam room is enough to start some children crying. It is not hard to guess their perception at that moment. Other times, strong, healthy adults become light-headed and even faint after having blood drawn for blood tests that they themselves may have specifically requested.

Fortunately, as we get older, we usually start to figure out how life works, often by trial and error. For example, you may notice that changing your attitude can change your experience of a situation, whether or not the situation changes. An example might be something like the day you decided that you were not going to be bothered by "so-and-so" any more, and—amazingly enough—you stopped being bothered. This kind of self-awareness is priceless, because it can help you reduce your personal suffering and actually create more opportunities for happiness.

When you haven't yet learned how to readily influence your experience of life events, you can readily slip back into your previous and more passive patterns of thinking and forget your own role in influencing your personal experience of life.

In our most-common patterns, we live day to day, experiencing our minds mostly as thoughts about events in our lives, and we respond in perceptions that categorize this or that event as being good, safe, fun, easy, scary, difficult, etc. These kinds of thoughts are our perceptions about life, which—whether we realize it or not—are influencing our everyday experience of life. In a strict sense, these perceptions are *creating* our experience. *Our perceptions and beliefs create how we think, feel, and behave.* If we perceive something as scary, such as a rollercoaster ride, we will react very differently than if we perceive it as fun.

Perceptions and Personal Energy Levels

Let us consider some of the ways your pattern of thinking can influence your own experience of your life events. Besides creating the way that you experience your life, perceptions influence your moment-to-moment personal energy level. *Perceptions of having fun or enjoying an activity generate more-positive feelings and an increase in personal energy. In contrast, perceptions that are scary generate negative feelings and an energy drain.*

If your goal is to achieve a higher personal energy level, you will want to learn about the creative power of your perceptions. In this section, we will discuss perceptions and other mind-related variables that can influence your personal energy. Mental attitudes and behaviors that can increase energy levels (energy gain) include optimism, humor, "going with the flow," and various types of relaxation exercises. In contrast, attitudes and behaviors that decrease energy (energy drain) include pessimism, cynicism, anger, and worrying. For the sake of discussion, we describe these attitudes and behaviors first of all as being mind related, but of course it is understood that the energy fluctuations are experienced in the body as well.

In reviewing some of the mind variables that you can use to improve your personal energy, it is noteworthy that most people admit to more experience with energy-draining attitudes than those that cause energy gains. The good news is that you can learn to use your mind to increase personal energy, as with meditation and relaxation exercises. Positive mental attitudes and optimism can also be practiced to increase energy gain. If the goal is overall improved energy, then mental energy drainers, such as worrying, cynicism, pessimism, and blaming, become less attractive and more of a liability. The importance of the mind must be highlighted, because it is in the mind that perceptions, attitudes, and behaviors originate. *It is in your mind that you choose between unhealthful and healthful options,* decide to follow or ignore your own good advice, decide whether to eat fruits or pastries, decide to take time to ponder spiritual concepts, or just continue working on your to-do list.

The Life Formula

To better understand how the mind influences personal energy level, you must comprehend how perceptions and beliefs create your life experience. This creative relationship can be illustrated using a functional concept of mind and body called the Life Formula. Here, mind and body meet and influence each other. The Life Formula can be written as

Event → Assessment/Perception → Response

The Life Formula can be called the Life Management Formula because it can help you understand and modify your personal experience of life. *The Life Formula states that life is a series of events that turn on assessments or perceptions, which in turn create responses.* The responses one experiences to an event depend not on the event, but on the perception or assessment of the event. A good place to see the Life Management Formula in action is in the study of stress. Reviewing stress as a response to a perception will help clarify how you use the Life Formula to create your stress and your life.

It is in your mind that you choose between unhealthful and healthful options.

The Life Formula states that life is a series of events that turn on assessments or perceptions, which in turn create responses.

61

Stress and the Life Formula

Observing stress provides a chance to see the mind-body connection in action. Try to remember that *in essence, your Stress Response is a response generated by your perceptions.* Where your mind creates stress, *you can learn to use your mind to create flow and peace of mind instead.* If you are like most people in our culture, you have learned to turn on the Stress Response to life events so well that you do so automatically, without conscious thought. Yet, the Stress Response itself is often one that your body has learned to turn on, through frequent, long-time practice.

One all-too-common example is the "worry" response. For some people, worrying has become an automatic, matter-of-fact response to common situations. Many people act as if worrying is supposed to be a part of life. They will even defend their worrying. Yet, worrying, too, is a learned response. Many people are caught up in negative patterns of responding to life, which they have learned. Too often, they have forgotten that there are other possible responses, besides the usual stressful ones.

So, with these ideas in mind, consider for a moment: What is stress to you? Think about it. Jot down your thoughts and note some examples for yourself on the lines below.

....

....

....

....

....

This question begins the process of examining what you mean by stress. *Stress is something that everyone experiences, yet it is different things to different people.* When asked about stress, many people describe it as something outside themselves. Stress is the boss, spouse, bills, traffic, or health.

One of the difficulties with these explanations is that if your concept of stress is that it comes entirely from outside yourself, it will seem to be much harder to manage than if you recognize that some of it comes from within. You have a better chance of managing what is within your sphere of influence—in this case, what is actually inside you. We can envision how many people understand stress by using a mechanical formula, illustrated as follows:

Stressful Event → Stress Response

This formula states that life is a series of stressful events, which cause Stress Responses. This mechanistic formula is more applicable to objects like billiard balls than to people. If the event is striking a ball with another ball, you can get an entirely predictable response. *With people, however, responses to an event may be quite varied.* For example, consider how different people think/feel about a rollercoaster ride. For some the response is joy and fun, while for others the response is fear and dread. The fact that a rollercoaster ride causes such different responses in different people suggests that the roller coaster ride (the event) itself is not the actual cause of the response. One or more other factors are creating the positive or negative response.

What do you think? What causes the different responses to the rollercoaster ride (event)?

....

....

....

....

....
Your perception of the rollercoaster ride.

You can easily recognize that what creates the response is the perception or assessment that a person makes of the rollercoaster ride. Your perception or assessment is what creates the difference between a positive or negative response to the same event. Thus, if you believe that you may get hurt on the rollercoaster ride, the accompanying response will be fear and avoidance. If you believe that the ride will be fun, the response will be a positive one and, perhaps, even a willingness to wait in a long line to get on the ride. A more accurate formula for describing this relationship between life events and your response will look like this:

Event → Assessment/Perception → Response

Rollercoaster ride → I could get hurt → fear, avoidance
Rollercoaster ride → This will be fun → excitement, wait in line

This relationship between event, perception, and response we have called the *Life Formula*. We will use it throughout this course to help you understand and modify your personal experience of stress and life events. The Life Management Formula states that life is a series of events that *turn on* an assessment or perception, which in turn *create* a response. *The response one experiences to an event depends not on the event, but on the perception or assessment of the event.* This statement is pivotal to understanding how life works and how you create your own reality, as well as your own stress.

Event—turns on → Assessment/Perception—creates → Response

This is one of the most important concepts in this course. When Balancing Act is presented as a six-week course, the first two weeks focus on understanding the Response part of the formula; the following three weeks focus on the Assessment/Perception, but no time is spent on the Event part of the formula.

What do you think? Why is no time spent discussing the "Event" part of the Life Management Formula?

....

....

....

....

....

No time is spent discussing the "Event" because usually you cannot control the events.

It is probably clear to you by now that no time is spent discussing the event part of the formula because, usually, the event has already occurred and, frequently, you cannot control life events. *However, you can influence your assessment and your response to your life's events.*

Though we may at times be able to influence events in our lives, most of our life events occur in an uncontrollable fashion. A quick review of the daily newspaper reveals the scope of this reality. From the weather to the economy to world events, we are met each day with the environment in which we live—like it or not. We are much more often in a better position to influence our responses to the event than the event itself. *Unfortunately, all too often people spend a great deal of time and energy analyzing and replaying an event that has already passed.* Reviewing and replaying how an event such as an illness, financial loss, or breakup of a relationship occurred may be invaluable to promoting growth and maturity and preventing further losses. However, people who repeatedly replay events may find themselves stuck and unable to move on. More answers are to be found by looking into the other parts of the Life Formula. *Highly effective people look more at their Assessments and Responses to create options for future actions.*

A common scenario in which you can see the consequences of people getting stuck on the event occurs when someone close to you goes through the breakup of a relationship. When your friend first talks about such problems, he or she is more apt to talk about the event (i.e., what

---

You can influence your assessment and your response to your life's events.

People spend a great deal of time and energy analyzing and replaying an event that has already passed.

happened and how it happened). After a while, the person will probably talk about his or her response to the breakup, how he/she is affected by it, such as feeling bad, can't sleep, etc. Talking about the event or the response to the breakup can go on for a long time, draining a lot of energy. As time goes by, time itself can help the healing process, even without the person gaining any more understanding of why the breakup was so difficult. However, if you want to speed up the healing process and increase your friend's understanding, you can encourage your friend to begin talking about her/his assessment of the event that created the painful response. Talking about the assessment of the event can help people understand why they are responding to the personal event as they are.

Highly effective people look more at their Assessments and Responses to create options for future actions.

In a more specific example, consider a young woman who was emotionally abused as a child. As a consequence, she has had difficulty trusting and engaging in healthy, long-term relationships. So she decides to see a therapist for counseling. During the early therapy sessions she describes the difficulties of her childhood and how traumatic her life at home was. In later sessions she will describe how her past has affected her and how it interferes with her developing healthy and lasting relationships. This phase can go on indefinitely, but it may produce changes.

Talking about the assessment of the event can help people understand why they are responding to the personal event as they are.

After many therapy sessions, the young woman is doing better and is capable of maintaining healthy relationships. What changed? Was it the event, the assessment, or the response? Obviously, the events of the past will remain the same. For healing to take place, what will have to change is how she perceives and understands the past events. She cannot change what took place at home during her childhood. However, she can learn to see it differently, perhaps to forgive her parents and, thereby, change her assessments of what happened. The new assessments will in turn create a more desirable response, which allows her to move on to healthier relationships.

Your Personal Stress Warning Signals

Rather than something outside you, your experience of stress is a response that occurs inside you. Your Stress Response is an individual response based on your personal interpretations of specific events. As you will see below, your Stress Response is also composed of a unique combination of your different responses. This becomes evident when you reflect on how your body lets you know when you are "stressed out."

Your stress response is composed of a unique combination of your different responses.

How does your body let you know when you are stressed? Give some examples.

....

....

....

....

....

Less often, people note mental thoughts and feelings as part of their response to stress.

When asked how they know they are stressed out, class participants usually describe their Stress Response in terms of different physical and mental responses. Most commonly, they mention body sensations like headaches, palpitations, muscle spasms, and even hunger. Some mention negative or pessimistic thoughts. Others feel nervous or irritable. Still others bite their nails or smoke more. When asked about their responses to stress, class participants usually describe two or three ways their bodies respond to stress. More often, they cite physical symptoms and behaviors, and *less often, they note mental thoughts and feelings as part of their response to stress.* Take a few minutes to find out: What are your personal stress warning signals?

Stress-Warning-Signals Exercise

Using the Stress Warning Signals worksheet below, take a couple of minutes to look over the various ways that people respond to stress. Check all the choices listed that describe the many ways that you can recall responding to stress in the past. If your own personal responses are not listed, like "biting finger nails," write them in, under "other." Add up your total number of stress warning signals.

B

BEHAVIORS

- ☐ Excess smoking
- ☐ Bossiness
- ☐ Compuolsive gum chewing
- ☐ Inability to get things done
- ☐ Grinding of teeth at night
- ☐ Overuse of alcohol
- ☐ Compulsive eating
- ☐ Attitude critical of others

E

EMOTIONS

- ☐ Crying
- ☐ Overwhelming sense of pressure
- ☐ Boredom—no meaning to things
- ☐ Edginess—ready to explode
- ☐ Easily upset
- ☐ Nervousness, anxiety
- ☐ Anger
- ☐ Loneliness
- ☐ Unhappiness for no reason
- ☐ Feeling powerless to change things

S

SENSATIONS

- ☐ Headaches
- ☐ Indigestion
- ☐ Stomachaches
- ☐ Sweaty palms
- ☐ Sleep difficulties
- ☐ Dizziness
- ☐ Back pain
- ☐ Tight neck, shoulders
- ☐ Racing Heart
- ☐ Restlessness
- ☐ Tiredness
- ☐ Ringing in ears

T

THOUGHTS

- ☐ Trouble thinking clearly
- ☐ Forgetfulness
- ☐ Lack of creativity
- ☐ Memory loss
- ☐ Inability to make decisions
- ☐ Thoughts of running away
- ☐ Constant worry
- ☐ Loss of sense of humor

Do any seem familiar to you? Check the ones you experience under stress. These are your stress warning signs.

Are there any additional stress warning signals that you experience that are not listed? If so, add them here:

....

....

....

....

Knowledge and awareness of your personal Stress Warning Signals are useful so you can intervene to avoid a full Stress Response.

When this exercise is done in class, the number of stress signals recognized usually ranges from under five to over thirty. Ten to fifteen stress warning signals are the average. During this exercise many people are surprised at the many different ways that their bodies signal them that stress is increasing. They did not recognize that negative thinking, memory loss, or overeating could be signs of stress.

This exercise gives you a snapshot of the varied ways that your body gives you early and late signals of your personal Stress Response. Whatever your number, this is a measure of your personal mind-body response to stress. *Knowledge and awareness of your personal Stress Warning Signals are useful, letting you know, as early as possible, that you are becoming stressed so you can more easily intervene to avoid a full Stress Response. For the sake of discussion, the stress warning signals can be divided into four interrelated groups of responses: Behaviors, Emotions, Sensations, and Thoughts.* We refer to this four-part response as the **B.E.S.T.** Response.

☯ **Return to breathing.**

Summary

The stress warning signals can be divided into four groups of responses: Behaviors, Emotions, Sensations, and Thoughts.

From childhood on, you are occasionally reminded that your mind can influence your life. Now you are being told that your mind creates your reality. Your patterns of response to your life events are individual and unique. Studying stress reveals the importance of your perceptions in creating your stress as well as your experience of everyday life. The Life Formula provides a tool for understanding the relation between perceptions of events and your responses. With awareness of your perceptions of life events, you have an opportunity to influence how you will respond. The way you respond to life can be described as Behaviors, Emotions, Sensations, and Thoughts. This four-part response can be called the B.E.S.T. Response. You have a personal BEST response to both positive and negative events.

Your B.E.S.T. Response

Your everyday life is experienced as (B)ehaviors, (E)motions, (S)ensations, and (T)houghts. These four variables that make up your everyday experience are called your B.E.S.T. Response. The B.E.S.T. Response occurs with both positive and negative perceptions but is often easier to observe in your response to stress. Your Stress Response provides you with the opportunity to witness your mind-body connection and the very individual and personal nature of your response to stress and life. The four parts of your B.E.S.T. Response are interrelated. You can influence the responses that you make to your life. By making changes in any one of the four areas of your responses, you can influence change in the other response areas and thus actually influence the way that you experience your life, including how you experience stress. Numerous mind body interventions are readily available to you and can be used to modify your B.E.S.T. Response.

☯ **Bring your attention to your breathing.**

In the Life Formula, life is a series of Events, and each event turns on an Assessment, which creates a Response. The Response part of the Life Formula represents your experience of the life event as your behaviors, emotions, sensations, and thoughts. The mnemonic BEST is useful for remembering these four interrelated parts of the Response: BEST stands for Behaviors, Emotions, Sensations, and Thoughts. These four types of responses occur regularly in your daily responses to everyday life events. Because stress is a common, important response that you experience to life events, it is a good place to study your B.E.S.T. Response. Effectively managing stress and increasing your personal energy can be accomplished much more easily when you learn to become aware of your own B.E.S.T. Response to stress.

Examples of the B.E.S.T. Response

Behaviors are physical actions, such as smoking, eating, pacing, talking, or napping.

Emotions are mental feelings, such as anger, frustration, fear, love, or joy.

Sensations are physical feelings, such as headaches, muscle spasms, or hunger.

Thoughts are mental self-talk, such as "Why me?," "I'm in trouble," or "I'm so lucky."

Stress management is about life management. Life is an ongoing process in which knowledge and awareness of your personal B.E.S.T. Response to the varied events that make up your life can help you in understanding yourself. Though much of the following discussion on the B.E.S.T. Response is about responses to stressful situations, it is important to see how this four-part response occurs in positive everyday situations as well.

In the Life Formula, life is a series of Events, and each event turns on an Assessment, which creates a Response.

The Life Formula and the B.E.S.T. Response are just as applicable for your use in observing positive situations as they are for your study of stress. For a positive and pleasant life situation, such as falling in love, you can easily predict a general B.E.S.T. Response. You can review a very specific response by recalling the last time you fell in love. For a person who is falling in love, the B.E.S.T. Response may look something like this:

Behavior: *acting and talking romantically*
Emotions: *feeling happiness, bliss*
Sensations: *feeling physically energized and alert, having little appetite*
Thoughts: *thinking optimistically about self, life, and surroundings*

The B.E.S.T. Response illustrates the mind-body connection in the closely coordinated sequence of both mind and body responses to life events.

Behaviors and physical sensations are categorized as "body" or physical responses. People with uncomfortable, painful, or uncontrolled body responses to stress are apt to seek help from medical providers with sensations like headache and fatigue or harmful behaviors like smoking or overeating.

Stress management is about life management.

Emotions and thoughts are categorized as "mind" or mental responses. People with "mind" or mental health concerns are more apt to go to psychiatrists, psychologists, or medical providers for help with anxiety or depressed moods/negative thinking.

It is important to recognize that the presence of this mind-body connection means that *body responses accompany mind responses, and mind responses accompany body responses.* If a response is present in the physical realm of the body, you can reasonably expect that a response will also be present in the mental realm of the mind.

As a family physician I often see patients for anxiety or depression. These patients generally do not come in saying they are feeling anxious or depressed. More often, patients with these mental disorders come in with physical symptoms such as fatigue, insomnia, or palpitations. In fact, one of the clues that a patient may be suffering from chronic anxiety or depression is frequent visits to the doctor or recurrent physical complaints for which no physical cause can be found. Needless to say, this can be frustrating for both the patient and the physician.

Understanding Your B.E.S.T. Response to Life Events

A closer look at how the four parts of the B.E.S.T. Response are interrelated can be provided by reviewing some examples from past workshops.

The first example is from the mother of a teenager.

The event: It is late at night and the teenager has not yet arrived home. The parent's assessment is that her child is delayed, perhaps because of a car accident. This assessment will usually elicit thoughts that her child is hurt and in danger. The thoughts will generate emotions like fear and worry. With these emotions, the body will produce physical sensations such as increased muscle tension and nervousness. As her nervous muscle tension builds up, her behavior includes pacing, trouble falling asleep, and venting anger when the teen arrives.

As is most often the case, this common scenario had a safe ending. A flat tire had delayed the teen. The parent's response was energy draining and reinforced an unhealthful pattern of reacting in a way that was potentially harmful to the mind and body. Most but not all parents would worry and respond in a similar manner. For your health's sake, you need to become aware of the harmful effects of worrying upon your mind and body.

Worrying and concern are not the same. Concern is having an interest in a desired outcome. This can lead to actions that will facilitate that outcome. Worrying, on the other hand, is closer to fear. Fear is a trigger for the Stress Response, and for that reason alone it must be checked. Unchecked fear leads to replaying negative consequences and inhibits constructive actions. One can be very concerned yet not give way to uncontrolled worrying. Not worrying does not mean that one doesn't

Body responses accompany mind responses, and mind response accompany body responses.

Unchecked fear leads to replaying negative consequences and inhibits constructive actions.

Not worrying does not mean that one doesn't care.

care. While concern can give direction, worry can drain energy without helping matters at all and, in fact, often makes matters worse. We need to work to avoid worrying, as we would avoid getting dirt on an open wound.

The second example is borrowed from my medical practice.

I called a patient after a routine mammogram to notify her that the radiologist had requested extra views. There were no specific abnormalities, but often, for the sake of being thorough, the radiologist asks for extra views of the areas in question. I left a brief message saying that we needed to get extra views with the mammogram. Two weeks later I saw the patient for a routine follow-up visit. She appeared tired and distraught. She told me that after my phone call, she had been extremely upset (emotion) because she was sure she had breast cancer (thought). Fatigue and nausea (sensations) accompanied her emotional response. As a result, she had trouble sleeping and lost weight due to poor eating (behaviors).

The extra mammogram views turned out to be quite normal, and the patient was then able to relax and to feel reassured. This is a common scenario where unchecked worrying causes unnecessary suffering. This is another example of a potentially harmful B.E.S.T. Response to a benign event. This scenario is replayed often in medical practice. Fear and worry can be debilitating, energy-draining responses that repeatedly reduce quality of life needlessly for many. A comprehensive mind-body approach to health must address the management of fear and worry. (I no longer leave any messages that can be misunderstood. I tell the patient that everything is okay and to please call me.)

In the above examples, **fear and worry could easily turn on the Stress Response with all its energy-draining consequences**. Considering the numerous negative effects of turning on the Stress Response, it is of utmost importance to reduce fear and worry. **If you can reduce the number of times that the Stress Response is turned on, you will experience less fear and worry.**

This can be health enhancing. The more you understand your B.E.S.T. Responses, the more options you have for influencing how you respond to life events.

Exercise

In the table listed below, review the B.E.S.T. Responses drawn from the examples discussed above. Use the rest of the table to insert B.E.S.T. Responses from your own experiences.

Event	Behavior	Emotion	Sensation	Thought
Teenager out late	Pacing	Fear, worry	Muscle tension	Danger
Mammogram report	Not sleeping	Fear, worry	Nausea, fatigue	I'm dying

Characteristics of the B.E.S.T. Response

The usual sequence of the B.E.S.T. Response is TESB.

Working with the B.E.S.T. Response table above, you can start to see characteristics of the interaction between the four parts of this response. You can begin to describe time sequence, congruency, connection, and interrelatedness.

What is the sequence, in time, of the four parts of the B.E.S.T. Response?

....

....

....

....

....

The actual sequence is TESB, but BEST is easier to remember.

We use the mnemonic BEST to help recall the four parts of our response, but *the usual sequence of the B.E.S.T. Response is TESB. Thought* is the first response to occur, followed by *emotion*, which is immediately associated with a body sensation. *In the B.E.S.T. Response to stress, the behavior occurs last, and it may be an attempt to reduce uncomfortable body sensations.* The behavior may be delayed, as in bingeing on ice cream or yelling at one's spouse when getting home after a stressful day.

In the B.E.S.T. Response to stress, the behavior occurs last, and it may be an attempt to reduce uncomfortable body sensations.

> *For example, a thought of danger turns on an emotion of fear. The fear is accompanied by a sensation of nausea. Due to the nausea, there will be food-avoidance behavior. Note that the behavior (in this case, food avoidance) is itself a response to the sensation. Likewise, when one is feeling very tense, the accompanying sensation may be a craving to practice behaviors like eating, smoking, and drinking. Pent-up tension may also lead to hitting someone or something (a wall, a pillow, etc.) to decrease the uncomfortable sensation within. In working with patients who are practicing unhealthy behaviors as described above, it is useful to reframe those behaviors as "attempts to self-medicate," in order to reduce their uncomfortable sensations and emotions. This reframing suggests that we strategize on ways to modify the thoughts and emotions,*

so that negative sensations do not build up, and the undesirable behavior is then less necessary.

In addition, other behaviors may be prescribed, such as breathing exercises or aerobic exercise to dissipate the built-up tension and avoid the unwanted behavior.

As you work with, and learn about, B.E.S.T. Responses, some of the following attributes of the four-part response will become apparent to you:

1. *Congruency. The four parts of the B.E.S.T. Response are congruent.* They have a similar quality and go together. If the thought or emotion is negative, the other parts of the B.E.S.T. Response will be negative as well. For example, if the thought is "They're trying to hurt me," the emotions will probably be fear and anger, rather than joy and fun.

   If the thought is "This is fun," the emotions and sensations that follow are likely to be pleasant.

2. *Connection. The parts of the response are usually connected—held together—like four mountain climbers.* If one goes up, it makes it easier for the others to go up. If one goes down, the others are also pulled down. For example, if your anger is lightened with humor, your thoughts will lighten up, and body tension (negative physical sensation) will decrease. If your body tension is decreased with a hot bath, your negative thoughts and emotional feelings will become less negative and move toward the positive.

3. *Interrelatedness. Changing the quality of one part of the B.E.S.T. Response will change the other parts of the response.* For example, if you are feeling very upset (emotion) and go for a walk, or take a hot bath (behavior), your emotional and physical tension will probably decrease.

Understanding the B.E.S.T. Response model reveals your unique and personal response to life events. In a stressful situation, some people respond with humor, while others will respond with cynicism or criticism. When worried, some people get headaches, while others experience a sensation of hunger or an urge for a cigarette. The "Stress Warning Signals" exercise in the previous chapter of this book helps reveal your personal pattern of responding to stress and supports a similar B.E.S.T. Response to positive events in your life as well. Awareness of the TESB sequence and knowledge of your stress warning signals allow for early recognition of stress so that you can intervene.

Knowledge of the interactive characteristics of the B.E.S.T. Response gives you functional tools to transform your B.E.S.T. Responses in everyday life. The following personal anecdote describes a stressful B.E.S.T. Response and how to turn it into a more positive experience.

The four parts of the B.E.S.T. Response are congruent.

Changing one part of the B.E.S.T. Response will change the other parts of the response.

Behaviors, such as my avoiding eye contact, are a late stress warning signal.

Recently, during a hectic day in my medical office, I noticed that I was avoiding eye contact and acting short toward the nursing staff. Concurrently there was a feeling of pressure in my chest. In addition there were fleeting thoughts like, "They're dumping on me," "They're giving me all the extra patients," and "Maybe that wouldn't happen if I weren't so nice." It finally occurred to me that these "feeling-sorry-for-myself" thoughts were my own early stress warning signals. The anger, chest pains, and avoidance behaviors were part of my personal B.E.S.T. Response. The pressure in the chest was the physical component of the anger I was experiencing. The avoidance of eye contact was a behavior consistent with the negative thoughts and feelings I was having. Once I became aware that these were signs of stress, I left the office for a walk around the block. Focusing on my breathing while I walked for ten minutes was enough to reduce my stress level from a high of nine out of ten to a more manageable level, of about six out of ten, which allowed me to return to work in a more comfortable state. Once my Stress Response had been reduced by walking, the negative Behaviors, Emotions, Sensations, and Thoughts disappeared.

I understood that the nurses were not being unfair to me. I wasn't being picked on. They were doing the best they could to get through a very busy day. Now, whenever I find myself feeling picked on, I know to look for other signs of stress. As I have found thoughts to be the first part of the B.E.S.T Response, these "they are picking on me" types of negative thoughts are an early warning signal of stress. Behaviors, such as my avoiding eye contact, are a late stress warning signal. Now, when I notice those negative "victim" thoughts, I interpret them as an early warning signal of stress. Knowing that the components of the B.E.S.T. Response are connected and interrelated, I know if I change one of the four parts, the rest will change. I have found changing behaviors more effective in changing my B.E.S.T. Response, especially if I am feeling overwhelmed. In the "victim" situation above, I chose an adaptive behavior like a short break to walk around the block or a relaxation exercise as soon as possible. In this way, I was able to change my B.E.S.T. Response and avoid those negative sensations (chest pressure) and behaviors (avoidance). Changing my B.E.S.T. Response had a positive effect on my experience of an otherwise difficult day, as well as on the hardworking staff and the patients seen that day.

The attributes of your B.E.S.T. Responses to life events create possibilities for changing your response to any event. *You can influence the response you have to life—at any time. You always have access to changing your response to a given situation.* Your personality and present circumstances will guide you to which of the four BEST components you should try to change first. The basic idea that "learning requires repetition" is applicable to whichever of the four responses you try to change. It may not be easy to change a behavior, emotion, sensation, or thought, but *every attempt facilitates future attempts. Just knowing that it can be done creates an opportunity and an option.*

Negative "victim" thoughts may be an early warning signal of stress.

You can influence the response you have to life— at any time.

You always have access to changing your response to a given situation.

*Just knowing
that it can be
done creates an
opportunity and
an option.*

Changing Your B.E.S.T. Response

It is not possible for any of us to understand everything about life. Often, it may be enough to know that life has certain basic characteristics, such as that described by the "Law of Action and Reaction"; that is, an action will always lead to a reaction.

New or different actions produce new or different reactions. We can consciously and intentionally apply this law of physics, or law of life, to create more-adaptive—and more-useful—responses (reactions).

Remember: the mind-body connection exists, and it is a two-way street. An action in the mind (thought/emotion) will cause a reaction in the body (sensation/behavior). Likewise, actions of the body will influence the mind. In order to use the mind-body connection for influencing change, remember that each part of the B.E.S.T. Response can itself be used as an action that will produce a reaction. For example, you can change your thoughts, and your emotions will change. Change your emotions with humor, and your thoughts and sensations will change. Change your sensations with a hot bath, and the other components will change too. With this insight into the interrelatedness of the four-part B.E.S.T. Response, let's review some useful ways that you can change your behaviors, emotions, sensations, and thoughts.

Influencing the Mind: Thoughts and Emotions

Thoughts and emotions are easily grouped together because they are both mental and closely intertwined. In some ancient teachings about the wisdom of life, thoughts and emotions are depicted as complementing each other. In one tradition, a very wise but very weak old man who is so weak that he cannot even walk represents the mind.

A very strong and powerful young man, who is blind, represents the emotions. Alone, neither one of them will do well in the world, in spite of their individual strengths. The wisdom in this story is made clear when the strong, young blind man places the wise, weak old man on his shoulders, and they go through life together. The wise old man is the eyes for the strong, blind young man, who in turn is the old man's strength.

This ancient story is meant to tell us something about how to manage our thoughts and emotions in life. Thoughts are quick and insightful, but they lack the power to get things done. For example, most people know what they have to do to be healthier, but they may not have the power to do it. Emotions, on the other hand, have a lot of power but often lack the light of awareness for making decisions. Lacking direction, you often invest a lot of energy into activities or relationships that are not good for you. *Thoughts without emotions are as unbalanced as emotions without thoughts. I think we do best when we use them together. Separated, both can lead you astray.* Learning to influence your thoughts and emotions, to help them work together, improves your chances of success in life.

Changing Thoughts

Thoughts are the most accessible of the four B.E.S.T. Responses. They are ever present and are often experienced as self-dialogue. Introducing other thoughts in the forms of positive self-talk, affirmations, or humor can be used to influence thoughts. Use Breath Awareness to help you as you observe your thoughts, so you can slow them down and make it easier to influence them with your self-talk.

Self-talk. You use self talk when you reassure yourself with internal—and verbalized—thoughts, such as "That chest pain is just gas and not a heart attack." You use it when you catch yourself worrying about being late and remind yourself to stop worrying about it. You use it when you remember the phrase "When life gives you lemons, make lemonade."

An important thing to recognize about self-talk is that you are already very practiced with it and have probably been using it since you were a small child—even though it may more often be negative than positive.

With a little more awareness you can soon be practicing much more positive self talk. Like most things you practice, it gets easier the more often you do it. *The mind-body connection will ensure that your positive self-talk has a positive influence on your B.E.S.T. Response.*

Here's an example of changing thoughts.

> *Years ago, after I had gotten into bed for the night, my wife, Ann, who was already in bed, asked me if I would go downstairs and get her a glass of water. My first thought was "Why don't you go? You are closer to the door." Fortunately, I didn't say anything. My thoughts were saying that it was a big hassle to go downstairs and get the water. I thought about it and asked myself, What's the big hassle, anyway? I figured it would take me about a minute or so to get her the water, so it was no real hassle. The benefit would be the brownie points I would get from Ann for doing it, and from the universe for helping someone. So, I ran downstairs and got the drink. She was happy. I felt good about it too. I thought I was learning how to get around the voice that tells us that things are harder than they really are. That voice doesn't really help much and actually creates unneeded negativity for me. A lesson from this experience is that a good way to change thoughts is to introduce a question, which challenges the thought you wish to change. Attempting to answer the question creates new thoughts and new possibilities. Once the thought is changed, the rest of the B.E.S.T. Response will change.*

We do best when we use them together. Separated, both can lead you astray.

Thoughts are the most accessible of the four B.E.S.T. Responses.

The mind-body connection will ensure that your positive self-talk has a positive influence on your B.E.S.T. Response.

Which occurs more often, negative worry thoughts or positive affirming thoughts?

....

....

....

....

....

....

Most class participants admit that a lot more time is spent replaying negative thoughts and feelings than positive ones.

Learn how to get around the voice that tells us that things are harder than they really are.

In class, when participants are asked how many have spent time worrying the previous day, most of them raise a hand. When asked how many of them spent time expressing gratitude for the good things in their lives, only a rare hand goes up. Most people practice indulging in more negative than positive self-talk. Change may seem difficult, but often it may just be a matter of practicing more positive self-talk to undo the tendency toward negative self-talk. If you accept—and internalize—the idea that negative self-talk drains energy and health, you are more likely to practice reducing negative and increasing positive self-talk.

Some experts recommend monitoring the number of times you engage in negative self-dialogue. Just the process of taking note of your negativity makes you more conscious of this tendency. Another idea is talking to yourself in a positive and supportive way. One easy way to do this is to point out to yourself the things that you are good at.

For example, I can say that I am a good dad, that I take good care of my car, that I give very caring medical service to my patients, that I make time to call my mom and visit often, and that I make time to pray and give thanks. Another technique is to try to express yourself as positively as you can. Instead of saying, "I'm an okay person," I can say that "I like myself!"

You can benefit from reminding yourself of the things you are good at doing.

Often, when I recommend that a client describe herself or himself in terms of something they are good at, the initial response is that they do not want to sound arrogant. I remind them that being arrogant is when people think they are better than someone else. Saying you are a good mother or a good worker is not arrogant. Saying you are a better parent than your brother or sister, or a better worker than your spouse, may be arrogant (as well as risky!). You can benefit from reminding yourself of the things you are good at doing. That is a reflection of self-acceptance and love.

Ways You Can Increase Positive Self-Talk

- Challenge negative self-talk with questions.
- Monitor the number of daily negative self-talks.
- Mentally or audibly list the things you are good at.
- Speak positively to yourself, as much as you would to encourage someone else.
- Speak positively to your mirror image.

Affirmations

Affirmations are simply expressions that are positive and validating. They are usually repeated either aloud or silently, mentally, to oneself. Some examples of affirmations are

- "The Universe provides all that I need."
- "Love is with me always."
- "Everything will work out as it is supposed to."
- "Each day I grow in love and awareness."
- "I choose peace instead of conflict."

Depending on your belief system, you can substitute the word "God," or "Spirit," for the words *The Universe* and *Love*, above. Any such word that has special meaning to you gives you the added bonus of a powerful, positive, and soothing effect. Affirmations are an effective way to change thoughts, because the constant repetition of them introduces and reinforces more-desirable thoughts and feelings into your everyday experience. *The mind-body connection will then see to it that these more-desirable thoughts and feelings will positively influence your physical sensations and, eventually, your behaviors.*

> *Years ago, the Reverend Jesse Jackson was shown on television giving a talk to a group of youngsters. He was urging his young audience to repeat the phrase "I am somebody!" As I listened to the segment on television, I realized that his simple phrase could be used to help people of all ages who are hampered by low self-esteem. It had to work. The mind-body connection would ensure that the emotions, sensations, and behaviors of those using that affirmation would be influenced, if they kept repeating and believing it. Reverend Jackson was using an affirmation to influence the young people in a positive way.*

You can be comforted that affirmations like this one, especially with the added support of group reinforcement, do work, because you are always on a continuum between low and high self-esteem. Practicing affirmations like this one will inevitably move you in the direction of higher self-esteem.

Challenge negative self-talk with questions.

Speak positively to yourself, as much as you would to encourage someone else.

The mind-body connection sees to it that desirable thoughts and feelings will positively influence our physical sensations and, eventually, your behaviors.

Humor

Humor is a quick and effective way to modify thoughts and emotions and the rest of the B.E.S.T. Response. One way to find humor in a thought is to magnify it, or to make it so irrational that it becomes nonsensical. Once you change the original sense or rationale of the thought, you change the thought and its accompanying emotion. The humor inherent in the new irrational thought usually will help mitigate any originally negative effect.

If you can find a humorous twist to whatever event you are facing, your thoughts and their accompanying emotions and sensations will change immediately. This may even influence your behaviors. As your response becomes less fearful and tense, there is less of a trigger of the Stress Response. Research has repeatedly shown that laughter and good humor are health enhancing and stress reducing. You will recall the mind-body research cited earlier, on the health benefits of humor.

While thoughts may be quicker and easier to influence, they may not have the sustaining power that emotions have. *A good laugh can move the emotions quickly away from fear and worry.* As stated earlier, there is power in emotions. Any time you can get your emotions behind an inspired thought or personal goal, you will find it is easier to persevere and follow through.

Changing Emotions

Emotions can be sweeping, strong, and overpowering. Their close relation to thoughts is undeniable. *If thoughts are the lines in a drawing, emotions provide the color.* The phrase to "get emotional" suggests thoughtlessness, being out of control, and irrationality. It can also mean vibrant, energetic, and full of life. While emotions can sometimes be difficult to control or change, there are various ways to influence them. Emotions can be changed by quickly challenging them with questions ("Why am I upset?"). Humor can also be very effective in modifying emotions. By using behaviors like walking, or running in place, to create different sensations, you can bring about change in your emotions too. Because emotions have close ties to thoughts, anything that changes our thoughts can also influence emotions.

Sometimes, you may be feeling so bad that a simple positive thought or affirmation is of little help. *In the face of a difficult emotion that needs to be changed, we can use emotionally charged thoughts, thoughts that evoke desired emotions.* Think of a time when you were very nervous and worried about a future outcome. It could have been whether or not you got a job or passed a test. It could have been whether a medical test result was normal or not normal.

In situations where the stakes are high and emotionally charged, telling yourself "don't worry" may be of little help. In these kinds of situations, using an emotionally charged thought to challenge the present emotional

Humor is a quick and effective way to modify thoughts and emotions and the rest of the B.E.S.T. Response.

A good laugh can move the emotions quickly away from fear and worry.

If thoughts are the lines in a drawing, emotions provide the color.

feelings would be more helpful. Emotionally charged thoughts such as spiritual or religious beliefs are related to one's personal core values, what one really believes in. To change worrying feelings, one can reframe worrying as not trusting that God or your Higher Power will provide.

Another option is to ask yourself, "How would Jesus or the Buddha (or any other strong positive influence in your life) handle this?" This may lead to lofty reflections on the meaning of the present difficulty and a shift in emotions, from worrying to considering the purpose and meaning of what you are experiencing. This kind of thinking, more correctly called *reflecting*, often leads to letting go (of the attempt to sustain perfect control on your own) and putting your trust in your Higher Power. *Recurrent and persistent feelings of anger may be reframed as energy draining and, therefore, harmful to your health.* You can focus your effort on acknowledging the anger that you are feeling and letting go of it.

Anger is an important emotion. We can do well to understand its benefits, and not just its dark side. In a given day, one is apt to experience anger numerous times. Anger serves an adaptive purpose. Like pain, it acts as a warning signal that something is not right and that your attention is needed to address an issue important to you. Anger is important because it points out your values and the things that matter to you. Your values may not always be the best, but even when angered because of selfish immaturity, anger is still a signal, which helps you learn more about who you are. Observing angry responses has helped me come to a realization about two basic reasons why I get angry with people or situations.

In simple terms, why do you think we get angry with people or situations?

....

....

....

....

....

We get angry when people don't do things our way,
or situations don't turn out our way

The Basis of Anger

Simply put, the basic reason we get angry at people is because they do not do things the way we think they should be done. They are not appreciating you the way you think they should appreciate you. They are not giving you the help or support you think they should be giving you. They are not giving you the respect or deference you think you should be getting from them.

In the face of a difficult emotion we can use emotionally charged thoughts that evoke desired emotions.

Recurrent and persistent feelings of anger may be reframed as energy draining and, therefore, harmful to your health.

This perspective on anger allows you to see how you want things to be, what outcomes are of value to you. This also gives others a picture of what your values are. The stronger your attachment to a value, the more anger you will experience when your expectation is not fulfilled.

The other reason for anger is because you think you have been hurt or caused to lose something important. An expected behavioral response to anger would be to attempt to control life and others. Trying to control others is a sure formula for suffering, for those you try to control as well as for yourself.

In many cultures, wise men and women have acknowledged that *suffering in life is an inevitable consequence of attachment to possessions or ideas, including emotions.* Those who can learn to live with fewer attachments are likely to experience less anger and less suffering in life. This is not to say that you should not have interests, likes, and preferences. Rather, you are served best by understanding the difference between preferences and needs. You define yourself by your preferences and your needs. Your preferences are the things you would like to have but do not need to have. Your needs are those things that you must have, such as love, food, water, and shelter. The more needs you have that are tied to other people's behaviors, the more it is possible for frustration and anger to follow when those needs are not met. It follows that the fewer needs you have, the more self-sufficient you become.

There is a saying that the person who wins is the one with the most toys. Perhaps it is better to say that *the person who wins is the one who needs the fewest toys, or—essentially—the one with the fewest attachments.* Reframing your anger, and looking at it as an attempt to impose your values upon others, may help you let go of the anger by giving up that selfish expectation.

When I am allowed, as a physician, to explore with a patient the story behind a set of chronic or recurrent medical symptoms that brought them to the doctor, anger is a frequent issue. *Many patients experience recurrent and chronic anger at work and at home.*

JM is a fifty-two-year-old woman, referred to our mind-body programs by her physician for help with fatigue and increasing body aches. The medical workup and testing revealed no treatable medical causes for her symptoms. JM was an attractive, well-dressed, and articulate person with a warm and gentle manner. In getting to the story behind the symptoms, we found a very hardworking, giving people-pleaser. The main frustration, she eventually admitted, was that her elderly mother was a constant aggravation to her.

Because her mother had been sick recently, JM made it her duty to drive from Chicago to northern Indiana three or four times a week to help her mother with shopping, cleaning, and household chores. The hardest part was that no matter what JM did, her mother was always complaining and critical of JM. During the initial consultation, JM was able to acknowledge that what she was doing was above and beyond the call of duty for being a good daughter. Her frustration and anger could be tied to her wanting her mother to change and behave in a sweet, grateful, and loving manner toward her.

JM was also able to acknowledge that her mother did not possess these nurturing personality traits, and that even at her worst, the mother was simply being her usual self. Rather than trying to change her mother, it was easier for JM to detach herself from the view that her mother had to be grateful. This was not easy, but it was made simple when JM could shift the problem from something that her mother was not doing to a solution that JM herself could achieve.

In this case, it was possible to make the shift, because JM considered herself a strongly spiritual person and a follower of Judeo-Christian teachings. By reframing her anger and frustration with her mother as a need to control her mother's reaction, she chose to let her mother be what she was. She chose to follow the spiritual idea that true love accepts others as they are. Acting from a higher purpose of love and charity, she was able to forgive her mother and release the anger that was tensing her mind and her body.

At her next two-week follow up visit, she reported more energy, less pain, and better sleep. In addition, she was able to plan her visits to her mother to fit better into her schedule, without having to act out of guilt or the need to please her mother. Visiting her mother was no longer painful. With the change in her attitude and supported by the use of daily relaxation exercises, JM gained health and well-being without changing her mother, who probably could not be changed anyway.

Chronic or recurrent anger can be debilitating and illness enhancing. When angry at others, you may try to control their behavior, to make it more your "right" way. *In truth, we are actually able to control very little in life, especially when it comes to others.* At best, you may sometimes be able to influence others somewhat, but *control* is a term best removed from relationships.

Try reframing anger as the desire to control others for not doing things your way. If you choose *not* to control others, you may become more open to accepting people as they are, and this acceptance leads to a significant reduction in anger. Controlling others does not fit into any whole-health plan. Giving up the attempt to control can free you from focusing on others' behaviors and allow you to turn toward focusing on your own energy balance. Your energy can be better spent developing your own strong habit of letting go, forgiving, and letting people be. This change can open the door to understanding the power of letting go and of forgiveness. Acknowledging emotional feelings, and then letting them go, is a powerful way to influence

Many patients experience recurrent and chronic anger at work and at home.

In truth, we are actually able to control very little in life, especially when it comes to others.

emotions and avoid much of the pain and energy drain of negative emotions. We will discuss more on forgiveness later, in the section on "Spirituality and Health."

Influencing the Body: Sensations and Behaviors

Sensations

Personal experience reveals how closely emotions are accompanied by changes in the body that we call sensations. The five senses of sight, hearing, smell, taste, and touch (including painful as well as pleasant touch) are the means by which the body receives its sensations. The sensations of perfect temperature on a beautiful day, the smell of cinnamon, or the taste of sweet watermelon all come to us through our physical senses. Due to the close relationship between emotions and sensations, described earlier in the section on "Stress Warning Signals," you can expect that changing your emotions will also change your sensations.

A humorous twist to a difficult situation can quickly change the sensations you are experiencing. Behaviors, as actions of the body, will influence the senses as well as the rest of the B.E.S.T. Response. When you go for a walk, you are creating sensations that are different from those you experience if you continue working. Some simple activities that change your sensations include a hot shower or bath, touch stimulation like a hug or massage, and

Try reframing anger as the desire to control others for not doing things your way.

Personal experience reveals how closely emotions are accompanied by changes in the body that we call sensations.

movement activity like aerobic exercise, yoga, or dance. Research has found physical activity, such as walking, jogging, and biking, to significantly reduce depression and anxiety and to enhance general well-being. Many of the mind-body interventions listed below are simple behaviors that stimulate the senses and positively impact emotional feelings and thoughts.

Changing Sensations

Sensations can be described as body responses. Sensations refer to the feelings of the physical body through the senses and nervous system. Palpitations, hunger, muscle tension, and pain are some examples of common sensations. *Sensations can be influenced by stimulating the senses of sight, smell, taste, hearing, and touch to produce different sensations* (see "Mind-Body Interventions," which follows). Awareness of your personal preferences in the use of your five senses can help you make substituting sensations an effective tool. Some people respond best to visual stimuli. Others may be more auditory and will respond better to certain sounds, like music. Since emotions are closely tied to sensations, activities that change emotions, such as humor, can also change sensations, as described above. Studies have found that laughter can increase pain tolerance, reduce muscle tension, and increase immune system competence. Emotions and sensations are also affected by scents. For some people, experimenting with scents has become popular, and aromatherapy can be an easy way to alter your energy and mood at home or work.

Pleasant or unpleasant scents can have a sudden and significant effect on our mood, and thoughts. The scent of freshly baked bread or a particular perfume is likely to conjure up thoughts and feelings related to past memories associated with those scents. The aroma of cinnamon and spice potpourri boiling in water may bring to mind memories of past holidays. You can easily experiment with favorite scents to find what works for you. Visit a fragrance shop and choose essential oils with fragrances that appeal to you or that are recommended for specific ailments. In the meantime, you might simply stop at your corner drug store and pick up some scented candles to start improving your energy with scents.

Behaviors

In the B.E.S.T. Response, behaviors are described as voluntary actions that attempt to lessen a sensation or restore it toward balance, or equilibrium of the body. When the emotion of anger is combined with the sensation of increased muscle tension, the behavior that follows may be throwing something breakable or punching a wall. The emotion of fear may be combined with a sensation of nervousness, and the behavior that follows may be increased talking. *Although these behaviors appear to be directed outwardly, they are seen here as being directed inwardly, to reduce the tension buildup.*

Sensations can be influenced by stimulating the senses of sight, smell, taste, hearing, and touch to produce different sensations.

Behaviors are seen here as being directed inwardly, to reduce the tension buildup.

The behavior may occur hours after the stress-producing stimulus.

It is easier to work with an individual once we label the undesirable lifestyle behaviors as energy-draining, maladaptive attempts to self-medicate.

When an emotional response like worry creates a hunger sensation, the balancing behavior is eating. *Note that the behavior may occur hours after the stress-producing stimulus.* That may explain the craving for ice cream or a cocktail once you get home after a difficult day at work. It is easier to understand unhealthful lifestyle behaviors if they are seen from the perspective of "attempts to self-medicate"; that is, a way of easing the uncomfortable buildup of emotional and physical tension, in response to everyday events.

As a physician coaching patients on lifestyle modification, *it is easier to work with an individual once we label the undesirable lifestyle behaviors as energy-draining, maladaptive attempts to self-medicate.* This way of reframing your perception of the behavior opens up possibilities to practice energy-gaining attitudes and behaviors to make you feel better. *Perhaps the most effective way to change behavior is to act or behave differently.* Actions create reactions. Behaving differently, practicing the new, desired, more adaptive behavior, is an effective way to influence the old, unwanted behavior. The essence of learning is repetition. Thus, the behaviors you practice, both the healthful and the unhealthful, are those that become easier and more automatic. *There are certain behaviors that are particularly useful for creating more- positive responses.* Among these are physical activity and relaxation exercises, which are simple, effective tools for improving energy and well-being, no matter what the original problem.

Perhaps the most effective way to change behavior is to act or behave differently.

In Balancing Act, *Breath Awareness (BA) is recommended as an essential tool and health-enhancing behavior for changing your B.E.S.T. Response. It requires no special equipment, can be done anytime and anywhere, and has low risk for injury. BA allows you to modify your B.E.S.T. Response instantly, by detachment.*

Anytime you are able to bring all your attention to your breathing, you must necessarily detach from the negative thoughts and emotions of the B.E.S.T. Response at hand. Recalling Father Link's words "If you can't stop doing bad things, do more good things," with practice you find yourself moving more easily and quickly toward a state of instant calm. There you become an observer, free from the consequences of judging others' actions, which most often do not require judgment on your part, anyway. As an observer who willingly suspends judgment, you receive two essential benefits: the practice of being in the present and the openness of mind to receive new impressions for future assessments.

There are certain behaviors that are particularly useful for creating more-positive responses.

The second best choice I recommend is walking. It also requires no special equipment, or expense, and is quite safe. We recommend starting with twenty-minute walks three times a week and then building up to seven days a week. The important thing is to develop the habit of taking time out for physical activity. From a mind-body perspective, walking's greatest benefit is in reducing built-up emotional and physical tension. Walking is generally quite effective in changing your overall B.E.S.T. Response. The next time you are very upset or stressed out, take a subjective measure of how you feel on a 1-to-10 scale (10 being the best). Then go for a twenty-minute walk. After the walk, you'll usually find a significant improvement in your tension score. Although this improvement in energy and feelings may be temporary, it is worthwhile. It is reassuring to know that there is a natural remedy that is readily available, which works to make you feel better. It also gives you hope that there is a way out of your present difficulties. If you cannot walk, there are other physical activities that you can choose from.

☯ **Return to your breathing.**

Summary

Much of your response to everyday life events can be described as a combination of behaviors, emotions, sensations, and thoughts. You can help yourself to remember this sequence by using the mnemonic acronym BEST. This four-part response is present in both positive and negative experiences. The four parts of your B.E.S.T. Response are interrelated; changing one can change the others. Thoughts are often the easiest part to change, but you may find that changing your thinking is hard to maintain. Emotions and sensations are harder to change initially but ultimately will have more influence on the other parts of your response. Behaviors may be the most difficult to change initially but can have a very strong and lasting influence on your overall response to life. Breath awareness is an especially useful behavioral change for modifying the way that you experience life events, because it can help you avoid quick, knee-jerk responses and make you more relaxed and calmly receptive.

The important thing is to develop the habit of taking time out for physical activity.

Much of your response to everyday life events can be described as a combination of behaviors, emotions, sensations, and thoughts.

Your Assessments Create Your Life

There is wisdom in understanding that your perceptions influence your life. The Life Formula explains this relationship between life events and your experience of them. The response or experience you have to an event in your life is created not by the event itself, but by the assessments or perceptions you make of the event. What is going on within you, in turn, influences what perceptions you make. Within you are your past experiences, genetics, culture, religion, and many other permanent variables. Temporary variables like hunger, pain, and illness also influence your assessments. The perceptions you choose, whether right or wrong, will create personal responses that are consistent in quality with the perceptions. Verifying an assessment reduces the energy-draining responses of false assessments. As your assessments are created in language, so the words or language that you use about yourself, about others, and about life itself creates much of your everyday experience of life.

☯ Bring your attention to your breathing.

The idea that you create your own reality, and thus your experience of life, is a provocative concept. During my late teens and college years I often heard this idea, yet no one really explained it to me. To some it may sound reminiscent of other times and philosophies—of the 1960s, or of New Age thinking, or of Buddhist philosophy—and it is true that we can find references to this idea in most paths to enlightenment. The truth in this concept is a powerful aid to a self-improvement program like Balancing Act because it supports the possibility of change for the better. The Life Formula describes this creative relationship between your perceptions of life events and life experiences.

The Life Formula

Event—turns on → Assessment/Perception—creates → Response

The Life Formula states that life is a series of events, which turn on your assessments of the events, and these assessments, in turn, create the responses you experience as life.

Usually, the responses to life events happen so quickly that you may have the illusion that the responses are caused solely by the events. Recall the previous discussion about how an event, such as a rollercoaster ride, can elicit two opposite responses: fear and fun. While for some, the response to a rollercoaster ride might be that it is fun, for others the response to the same ride might be that the experience is one of terror. This simple observation suggests that the response to the rollercoaster ride is not the result of the event itself. So, if not the event, what is it that creates the response? It seems clear that the creator of the response to the event is the perception of the ride that is held by the person who is experiencing it. The different perceptions create the different responses.

There is wisdom in understanding that your perceptions influence your life.

The word "perception" refers to the way you see things, to the meaning that you give to them. The significance of perception is that the meaning you give to an event or situation creates how you think about, feel toward, and react to the event. *There is wisdom in understanding that your perceptions influence your life.* Your responses to life events are not as spontaneous as they appear. They are usually preceded by your perceptions. Other closely related terms to the word *perception* are *belief, perspective, understanding, evaluation,* and *assessment.* I prefer the word *assessment* to the word *perception* to describe the interpretation or meaning that a person gives to an event or situation, because it emphasizes the role of the person's thought processes in how they will experience an event. *Here, in describing the thought processes, perception and assessment may be used interchangeably.* Assessment implies an active interpretation of an event that is based on personal knowledge and experience. As such, *assessments may change* as knowledge and experiences change.

Here, in describing the thought processes, perception and assessment may be used interchangeably.

In modern medicine, the word *assessment* is used to describe the diagnosis of a medical problem. The assessment, or diagnosis, is the doctor's best interpretation of the signs and symptoms found in the patient. The symptoms, such as fatigue, chills, pain, or dizziness, are what the patient experiences. The signs are the additional objective, observable findings, noted by the physician examining the patient, such as fever, wheezing, open wound, skin rash, etc.

The interpretation—or assessment—of the signs and symptoms will depend on the physician's level of medical knowledge and experience. It is important to emphasize this point. The medical assessment depends ultimately on the diagnostic abilities of the clinician—and not on the simple existence of the signs and symptoms that the patient presents to the clinician. The symptoms and signs constitute the *event* being interpreted. A different clinician might make a different diagnosis of the same history of symptoms and physical findings. The important thing is that whether the assessment or diagnosis is right or wrong, the actions taken to care for the patient will depend on the assessment the physician has made. *In life, as in medicine, the responses to events depend on the assessments made of those events.* Just as the assessments made in medicine are a creative force, the assessments you make in life to daily events are of major importance in creating your experiences of life.

Why are perceptions/assessments important for you to understand?

....

....

....

....

....

....

Perceptions/assessments are your interpretations of an event or situation.
They create your responses to the event.

Physicians are trained to write notes in your medical chart, using a method called the SOAP method. The SOAP method is a comprehensive way of recording the doctor-patient interaction. Each letter stands for a different part of the interaction.

S *stands for* **Subjective**. *This is what the patient describes as the medical problem or symptoms: "I feel miserable, my head hurts, and I feel chilly."*

O *stands for* **Objective**. *This refers to the physical findings that the physician observes during the physical exam. This includes temperature, blood pressure, and the physical appearance of the patient. It includes the results of laboratory tests, EKGs, x-rays, and other tests, which provide objective information.*

A *stands for* **Assessment**. *This is the interpretation, or analysis, which the physician makes of what the patient has said and what the physician can observe by listening, examining, and testing. The assessment is the physician's best explanation of the signs and symptoms and test results. It is not necessarily the truth or the correct assessment. The assessment or diagnosis is the best interpretation the physician can come up with, given the available information and the physician's medical experience and diagnostic skills.*

In life, as in medicine, the responses to events depend on the assessments made of those events.

P *stands for* **Plan.** *The plan, or response to the patient's medical problem, is based on the assessment. The plan is a reasonable and often-predictable response to the assessment made by the physician of the patient's subjective and objective information.*

Example

S: *A twenty-five-year-old man complains of a runny nose and feverish feeling.*

O: *On exam, the patient exhibits a temperature of 100.4°F, and a clear nasal discharge. The rest of the exam is normal.*

A: *The patient has a cold or upper respiratory infection.*

P: *Rest, fluids, and symptomatic treatment.*

If, the next day, the patient returns with facial pain, green nasal discharge, and a higher fever, plus the above findings, the assessment would change to bacterial sinusitis. As the assessment changes from viral infection to bacterial sinusitis, the plan changes, too, and now includes an antibiotic. As in medicine, our assessments create the responses we make to our lives' events.

Why is it so important to understand that the assessment creates the response?

....

....

....

....

....

If the assessment creates the response to your life event,
it creates your life too.

Our assessments
are important
as the cause of
how we think,
feel, and
behave.

If our assessments, rather than external events, create our responses to life, then *our assessments are important as the cause of how we think, feel, and behave.* In light of this fact, we would be wise to become knowledgeable about how assessments are made, what influences them, and how to use them to our advantage.

Our assessments may not be the truth, but our best interpretations of events, at any given point in time. Another important concept is that while any given event could trigger many assessments, once an assessment has been made of an event, the field of responses is narrowed down significantly. To emphasize the dynamic aspect of this relationship between assessment and response, we can say that the assessment *creates* the response.

The *Event-Assessment* half of the Life Formula is more variable and less predictable than the Assessment-Response half.

Event → triggers → Assessment
                         (less predictable, more variable)

Different people assess an event in different ways, and any two people may have similar assessments, but for different reasons. When an event occurs, there are at least as many different ways to assess it as there are different people.

> *If a loud noise is heard outside (the Event), it can trigger numerous assessments. Some may interpret it as a car backfiring, while others hear a gunshot or fireworks. The assessments made will depend on expectations and past experience. Of course, if a person is totally deaf, no assessment is triggered. Or, two people may appear to have similar assessments, but for very different reasons. Two friends may like a particular music group, but for different reasons. One likes the voice of the lead singer, while the other one likes the band's driving rhythms.*

In contrast, the Assessment-Response half of the Life Formula is more predictable and less variable than the Event-Assessment half.

Assessment → creates → Response
                         (more predictable, less variable)

Once you know the assessment, the nature of the response may be more predictable. *The response that follows will usually be appropriate for the assessment.* Conversely, you can look at a response and get an understanding of what kind of assessment had to take place to create that response. *Once you understand the kind of assessments people around you are making, you may choose to work with their assessments rather than focusing on their responses.*

> *While an event may trigger many assessments, once an assessment is made, the number of appropriate responses decreases. This part of the Life Formula is mechanical and constant. When an assessment is made, the response that follows is usually congruent in quality with that assessment. The assessment itself may be incorrect or false, but it will still create a response that is consistent with the assessment.*

> *For example, you see a friend at a distance, and you wave hello. Your friend appears to look your way and then looks away without waving back. If your assessment is that she is ignoring you, your feelings may be hurt, and your behavior might be to withdraw from her and even to criticize her. If your assessment is that she is so preoccupied that she did not notice you, your response may be more caring. You may stop later to ask how she is, to offer support, or to invite her to go somewhere to talk.*

Our assessments may not be the truth, but our best interpretations of event, at any given point in time.

The response that follows will usually be appropriate for the assessment.

The Nature of Assessments

Once you understand the kind of assessments people around you are making, you may choose to work with their assessments rather than focusing on their responses.

As you begin to examine the assessments made by you and those around you, you may find yourself feeling more understanding of yourself and others. That is good for your health and energy. Here is another example to help understand how your assessments, and not the events, create your responses.

> *One day, you are walking down the street, feeling good, minding your own business, and someone bumps into you. You sort of bounce off the person and keep going. Maybe you mumble, "Pardon me," but you don't even look back to see who it was. You just go about your business and don't give it another thought. Another day, you're upset about a previous argument and preoccupied with your negative thoughts, and someone bumps into you. This time you stop, give them a big scowl, and maybe even say something like, "Why don't you watch where you're going!" It's the same event, but with a different response.*

What caused the different response?

....

....

....

....

The inner state or mood you are in creates a different response to a similar event.

The way you are thinking or feeling before someone bumps into you is setting up the way in which you are going to respond. The bump, or the person bumping into you, did not cause the response. Since your assessments determine much of your life experience, let's look at where assessments come from and what influences them. The following example can help illustrate an insightful aspect of the nature of assessments.

The way you are thinking or feeling before someone bumps into you is setting up the way in which you are going to respond.

Picture of 3 balloons with air, water, and ice

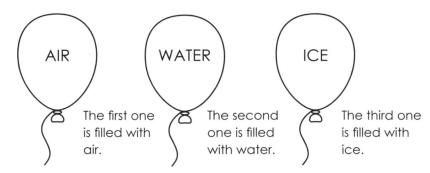

AIR — The first one is filled with air.

WATER — The second one is filled with water.

ICE — The third one is filled with ice.

The event is going to be the piercing of each balloon surface by a sharp needle. This event is the same in all three cases.

What is the response, in each case, to the same event?

No. 1: ....

No. 2: ....

No. 3: ....

The balloon with air pops. The one with water leaks.
The frozen one doesn't change.

The event in all three is the piercing of the balloon surface, yet there are three different responses. The one with air pops, the one with water leaks, and the frozen one has a little hole but doesn't change much.

So, although the event was the same—the piercing of the balloon surface—there were three different responses.

What caused the different responses in the three balloons?

....

....

....

....

....

The different responses are due to what was inside—
the preexisting contents of the balloons.

What is inside each balloon—its preexisting content— affects how it will respond to a particular event. This example suggests that *the internal makeup of the object experiencing the event is what creates responses, not the event itself.* Applied to people, this means that *what is inside a person is important in influencing how a person will respond to events in life.*

> *At a conference I attended years ago, Deepak Chopra related an old teaching story that I still use in my workshops. A student asked his teacher, "Master, do we live in the same world?" This was a good question, because the student had noticed that the Master acted differently from the student in various situations. When the monsoon rains came for weeks, the Master handled it differently from the way the student handled it. When the famine came, the Master handled it differently. When thieves raided the monastery, the Master responded differently from the student. So, the student was asking a good question; namely,*

The internal makeup of the object experiencing the event is what creates responses, not the event itself.

"Do we live in the same world?" The Master answered, "Yes, we live in the same world. But you see yourself in the world. I see the world in me."

What did the Master mean?

....

....

....

....

....

What is inside a person is important in influencing how a person will respond to events in life.

The Master was trying to explain to the student why they appeared to be living in different worlds. The student responded to outer events. If it was sunny, the student felt *up*; if it was rainy, he felt *down*. The Master responded to his own inner interpretations of the events. If it was rainy, he saw an opportunity to read or write indoors. The Master knew that his experience of the world was subject to his inner assessment of the events occurring around him.

This brief story illustrates the essence of the Life Formula, that the assessments you make of life events create your experience of life. In this teaching story, the student lacked awareness of the truth that perceptions create our reality. To "see yourself in the world" is to react automatically to events, without awareness that in a fraction of a second our very personal assessments are determining our reaction. To "see the world in me," as the Master did, is to realize that our interpretation of the event is the final arbiter or creator of our experience.

With this newfound awareness of how we create our lives, we can see that it is possible to create new experiences. Knowing this, the Master could see the rainy day as a happy event, rather than a sad one. Knowing that it is possible is not the same as doing it, however. Learning "to do" requires practice. With practice, this awareness of how we create our lives becomes an opportunity for creating a more balanced life. It is not easy, but it can be done. In adult life there are few things as effective for easing the burden of everyday life as this lesson of learning to create your life from within, by managing your assessments.

The Variables That Influence Your Assessments

Your assessments are influenced by numerous variables. We can divide the various influences on our assessments into two groups—*the permanent* and *the temporary.*

Permanent Influences	Temporary Influences
Genetics	Hunger
Past experience	Pain
Culture	Mood
Gender	Finances
Age	Illness
Education	Energy level

What kinds of general variables influence your assessments?

....

....

....

....

....

Numerous factors, such as culture, gender, age, education, experiences, hunger, pain, and finances, influence your assessments.

The permanent variables include genetics, culture, gender, past experiences, education, and age. Temporary variables change from moment to moment and include hunger, pain, mood, finances, illness, energy level, and finances. Some variables, such as your age and experience, change with time and exert different influences on your assessments over the years. You generally can't change the permanent variables, but you can effectively change temporary variables, such as your energy level.

Generally, activities that improve your personal energy will make it easier to choose more-positive assessments. When you are tired or hungry, you are more likely to become frustrated and irritable. Taking time for a short nap or meditation can boost energy and increase the likelihood of a more positive assessment. A small amount of high-quality food can have a similar effect. Taking pain medication early in the development of a painful condition can influence the quality of the whole day. A brisk walk for twenty minutes increases alertness and reduces the tension of a difficult day. The idea is to be aware of temporary variables that you can alter to help yourself feel better.

With practice, this awareness of how we create our lives becomes an opportunity for creating a more balanced life.

Your assessments are influenced by numerous variables.

Choosing activities that increase your personal energy can positively influence assessments.

Feeling better and with more energy, you are more likely to choose more-positive assessments. Due to the correlation between personal energy level and well-being, *choosing activities that increase your personal energy can positively influence assessments.* The energizing mind-body interventions discussed in chapter 4 can also be used to positively influence your assessment-making process. As you become familiar with how energy influences your assessments, you can practice shaping your assessments and your responses to life.

Your Assessments Reflect You

The combination of permanent and temporary variables that influence assessments can be very different from moment to moment and from day to day. *Your assessments thus reflect a combination of these variables at any given point in time.* More succinctly, your assessments reflect what is going on within you, and, likewise, the assessments that others make reflect what is going on within them. If people are living according to their assessments, then they are doing what they think is right. This leads to another pearl of awareness that has saved me much aggravation and suffering: *most people are functioning at their best level.*

To say that someone is functioning at her or his best level means that at a given point in time, like you, that person is doing the best that he or she can, according to the assessments and skills that they have available at the time. This does not mean that they would not do better with more training or counseling. It means that at a given point in time, *most people, like you, are doing the best that they know how.* Even if, to you, they are doing a shoddy job, on some level, they think that it is okay to do it the way they are doing it. A person who steals from you or cheats you has decided, on some level, that this is what he or she should be doing to provide for him—or herself. That person who does not return your call is probably returning whatever calls he can, given his criteria or priorities for which calls need to be returned. Until that person develops more awareness, or life management skills, that individual must necessarily continue to do things the same way; the way he knows.

Having this view of others can reduce your stress and save you energy by freeing you from having to judge and react negatively to people who are usually just doing what they think is right. Interestingly, even if they say they know it is wrong, they are doing it because on some level they think it is OK to do so—they are making choices based on the pressures in their own lives *as they perceive them.* This perspective allows you to see that *the people who disappoint you are usually not trying to disappoint you. They are just trying to get through life.* They are just doing things their way, just as you do things your way.

When despite your disappointment you accept that people are doing their best at the moment, you are not excusing people's behavior. Rather, you are acknowledging that you don't know the whole story and that you are better off to avoid making an absolute assessment at all. If it is a situation where correction of a behavior is required, you may, instead, focus on communicating your request more effectively or teaching the person how to do the task differently. Other options are to focus on your breathing and leave the person(s) alone, or distance yourself from them. The point is that *you can save energy and pain if you accept people where they are, rather than constantly reacting to other people's way of living their lives or trying to change them.* Awareness of this point allows you to understand others better, especially when they disagree with you or don't meet your expectations. Even if you don't like or share their assessments, you can remember that their way of assessing a situation is as much a part of their uniqueness as your assessments are of yours.

> *Many times in a day I am tempted to respond negatively to people's behavior that I find disappointing or frustrating. One thing that used to infuriate me was when a taxi driver in front of me stopped abruptly to let out a passenger. Instead of pulling over to the curb, the driver would stop in the middle of the street, causing the traffic behind him to stop too. I would quickly respond in a loud tirade of choice words while leaning on my horn. With time, I reflected and noted that my strongly negative response to a common event in city traffic suggested that I had made some strongly negative assessment about the taxi driver stopping in traffic. When I chose to think that the driver may not have known better at the time, my response became less dramatic. Choosing to think that the driver was doing the best he knew, given his inner and outer conditions, allowed me to experience a less painful, less energy-draining reaction. I forgave the behavior without thinking of forgiveness. I was able to let it go. Later, when I had learned to practice Breath Awareness while driving, I could observe the taxi stopping as before, but with minimal, if any, reaction.*

An illustration of the fact that people react at their best levels according to what is within them can be found in the different ways people respond to an illness. *While some respond with fears and worries, others respond with positive attitudes and behaviors;* some respond as victims, and others take charge of their lives.

The different responses to an "illness" event can be accounted for by the significantly different assessments of the "meaning of the illness" to different individuals. Such assessments are reflections of the uniqueness and individuality of each person. Assessments are as unique to an individual as fingerprints. In the face of illness, some see danger and opportunity, while others see only danger. It is interesting to note that *the Chinese word for "crisis" includes two symbols: one means danger; the other, opportunity.* In the face of a perceived crisis, the perception of danger without opportunity is a reflection of the individual who is likely to turn on the Stress Response. Awareness of this point allows you to better understand your responses,

You can save energy and pain if you accept people where they are, rather than constantly reacting to other people's way of living their lives or trying to change them.

and also to better understand others, especially when they disagree with you or you don't like the way they respond to an event.

As a physician, I have had much opportunity to observe illness behavior for more than thirty years. Most patients appear to interpret illness as a bother, an obstacle to be removed, so they can go on with their lives. For them, a prescription is all that is needed to make things right and allow them to go on their way. For a few, illness becomes a time for reflection about life and where they are going. Some people are able to turn their lives in the direction they want, after grappling with illness. This is true with something as common as the flu and is even more striking in the face of life-threatening illnesses, such as heart attack or cancer. In serious situations, people respond according to their assessments. Those who see their illness "crisis" as an opportunity to get their lives on track respond positively. For these people, a mind-body-spirit approach to health enhancement becomes a journey that leads to a more meaningful life. Some have said that if it had not been for the heart attack or cancer, they never would have found their way to where they were supposed to be. As for me, I often tell my patients that I learn more about health— and life—when I am sick than when I am well.

How Assessments Create Your Stress Response

Assessments can be categorized as positive or negative, in terms of the quality of the response created. A positive assessment is one that creates a desirable, energizing, or health-enhancing response. For example, an assessment that "things are going to be all right" helps create a sense of peace and tranquility, as will an assessment that "you are a child of a God, who loves you very much."

A negative assessment is one that creates a threatening response, which is likely to turn on the Stress Response. Perhaps the most-common negative assessments are those associated with worrying. Clearly, much of our everyday Stress Response is preceded by negative assessments.

Most people have more practice making negative assessments than positive ones. So, by applying the Life Formula to our negative assessments, we begin to see how our everyday experiences (thoughts, feelings, sensations, and behaviors) of stress and worry are created by the way we look at life events.

The creative use of assessments is applicable to positive assessments as well. When you practice positive assessments with the use of affirmations, inspirational reading, or prayer, the response created will be along the lines of hope, love, and peace of mind. As you observe the various assessments you make of life events, you soon realize that *many of your everyday assessments are not true.* This is important because *whether your assessments are true or false, they are creating your life today,* through the thoughts, emotions, physical sensations, and behaviors you experience as living. Nonetheless, negative assessments are likely to create uncomfortable, and possibly painful, experiences. Too often, then, stress is a painful experience of life based on a negative assessment that you chose for yourself.

What kinds of assessments create the Stress Response?

....

....

....

....

....

The Stress Response is created by assessments of danger or loss of something important, such as loss of life, health, power, love, money, or energy.

Assessments: Maybe True, Maybe False

The assessments you make can be divided into verified or grounded assessments and unverified or ungrounded assessments. *Verified assessments are those in which there is reliable evidence or consensus that an assessment is true.* The unverified assessments are those for which there is little or no evidence. *Another word for unverified assessment is opinion.* The following are examples of each type of assessment.

Verified	Opinion
It's Monday.	It's a bad day.
The Dallas Cowboys are 8 and 2.	The Dallas Cowboys are the best team.
He fell.	He is clumsy.
I don't know the answer.	I am stupid.
She hasn't called back.	She doesn't care.
It is 85 degrees outside.	It is too hot.

Note that people don't usually disagree over verified assessments. People don't usually argue whether it is 85 degrees or not, if the thermometer says so. They argue about whether it is too hot or not. This is an opinion.

When you start thinking of your assessments as verified or opinion, which one is more common?

....

....

....

Rarely does someone describe stress as caused by her or his perceptions.

Stress is an inside job.

Verified assessments are those in which there is reliable evidence or consensus that an assessment is true.

....

....

We usually make more unverified assessments than verified ones.

If you look at most of the assessments you make during the day, you find that a large share of your daily assessments are simply opinion. This may come as a surprise because people commonly assume that they are working with thought-out, verified assessments. In truth, we most often are working out of old, automatic ways of looking at things. Some very common ungrounded assessments include the following:

"I'm going to be late."
"This is going to be awful."
"It's going to be a terrible day."
"I've lost my … forever."

Unverified assessments like the ones listed above usually turn out to be incorrect or false. You get there on time. You survive the difficult situation. Your day turns out okay. You find whatever you lost. However, it is also true that every time you indiscriminately think or express these ungrounded ideas, your body must necessarily respond to them as if they were true. *The body dances to the music of the mind.* Since your assessments are creating your responses to your life situations, it is in your best interest to practice verifying the truth in your assessments as often as you can. Verifying assessments will help reduce the problems, misunderstandings, and unnecessary conflicts that you experience.

Verifying assessments can lead to less energy drain and suffering. If you don't acknowledge and avoid false assessments, they will keep you in a negative life-draining cycle that you think of as a "normal part of life."

The Importance of Verifying Assessments

Having recognized the importance of assessments in creating your life, it becomes more important to discern true from false assessments, especially since negative assessments tend to be more common than positive ones. When you assess everyday situations as threatening, you are exposed to potentially harmful physiological and psychological changes. If the threat is real, you must respond appropriately. However, in the more common situation when the negative perception is not true, you are likely to experience variations of the Stress Response that are unnecessary and can cause you needless suffering and energy drain.

The good news about life is that most of the negative assessments we make daily are false. *Most of the bad things we worry about never happen.* Since the body cannot always discern which assessments are true, it is important to be able to evaluate or verify how true an assessment is. Verifying your negative assessments quickly reveals many misleading, false assessments. Reducing the number of false assessments that we make can save energy, reduce stress, and improve the quality of everyday life.

When I was running late to the airport, I made the flight. When my daughter came home late without calling, she had not been in a car accident. When I worried about my patient's minor surgical wound, everything healed fine. Again and again, I see that most of the negative assessments I make do not turn out to be correct. More significantly, when I think about my major problems in the last ten years, I can see that almost all of them turned out quite well or at least a lot better than I thought they would. The abnormal mammogram Mom had was not cancer. My daughter Nicole's abdominal pain was not appendicitis. The changes at work were difficult at times, but they turned out fine. All the problems with finishing our basement resolved themselves. The sailboat was put away later in the season than I had hoped, but without any problems. Looking back at my life, I can't remember as many terrible things actually happening as I remember worrying about. Most of the bad things I worried about just never happened.

False assessments can often create unwanted, or even disastrous, outcomes. *Responding to false or ungrounded assessments is likely to create chaos and confusion in your life.* It will surely lead to more stress and a waste of energy and time. It is like building a house on sand, rather than on stone. Assessments that are correct or closer to the truth create possibilities for growth and awareness. Even when the assessment is a negative one, such as having a terminal illness, the possibilities for an enriching and deeper experience are still available. As sure as "the truth will set you free," verified assessments will free you from hardships and suffering that so often follow false assessments. The more truthful your assessments, the better you can see what is going on and the more likely you are able to respond appropriately. It is important to know how to verify your assessments.

How to Verify Assessments

Let's review a previous scenario to explore the benefits of verifying assessments. You are at work, and you see a colleague down the hall. You wave at her, and she looks your way but does not acknowledge your greeting. The truth is she is so overloaded with work that although she looked in your direction, she didn't really see you. Now the ball is in your court. If you decide that she is just being rude and ignoring you, your response will be to avoid or ignore her. If, however, you decide that she is so overloaded and stressed out that she could not even respond to you, your response will be more supportive. How do you decide which is the correct assessment?

Verifying
assessments can
led to less energy
drain and
suffering.

How could you verify your assessment?

....

....

....

....

....

You could ask her why she did not respond to your greeting.

You could verify your assessment by simply asking a question. *Asking questions has long been one of the paths to truth, knowledge, and wisdom.*

Questions are used to move you as close to what is true as you can be. Once you have a verified assessment, your response will be more correct than if you are misjudging a situation. It may mean admitting your mistake, at least to yourself. It may mean doing something you don't want to do, like firing someone. *When working with verified assessments, there is strength and comfort in going with what is true rather than with what is false.* If you made a judgment, such as "She's rude," your responses are likely to be negative and limited. There is not much room for discussion, if you choose the superficial negative assessment. She has been judged and found guilty. Verifying assessments creates more possibilities for growth and harmony. In the above example, if you are not able to ask your friend if she was ignoring you, it is best to suspend judgment for the time being and acknowledge that until you talk to her, you really do not know why she did not respond as you expected. *"I don't know why" can be used to avoid ungrounded negative assessments.* This phrase can also help you develop your acceptance of uncertainty, since uncertainty is so much a part of life.

Responding
to false or
ungrounded
assessments is
likely to create
chaos and
confusion in
your life.

The last time I reached for my wallet and could not find it, I noticed an immediate sense of panic welling up. My mind started to scan places where I might have left it. Then I experienced a series of thoughts about hardships and hassles that follow losing credit cards and my driver's license. What seemed most disheartening was the thought of wasting a half day at the secretary of state's office getting a new driver's license.

The scenario created instantly in my mind was quite dramatic and frightening. The tension and stress that accompanied such negative thoughts were building up quickly. Choosing to focus on breathing awareness, I was able to lessen the impact of this imagined stream of frightful consequences. Then I modified my assessment by deciding that I had not lost my wallet but simply misplaced it. This shift in perspective created a different, less stressful response and allowed for a reasonable approach to finding the "lost" wallet. After reviewing the activities of the previous evening, I remembered taking it out of my pocket in the car, while visiting the automatic teller. I found it lying on the front passenger seat. As usual, all the worrying and stress were unnecessary and could have been avoided by my questioning my assessment of the missing wallet much more quickly.

Modifying Assessments

There are several ways to modify your assessments. The quickest may be simply to resist making an assessment by shifting awareness to your breathing; a simple and effective way to suspend judgment. Practicing the Breath Awareness exercise allows you to observe the events for a few seconds before automatically turning on an ungrounded assessment.

Observing your responses to common events like losing your wallet or keys provides opportunities to witness how you have programmed yourself to react with an immediate Stress Response to situations that pose no significant danger. A similar scenario plays out repeatedly during the day with common events that turn on a Stress Response in you. *The breathing-awareness exercise places a pause between the event and those habitual worst-case-scenario assessments.*

Another way to modify assessments by suspending judgment is to say, "I don't know yet." This approach buys time to consider other interpretations of the event. When you have an experience and choose "I don't know yet" to interpret it, it leaves room for more information to come in, to shape a more correct and grounded assessment. The more factual information you have, the more reliable the assessment will be. *Assessments based on reliable information can make for more productive responses.* Unfortunately, in making assessments, people often confuse opinions with facts. It is important to remember this human tendency. By learning how to distinguish opinion from fact, you give yourself the option of acknowledging them without assuming that they are true.

Challenging your assessments with questions provides another way to effectively alter and ground your assessments. Questions work by leading you to other possible assessments, as well as by delaying a too-hasty judgment of the event. *They are effective tools for stimulating learning and redirecting your thinking.* Since learning creates change, new possibilities will follow. You can use the following questions to shift your perspective and open up different avenues for action.

Questions for Modifying or Verifying Assessments

What else could this mean?
What happened the last time this occurred?

Asking questions has long been one of the paths to truth, knowledge, and wisdom.

When working with verified assessments, there is strength and comfort in going with what is true rather than with what is false.

"I don't know why" can be used to avoid ungrounded negative assessments.

What does this assessment say about me?
Why am I looking at it this way?
How do I know this is true?
What's the worst that could happen?

It makes sense that whether you are asking "the Big Question" (Why am I here?) or simply trying to verify an assessment, you are best served by being as close to the truth as you can. That is where questions come in. Responding to these questions can move you toward more-critical thinking. This creates a space in time so you are less likely to respond in the old, automatic, stress-producing patterns. As you practice challenging your assessments, it becomes easier to choose assessments that are truer. With practice you learn that there are almost always other possible assessments, and you react less automatically.

In testing or verifying assessments I recognized an important, easy-to-use tool for reducing stress by reducing false alarms. As it became clearer to me that we create life with our assessments, verifying assessments quickly became a tool for reducing the number of stressful experiences of everyday life. At first, I verified assessments with questions like "How true is this?" Later, I questioned if an assessment was necessary at all. What if I did not make an assessment?

I realized that in many cases I didn't have to make an assessment of an event. I could just let it be. How liberating! If someone cuts me off in traffic, rather than making an assessment about the person's rudeness or incompetence as a driver, I can just observe my breathing and let it be. Had I chosen deliberate rudeness as the motivation of the driver, I would also have chosen anger and frustration for my experience. This anger would probably still be with me, even after the driver was out of view. When someone doesn't return my call in a timely manner, I can believe the person is taking me for granted. If I do that, I am left with a feeling of resentment, even if the person does call later. Both anger and resentment are stress-producing emotions. However, if I decide that I do not really know why the person has not called, perhaps they are ill or too busy, my inner response is subdued or neutral. Better yet, I can choose to not make an assessment and just let it go! By using either approach, I can feel at peace. Thus, it is important to me to verify my assessments, to get close to what is true, rather than just react to my first opinion. I have found that it is perhaps more important to learn to not make assessments. In the words of William James, the great American psychologist, "Wisdom is knowing what to overlook."

Modifying Assessments

1. Practice Breath Awareness.
2. Recognize that "I don't know yet."
3. Challenge with questions.

How Words Create Your Life

Your assessments of life events are pivotal in creating your life. Positive assessments increase positive responses. Learning to influence your assessments can take time. One way to accelerate your learning is to become aware of the language you use on yourself every day.

Like most people, you practice self-talk on a regular basis, often unaware that you are doing so. When you make one of many numerous ungrounded assessments, such as "I'm going to be late," you are practicing self-talk. Most assessments of life events are forms of self-talk, in which you tell yourself your interpretation of an event. Self-talk, like assessments, can have a creative quality. To access the creative potential of assessments and self-talk, understand that assessments and self-talk are made in language. *If assessments create responses, and assessments are made in language, then language creates responses.* Language creates your life. *Language is more than descriptive. It is creative.* Language is a form of action that, in turn, leads to a reaction or response.

Once you realize the creative power of language, or words, you become conscious of the potential effect of what you say to yourself and to others. The words you use with yourself will create a B.E.S.T. Response. The words you use with others will influence their B.E.S.T. Responses, as well, depending of course on their assessments of your words. If you are having difficulty solving a problem and say, "I am stupid," that will create a much more negative response in you than if you say, "I haven't figured out the solution to this problem." This second, more grounded assessment leaves you with options, such as getting help or trying something different. *Likewise, if you happen to trip while walking, are you clumsy, or did you just trip? You decide.* The truth is that the choice you make in language, whether it is true or not, has consequences for how you think, feel, and act. The language you use to refer to yourself and to others creates your experience of life. This may be why "if you think you can't, you probably can't." If you think you can, you have at least a chance to succeed. *We live in language, within a house of words.*

The concept that assessments create and as assessments are made in language—therefore, language creates—has been one of the most important lessons of my adult life. I am grateful to Matthew Budd, MD, who first taught me that language creates, in a mind-body workshop called "Ways to Wellness" that I attended in the early 1990s.
Back then, as a father of young children, I noted how we instinctively choose loving and positive words when we speak to our babies and toddlers. I realize it is just as important with them now that they are teenagers. I am old enough to know that it will be important for them as adults too. Yet, it remains that for many people, as they get older and their physical and emotional load increases, the loving and supportive language that they need to hear actually decreases in

As we create life with our assessments, verifying assessments quickly becomes a tool for reducing the number of stressful experiences of everyday life.

"Wisdom is knowing what to overlook."

If assessments create responses, and assessments are made in language, then language creates responses.

their life experiences. I came to realize the importance of using positive, encouraging, and supportive words when speaking to my patients, my friends, and myself.

Creating Life through Self-talk

Instinctively, most adults take advantage of this creative quality of language. When speaking to newborns and toddlers, most people use very gentle and soft tones and loving words. By the way they use language, they appear to be speaking as if they might influence the development and future life of the child. I think they are right to think that way. Even my oldest patients benefit from kind, loving, and supportive language. *So, too, do you and I benefit from speaking to ourselves with respect, kindness, and love.* Using "I love you" with children is a sure way to help children become stronger and more confident individuals. Even if they don't seem to be paying attention, on some level they hear it, and it can make a big difference in many lives, especially later during the hard times that are sure to come. Good teachers, pediatricians, and other professionals who work with children know this well. *Loving, supportive language benefits children, teens, and adults of all ages.*

When I learned of this creative quality of language at Dr. Budd's workshop, I experienced an epiphany. The idea that we create our own reality always seemed true, but now I understood how our personal reality is created. Through the creative role of language, I saw, for example, how hope and optimism could be practiced and made into habit for the benefit of the individual. "Habits make the man," but the actions that become habits are usually preceded by thoughts made in language or words. A quote I heard years ago, "As a man thinketh, so he is," always made sense to me. This "new" idea, that language plays an active role in how one thinks, made sense too. Two skills that I have found most helpful for managing life are the ability to remain calm within and the ability to change. With language I can persuade my mind and body to practice the ideas and activities that reduce my Stress Response and make inner calm possible during everyday life. If I want to change some behavior or attitude, language provides a starting point from which to build momentum and move forward.

This newfound realization, that language creates, makes it even more important that you use care when choosing assessments in everyday life. The language you use in your assessments will create your responses and, therefore, your life. This is where you can take an active role in creating your life. "Yes, I can" or "I have not yet learned how to… " will necessarily create more options for success than "I can't." Now it becomes more important to avoid using negative language, which engenders negative responses or experiences. *Life becomes more exciting with the realization that by actively using positive language, you can positively influence your life experience.* Words are symbols, and the words you choose have meaning for you. Use this knowledge to your benefit and the benefit of others. Encourage yourself and those around you to practice using more-positive language. Remember the aphorism "The mind is like a garden." The positive words you plant in it will take root and blossom.

If the mind is like a garden, what happens if you don't tend your garden?

....

....

....

....

....

An untended garden grows wild and fails to supply the hoped-for harvest.

When asked what happens to your garden (mind) if no one tends to it, class participants are often quick to say, "It dies." That is not true. If you don't tend your garden, it does not die; rather, it grows weeds (negative thoughts). The life force will continue to support life in some form, but it may not be what you intended. So it is with your thoughts. If you do not tend your thoughts, you will still have them, but more of the negative or unwanted ones. *If you tend your thoughts with love, acceptance, and self-respect, more positive thoughts will grow from your mind.*

Exercise

If you want to experience the creative benefits of language, look into a mirror several times a day and say, "I love you." It can be a moment of reckoning when you look into your own eyes in the mirror and say that to yourself. It does not matter if you feel it or not; just say it and note your inner reaction.

Remember the love that you have felt for someone else or that someone else has felt for you, and consider the meaning of also loving yourself. As you say the words "I love you" to yourself, remember that it is the affirming love for yourself that you can extend to others as well. As we'll discuss in the section on "Spirituality," love is more than just a feeling. Love will exert its benefits, even if one is not immediately aware of it.

☯ **Return to your breathing.**

Loving, supportive language benefits children, teens, and adults of all ages.

The realization that language creates makes it even more important that you use care when choosing assessments in everyday life.

Life becomes more exciting when, by actively using positive language, you can positively influence your life experience.

If you tend your thoughts with love, acceptance, and self-respect, more-positive thoughts will grow from your mind.

Knowing that assessments are made in language allows you to use language to restructure yourself and your life.

Summary

Your assessments have a significant impact on your experience of everyday life. In any given day, you make scores of assessments about many unrelated mundane events—the numerous events that make up your daily life. From the moment you wake up, you are bombarded with a great number of situations: the ringing alarm clock, the weather, traffic, running late, missing a bus, and encounters at work. You automatically make interpretations or assessments of these events, which influence how you think, feel, and act. These thoughts, feelings, and actions, in turn, become events in your life, which will trigger more assessments. This is part of the circle of life. In the midst of the numerous assessments that create the quality of your life experience, choosing assessments that are verified and grounded in truth provides an opportunity for improving your inner experience of life. *Knowing that assessments are made in language allows you to use language to restructure yourself and your life.* In choosing words that encourage and support you, you are choosing a creative force for a health-enhancing response to life's events. Start now to give yourself the benefit of the doubt and use positive self-talk to interpret everyday events and situations. With repetition and practice it will become automatic.

PART

THREE

THE
BODY DOMAIN

Nutrition for Energy

Food is first of all a source of energy for body and mind. What you eat can also promote health or illness. The basic building blocks for nutrition are carbohydrates, proteins, and fats. In order to maximize your chances of good health, you need a balance of these nutrients. Good nutrition also means eating more natural foods and fewer processed foods, and more fresh fruits and vegetables, and less salt, sugar, saturated fats and trans fats, and empty starches. In our fast-moving world, we often find ourselves consuming "fast foods" and "prepared" foods that contain too much sugar, salt, fat, chemical preservatives, and other additives. These are foods that not only do not give us adequate nutrition for good health but are actually implicated in the high incidence of all-too-common ailments of our consumer society.

One approach to food and weight control is based on the "glycemic index." The glycemic index rates foods on the basis of their simple carbohydrate content and how quickly and how much they make the blood sugar rise. High-glycemic-index foods that can quickly raise blood sugar include processed foods such as wheat flour products, white rice, potatoes, and sugars of all kinds. The complex carbohydrates that do not cause the unhealthful, rapid rise in blood glucose levels include whole-grain flours and whole-grain baked goods, most fruits, greens, and vegetables. High-glycemic-index foods are also associated with decreased nutrient levels, higher insulin levels, and weight gain. Higher insulin levels and excess weight gain are associated with many serious diseases. Low-carb diets include low-glycemic, plant-based foods, which typically provide increased nutrients, help regulate blood sugar, and avoid high insulin levels. Recently, foods thought to be healthful, like dairy and grains, have been found to promote inflammation and disease in susceptible individuals.

Weight management is possible because you are already on a continuum between normal weight and obesity. The goal in weight management is not just to lose weight, but to lose fat. Fat loss is more likely to succeed with a threefold approach of mind, body, and spirit to life management.

☯ **Bring your attention to your breathing.**

Food is more than an energy source. Hippocrates said, "Let food be your medicine." Centuries later, scientists continue to make discoveries supporting the role of nutrition in the prevention and reduction of disease, as well as enhancement of the healing process. What you eat can be helpful or harmful.

Like medicine, the food you eat and the food you don't eat may actually help lower blood pressure and cholesterol, thus reducing the risk of heart disease and stroke. Eating quantities of refined-flour and high-sugar foods can lead to harmful fluctuations in blood sugar, with alterations in mood and energy levels. Simply reducing the intake of these foods may alleviate these undesirable side effects and chronic diseases down the road.

High-fiber foods like bran and beans help lower cholesterol and keep blood sugar levels more even. They also help keep you feeling full and make it easier to avoid excessive eating. The foods you eat are important building blocks in your physical and psychological development. Obesity, which is reaching epidemic proportions in America, often begins in childhood and can have physical and emotional consequences. Using food for nutrition rather than for pleasure and emotional comfort is an important concept for those seeking to improve personal energy levels through food.

As adults, we are free to choose what we will eat. What we choose to eat or to not eat plays a major role in the development of certain diseases like diabetes, heart attacks, and cancer. What we choose to eat also impacts our moods and energy throughout the day.

Each culture has its own staple sources of nutrition. In the United States, much of the population still emphasizes meat and potatoes. Marketing of mass-produced, prepared food favors high sugar, high salt, saturated and trans fat, and refined starches. There are several reasons for this emphasis. Both sugar and salt are preservatives; foods with high sugar and high salt content last longer and can be stored and shipped relatively inexpensively. Flavor is enhanced by salt and sugar, and addiction to these ingredients can be counted on to help perpetuate sales. Our combination of carbs, fats, sugars, and salt may satisfy hunger, and do it very quickly, but is void of many essential nutrients.

The foods of other cultures, notably Mediterranean cultures like Italian, Greek, and Middle Eastern, have attracted attention as options for more healthful fare. Mediterranean cultures use more olive oil, consume more whole grains and fish, and eat less red meat and fewer processed foods. Studies find less heart disease in these groups. Traditional Japanese cuisine

---

The foods you eat are important building blocks in your physical and psychological development.

Water, fruit, vegetables, and oil-rich foods can positively affect our mental health by up to 80% while our typical "stress relief foods" such as sugar, caffeine, alcohol, and chocolate can actually negatively affect your mental health by 80%.

—Kristin Gustashaw, registered dietitian

is high in fish and fermented soy and low in processed foods as well. The Japanese have very little breast cancer, thought to be related to the protective effect of soy consumption and iodine in sea vegetables.

Clearly, foods have a role in causing, as well as preventing, disease. Today, we know more about the role of nutrition for preventing disease and altering moods. Research shows that water, fruit, vegetables, and healthful-fat foods can positively affect our mental health, while our typical "stress-relief foods" such as sugar, caffeine, alcohol, and chocolate can actually negatively affect your mental health.

Nutrition is an essential topic in Balancing Act, because the foods you choose, and the amount you consume, impact your immediate and long-term energy levels. This, in turn, impacts your daily physical and emotional experiences. Under increased stress and in a rush, we tend to eat more junk food. On a leisurely vacation, we are more apt to take our time with meals, and to include more fruits and vegetables. The resultant energy levels following a meal affect behaviors and self-dialogue about life.

In this chapter on nutrition, we will first present a brief review of the basics of nutrition. Then we will discuss three areas for positively modulating optimal energy level with food:

1. superfoods
2. the sugar-insulin connection
3. "healthy" foods that can make you sick

This information is drawn from many sources, notably the workshops in nutritional medicine of Jonathan Wright, MD, and Allan Gaby, MD, as well as the writings of medical doctors Steven Gundry, Terry Wahls, and Andrew Weil. What follows can be considered as "core-content" information, including practical applications to help you start influencing your energy with food.

Basic Nutrition

The building blocks of a well-balanced diet are proteins, fats, carbohydrates, vitamins, and minerals.

Proteins are necessary for muscle tissue and numerous biochemical components like hormones (such as insulin) and enzymes. In the American diet, protein is usually derived from meat and dairy (milk and cheese), fish, and eggs. Soybeans, legumes (beans), and nuts provide a second major group of protein sources.

Carbohydrates (CHOs) are made of sugars (glucose) or chains of sugars (complex CHOs). Complex CHOs, found in fruits, vegetables, and whole grains, are favored over simple sugars (table sugar, honey syrup) and simple starch

The foods you choose, and the amount you consume, impact your immediate and long-term energy levels.

Under increased stress and in a rush, we tend to eat more junk food.

CHOs (wheat, rice, corn). CHOs are the common and quick source of fuel for energy. The body also converts proteins and fats to sugar for energy, but this takes longer.

Fats are necessary for brain/nerve tissues, for cell membranes, and for storage of calories. Animal fats, as in meat and dairy, are called saturated fats. Saturated fats are generally solid at room temperature. They tend to be high in cholesterol and can promote heart disease. A high consumption of saturated fat is thought to be associated with a number of different diseases. However, not all fats are bad. Unsaturated fats (poly-a nd monosaturated), such as olive oil, and the fats in avocados, nuts, and sunflower seeds are better for the heart. Be cautious of your amount of any fat, however, since they all have 9 calories per gram of fat.

Fiber is the part of plants that is not digested by the gastrointestinal tract, and it helps food move through the digestive system. It also assists with feeling full. Since it is not digestible, it adds no calories. The two types of fiber are soluble and insoluble. Soluble fiber is found in most fruits, vegetables, whole grains, and beans. It helps reduce cholesterol levels and stabilize blood sugar. Insoluble (in water) fiber is found in whole grains, especially wheat, corn, and rice. This kind of fiber helps improve bowel movement regularity and prevent constipation. Constipation is associated with an increased risk of colon cancer. Diets high in fiber-rich foods are associated with reduced caloric intake, as well as reduced cholesterol, and decreased cancer risk. This makes increased fiber in the diet an easy way to reduce illness and improve health.

> Fiber is the closest nutrient to the "Magic Bullet" everyone is in search of to help them stay healthy.
>
> —Kirstin Gustashaw, registered dietitian

Vitamins and minerals are micronutrients required in minute amounts for numerous biochemical reactions that are essential to life and optimal health. Iron, for example, is necessary for the production of red blood cells. B vitamins are important for nerves and brain tissue. Lack of certain vitamins or minerals can cause diseases. Lack of vitamin C causes scurvy; lack of vitamin D may accelerate osteoporosis. These abound in fruits, vegetables, nuts, beans, and whole grains, as well as other foods. Fast foods and processed snacks are usually severely lacking in vitamins and minerals. In addition, they are often high in less healthful fats and sugar, leading to increased caloric intake with minimal nutrition.

Food is generally most beneficial when consumed as close to its natural state as possible. In its natural state, food contains more vitamins, minerals, and health-enhancing substances than when it has been processed. The processing of grains, for example, removes fiber, vitamins, and minerals. Even when scientists are able to isolate the important "active ingredients" of a food, such as vitamin C found in oranges, it is preferable to consume the "whole" food. While orange juice is a good source of vitamin C, eating a whole orange will provide more than the juice alone. The whole food provides nutrients such as vitamins, minerals, and fiber not found in processed extracts. It is reasonable to assume that the whole food also provides additional essential nutrients that may not yet have been identified and may have a synergistic effect when consumed as a whole.

Traditionally in the US, the foods recommended for daily nutrition have been classified into the four basic food groups: (1) dairy, (2) meat, fish, and protein sources, (3) fruits and vegetables, and (4) whole grains. The US government updates its dietary guidelines every five years to promote health and prevent disease. The key recommendations from the 2005 publication are as follows: consume adequate calories to meet your needs; maintain a healthful weight; be physically active; increase fruits and vegetables; limit total fat intake; focus on complex, fiber-rich carbohydrates; practice moderate sodium and potassium intake; consume only moderate amounts of alcohol; and follow the rules that provide for food safety. A brief description of these guidelines follows.

Dietary Guidelines

Variety in eating is essential for nutritional balance. Your body needs numerous nutrients to be healthy. No single food or group of food has all the necessary nutrients for good nutrition. This means we should try different foods for breakfast, not just the same cereal every morning. Dairy foods: good sources of calcium, vitamin A, vitamin D, vitamin B, and protein. Low-fat milk products include yogurt, skim milk, and low fat cheese. If you want to avoid milk, consider almond or coconut milk, available on the grocers' shelves or in the dairy section. Meat: high in protein, yet can be high in cholesterol. Red meat has more cholesterol and saturated fat than white, skinless chicken or turkey meat. Both ground chicken and turkey can be used for burgers, and in any way you would use ground beef, as in tacos, chili, and meatballs. Beans and nuts are relatively high in protein and low in saturated fats. Fruits and vegetables are a great source of vitamin C, beta carotene, and antioxidants. Most fruits and vegetables are complex carbohydrates, high in fiber, with little fat or protein. Grains are represented by wheat, oats, rye, rice, corn, and barley. In their whole state, grains are complex carbohydrates, providing fiber and many vitamins and minerals, before processing removes most of them. The important thing is to have a variety of all these foods.

Follow a diet with emphasis on increasing "good" fats and decreasing "bad" fats. Obesity and a high-fat diet are risk factors for cancers of the colon, breast, and uterus, as well as heart disease. Having high cholesterol is a risk factor for heart attacks and should be avoided. Diets high in saturated fat (found in animal products as well as processed foods) and trans fats (found in processed foods) can also increase your cholesterol. Trans fatty acids are dangerous to health because they unbalance the natural healing system and increase the risk of cancer. Trans fatty acids are produced when vegetable oils are hydrogenated to make them solid. This fat, though derived from plant oils, may act similarly to saturated fat, increasing the risk of heart disease. Trans fatty acids are found in margarine and packaged foods

Many of our common snack foods are high in calories and fat, high in salt, and lacking in essential nutrients.

Food is generally most beneficial when consumed as close to its natural state as possible.

In their whole state, grains are complex carbohydrates, providing fiber and many vitamins and minerals.

Trans fatty acids are dangerous to health because they unbalance the natural healing system and increase the risk of cancer.

and are added to increase shelf life of snack foods, baked goods, crackers, and cookies. Avoid fried foods, not just because of the increased calories (think food dipped in fat) but also because heating most oils to high temperature causes the generation of free radicals that can cause damage to cells, proteins, and even DNA. More-acceptable fats include extra virgin olive oil, olives, coconuts, avocados, and walnuts. However, for cooking, the recommended oils are unrefined sesame seed and coconut oils. Unrefined sesame seed oil and coconut oils can be heated to high temperatures, as in Chinese stir-fry dishes. Olive oil can be used for low-heat occasions, such as sautéing vegetables. Avoid regular use of sunflower seed, corn, and soy oils. For more on good and bad fats, see *Eight Weeks to Optimal Health* by Andrew Weil, MD, and Mark Hyman's *Eat Fat, Get Thin*.

Natural plant products in your diet can satisfy appetite and lower caloric intake due to the fiber and minimal fat in them.

Consuming more fruits and vegetables provides the maximum amount of vitamins, minerals, and fiber. Natural plant products in your diet can satisfy appetite and lower caloric intake due to the fiber and minimal fat in them. Eating high-fiber food results in a more filling sensation. A slice of white bread with zero grams of fiber may do little to dampen hunger. One medium-sized apple with about the same number of calories is much more filling. Increase your intake of fruits by making fruit salads and using fruit as a snack at work and home. For most people, increasing vegetable consumption is the hardest change in eating habits. Soups and smoothies are a good way to get more vegetables into your diet. Try adding frozen veggies to an egg-white omelet or your morning smoothie for a quick yet nutrient-packed breakfast.

Foods that are advertised as "low fat" often have increased sugar content to improve flavor.

Limit sugar intake. Start weaning yourself from sugar by cutting out table sugars, candy, and sweets that are mostly sugar. Foods that are advertised as "low fat" often have increased sugar content to improve flavor. Try substituting frozen yogurt for ice cream. Try fruit with fat-free whipped topping instead of cookies. One 12-ounce can of regular soda pop has about nine teaspoons of sugar, or 140 calories! A soda pop may give you a quick "sugar high" typically coupled with a "caffeine buzz" if the soda is a cola drink. This buzz of energy will dissipate quickly, however, and may leave you feeling more sluggish and dehydrated. Rather than waste your calories on trying to give yourself a jolt, consider a glass of water with fresh lemon, lime, or orange slices. People often confuse dehydration for hunger or lack of energy. Always try to grab water first, and wait about thirty minutes before heading for food or caffeine. While some people choose diet soda as a way to avoid sugar, most nutrition authorities do not recommend this option. Artificial sweeteners have not been shown to help people lose weight. In addition, they make the drink so sweet that it promotes a taste for sweet drinks and foods. It is better for you to wean yourself from your sweet tooth by gradual avoidance of sugar and artificial sweeteners.

One 12-ounce can of regular soda pop has about nine teaspoons of sugar, or 140 calories.

Limit salt intake. Even if you do not use a saltshaker, you may be getting an excessive amount of salt in your processed foods. They are usually very high in sodium and low in potassium. Conversely, fruits and vegetables are very high in potassium and very low in sodium. Moving to more-natural foods, and foods that you prepare yourself, will do much to reduce your salt intake, as well as the amount of preservatives consumed. A first step to decreasing salt intake is to avoid or severely limit prepackaged and fast foods. Instead, choose plant foods that are in their natural state and foods that you prepare yourself. Always read the ingredients to check for salt or sodium.

Limit alcohol consumption. Although one to two alcoholic beverages per day may decrease the risk of heart attack, more than that amount becomes a risk factor for heart disease and cancer. Alcohol is toxic to the stomach and liver, and, in excess, it is a carcinogenic risk factor for cancer of the head and neck, esophagus, and liver. Increased alcohol consumption may be a sign of alcoholism or of using alcohol to handle stress (self-medication). Also, alcohol is high in calories. If you wish to drink alcohol, consider small amounts of red wines, which are high in protective antioxidants. Remember, too, that alcohol is less toxic if combined with food, usually protein.

The basic nutritional information presented up to now may be summarized:

Eat natural foods, and foods you make yourself, as much as possible. This will provide needed vitamins and minerals, which will help increase and maintain better personal energy levels. Minimize fried foods and prepackaged foods to avoid harmful free radicals and unnatural trans fatty acids. Avoiding foods high in sugar and refined starches, and increasing whole grains, fruits, and vegetables, will decrease the energy drain associated with fluctuating blood sugar levels and will also assist with safety and weight control.

Superfoods

Here is a review of highly nutritional foods for those looking for food-based therapeutic options, which prevent disease and enhance healing. More-healthful foods will have a positive effect on overall energy balance as well. These foods are available at your grocery store and are easy to add to your current diet.

Vegetable and fruit juice. Freshly made vegetable and fruit juices contain abundant vitamins, minerals, and enzymes in a form that is easily assimilated. These juices or smoothies can be made with a juicer or a blender. One can make quite exotic blends of juices and vegetables by experimenting with different combinations. Many health clubs now have a nutritional drink bar where you can sample many delicious combinations of fruits and vegetable protein smoothies, before you try to make them at home. For more nutritional value, start with vegetables and greens in the blender or juicer and add low- sugar fruits like berries. Carrots, spinach, broccoli, cauliflower, asparagus, and green peppers are some of the vegetables that can be blended for a vegetable drink or added to the fruit drink. Just keep that blender or juicer on the counter and use it for a delicious breakfast or for a quick meal on

Processed foods are usually very high in sodium and low in potassium

If you wish to drink alcohol, consider small amounts of red wines, which are high in protective antioxidants.

Eat natural foods, and foods you make yourself, as much as possible.

the go. If you decide to just use a juicer, then plan to use the "sludge" in salad dressings, sauces, or soups so you don't miss out on the fiber.

Fruits and vegetables. Some common everyday fruits and vegetables stand out as excellent sources of vitamins and minerals and fiber. Vegetables are also a source of protein, as well as needed essential fatty acids, vitamins, minerals, and numerous yet-to-be-identified nutrients. One medium stalk of broccoli provides up to 5 grams of protein. Broccoli, one of the cruciferous vegetables, is known to have anticancer properties. Broccoli is often recommended for those with a family history of cancer or who are at risk for cancer due to lifestyle factors like smoking. Other cruciferous vegetables and relatives of broccoli with protective properties include cauliflower, cabbage, and brussel sprouts. Highly recommended greens at your supermarket include kale, chard, spinach, and collard greens. Healthful vegetables choices include asparagus, avocado, green beans, beets, carrots, celery, eggplant, onions, peas, green and red peppers, tomatoes, yams, and sweet potatoes.

Dark grapes and blueberries have very powerful, protective antioxidants and are highly recommended.

Legumes. Beans have often been described as a near-perfect food because of their abundance of B vitamins and minerals including iron and magnesium. In addition, they are a good source of protein and fiber. Soybeans are often the main source of protein for many vegetarians, with a cup of soybeans providing 15 grams of protein. That is as much protein as a small breast of chicken. A cup of kidney beans, used in chili, has a whopping 5.8 grams of fiber, while a cup of oat bran has 4 grams of fiber. Commonly available beans include red kidney beans, lentils, navy beans for soup, and chick peas for hummus.

Increasing Healthful Foods

Many of the patients who could benefit dramatically from improving their diet often have very little interest or experience in choosing, cooking, and consuming more-healthful, natural foods. Nutritional advice, which recommends a change to more-healthful, plant-based foods, will usually go unheeded unless there is a pressing medical problem already present, such as diabetes, cancer, or a recent heart attack.

In the majority of generally healthy patients, often described as the "worried well," the change to a more healthful diet can occur in small steps, which may be easily assimilated into the current lifestyle. I find the patient can be engaged more effectively if the trial of the new vegetables, fruits, and beans is made to be less disruptive to their usual eating habits. One very effective way to practice eating better is to go to a salad bar at your supermarket or restaurant. There you can choose a variety of raw vegetables, fruits, and beans to practice eating this more healthful way. Start with a small salad container, replacing lettuce with spinach leaves and cutting a variety of the vegetables into small bite sizes. More-extensive salad bars also offer legumes, like kidney beans and garbanzo beans (chick peas).

Generally, I am not too strict on the choice of salad dressing at the beginning, since the main goal is to increase the consumption of the vegetables and salads. Start with a dressing you like and try to wean yourself to more-healthful ones like vinaigrettes or olive oil. Another option for increasing vegetables is frozen vegetables, with or without a sauce. Again, my goal is to increase the positive behavior of increased consumption of these foods. Once you have acquired a taste and habit for the vegetables and fruits, it is easier to work on more-healthful choices and preparations within these groups.

Ways to Eat More Vegetables and Fruits per Day

- Make soup with vegetables or add vegetables to most soups.
- Complement any meat or fish dish with steamed or sautéed vegetables.
- Add whole vegetables to chili or pureed vegetables to sauces.
- Add vegetables to pasta dishes.
- Stir-fry or grill vegetables for a change in taste and texture.
- Add fruit to cereals and for dessert.
- Make fresh fruit salad every three days from at least three low-glycemic fruits.
- Use whole fruits or fruit salad for your midmorning and midafternoon snacks.

Once you make more healthful eating a goal, some of the previously discussed suggestions are used as short-term objectives to be worked into your eating habits. Remember, if you can't stop eating bad things, eat more good things. Even while you continue to consume unhealthful foods, begin making substitutions with more natural and whole foods.

The Sugar-Insulin Connection

The daily food choices you make influence your personal energy levels. While all foods provide calories for energy, different foods influence your personal energy level differently. You may have already noted that some foods may increase your energy and well-being, while others may make you tired or sleepy. The foods you choose, as well as how you combine them, are important variables for influencing your energy levels. One food that can have an immediate influence on your energy, mood, and mental clarity is sugar, a personal energy drainer.

One of the detrimental effects of modern civilization has been the change to processed foods. High on the list of unhealthful processed foods is the high level of sugar consumption. Increased sugar consumption and decreased fiber in the diet are associated with many diseases, notably heart disease, strokes, cancer, and diabetes. These four diseases are among the most

Beans are a near-perfect food because of their abundance of B vitamins and iron, plus calcium, magnesium, zinc, copper, and potassium, as well as protein and fiber.

One way to practice eating better is to go to a salad bar at your supermarket or restaurant.

Remember, if you can't stop eating bad things, eat more good things.

Some foods may increase your energy and well-being, while others may make you tired or sleepy.

common causes of premature death in our country. The good news is that decreasing sugar consumption and returning to whole foods can positively affect these and many other diseases.

For Americans of all age groups, the heavy consumption of "empty" calories from sugar is shocking. The average consumption of sugar in the US is now up to more than 150 pounds per year, considerably up from a few pounds per year a couple of hundred years ago. If 150 pounds of sugar is an average, then some people, especially adolescents, are probably consuming 200 pounds or more a year, or more than a half pound of sugar per day! Sugar is everywhere and disguised under many different names.

Other names for sugar: brown sugar, corn sweetener, corn syrup, dextrose, fructose, fruit juice concentrate, glucose, honey, maltose, and sucrose

The foods and ingredients making up a food product are listed on the nutritional label, in order from greatest amount to least. If you find any of the previously mentioned forms of sugar listed in the top two or three ingredients of, for example, a sweet breakfast cereal, there is a large proportion of sugar present in that food. Besides being heavily present in sweet rolls, candy, and deserts, sugar is in prepared cereals, salad dressings, ketchup, barbecue sauce, baked beans, and most snacks. Low-fat yogurt is often very high in sugar.

My initial introduction to sugar as a health problem was in 1999 at a nutritional-medicine seminar given by Jonathan Wright, MD. According to Dr. Wright, about one-third of the population is sugar sensitive. These sugar-sensitive individuals may experience an energy drain when they consume processed sugar in candy and sweets, or sugar in its quick-release hidden form, starch. These forms of sugar can have a negative impact on personal energy level, and thus on general health, due to their effect on the hormone insulin. The overload on the sugar-regulating mechanism and the resultant physiological imbalance is already being linked to modern diseases like heart disease, strokes, and diabetes.

Glycemic Index

The glycemic (*gly = sugar, cemic = blood*) index of a food is a relative measure of how much the blood glucose rises within a period of time after a specific amount of food is consumed. By agreement, the glycemic index (g.i.) of white bread is set at 100. Foods are rated in comparison to white bread. Carbohydrates that raise the blood sugar rapidly are said to have a higher glycemic index. Foods that raise the blood sugar slowly have a lower glycemic index. Interestingly, most of the healthful foods that are recommended, such as fruits, vegetables, and beans, have a lower glycemic index.

For a list of the glycemic index of various foods, you can go to the internet and search "glycemic index list." There you will find access to many lists with the glycemic index of hundreds of foods. In appendix III I have included a table showing the glycemic index of various food groups, from extremely high to low. In general, processed grains have a high g.i., while most fruits, vegetables, and beans have a lower g.i. I generally tell patients to "avoid or minimize wheat, rice, corn, and potatoes" to start lowering the g.i. of their diet. The main thing is to choose lower- glycemic-index foods as often as you can.

A higher glycemic index means a faster rise in blood sugar and a corresponding rise in blood insulin. If the repeated elevations of blood insulin levels are sustained, this can lead to hypoglycemia or low blood sugar and energy drain. A low-glycemic-index diet helps avoid a blood sugar rollercoaster. With low-glycemic carbs, glucose and insulin levels will be better managed. You will also have long-term energy and curbed appetite.

The following is a case taken from my medical practice. A twenty-eight-year-old woman came to see me, complaining of feeling faint and light-headed in the morning on her way to work. A detailed history revealed that she worked in a dry-cleaning plant. Due to the high temperatures at work, she generally drank six to eight cans of soda pop per day. (If one can has about 9 teaspoons of sugar, she was consuming about 64 to 72 teaspoons of sugar per day!) Based on her history and lack of physical findings, blood tests were done to determine the blood levels of insulin and c-peptide, a precursor of insulin. Both tests came back at more than three times the high normal level. She was educated on effects of a high-sugar diet and the glycemic index of foods. She started on a low-glycemic-index diet, with five smaller servings per day. Fortunately, she also agreed to give up the soda pop. She substituted water for the soda. Within two months, her blood tests were back to normal range, and she had no further symptoms. An added benefit was that she lost about 10 pounds simply by eating better and giving up the sugar water (soda pop).

After repeated peaks of blood sugar and insulin, susceptible individuals may eventually end up with a sustained elevated level of circulating insulin, even when fasting. This fulfills one of the precursors for adult-onset diabetes, elevated levels of circulating insulin. This may accelerate your shift toward developing diabetes. Even if you don't get diabetes, the high levels of circulating insulin have their own negative side effects. You will likely gain weight and increase your inflammation. Over time, chronic elevations of insulin can lead to major health problems. A low-glycemic-index diet can improve optimal energy levels by decreasing the energy drain of a high-sugar diet. This same, more nutritional diet can also help prevent several chronic diseases, not normally thought to be related to sugar in the diet. Evidence has shown that high levels of sugar consumption correlate with strokes and heart attacks. It is important to know that even if you have

Carbohydrates that raise the blood sugar rapidly are said to have a higher glycemic index.

A high-glycemic-index diet increases energy drain due to fluctuating blood sugar levels.

By eating low-glycemic carbohydrates, you'll have long-term energy and curbed appetite.

inherited a gene for diabetes or heart disease, the expression of that gene can be modified by a low-glycemic-index diet and exercise so you can avoid the disease.

Undesirable Side Effects of Insulin

Other than regulating blood sugars, insulin has other important effects on fat metabolism and weight that are of interest. When the level of circulating insulin is raised, the burning of fat or fuel is inhibited. Elevated insulin turns off hormone-sensitive lipase, the enzyme that allows you to burn fat for fuel. This will make it harder to lose weight. Last, the presence of insulin signals the body to turn the unused blood sugar from the last meal into fat. This makes it easier to gain weight, especially after large meals or excess snacking, even if you are eating low-fat foods. A nonmetabolic effect of insulin is that it promotes inflammation, which could worsen any of the inflammatory type of diseases like arthritis or asthma.

Over time, with chronically elevated levels of insulin, the body becomes less sensitive or resistant to the effects of insulin. This is insulin resistance. As a result, progressively higher insulin levels are needed to keep the blood sugar normal, causing the pancreas to work harder. Eventually, even with higher levels of insulin, the blood sugar levels begin to rise above normal, and the diagnosis of diabetes is easily made with a blood sugar test. High insulin levels, plus insulin resistance often found in obesity, are the two main abnormalities associated with the development of adult-onset diabetes mellitus (also known as type II diabetes). Health researchers point to our high-sugar, high-processed-starch diet as a significant contributing factor in the severe rise in new cases of adult-onset diabetes. A diet low in sugar and starch is strongly recommended for preventing diabetes and maintaining higher energy levels.

Eating for Lower Insulin Levels

Smaller sugar/carbohydrate feedings with resultant smaller blood sugar loads promote lower, more normal insulin levels. Foods with lower glycemic index do the same by avoiding the quick blood sugar rise that can trigger high insulin levels.

Keeping your blood sugar in the middle range, and avoiding the extreme peaks and valleys, will give you more energy and help you lose weight without excessive hunger. Better yet, such a diet can reduce the risk of getting adult-onset diabetes and heart disease. A low-glycemic-index diet can stabilize blood sugar and insulin levels. In addition, through its effect on keeping insulin levels lower, low-glycemic-index eating helps lower cholesterol and reduces body fat, all while you eat more healthfully than ever. Weight loss is easier without going hungry or following fad diets.

Protein, fiber, and fat in food can delay the digestion and absorption process.

Slowing down the absorption of food slows down the conversion of food into blood sugar. Protein in your meal or snack takes longer to digest and leads to a slower rise of the blood sugar, with little stimulation of insulin secretion. Fiber in apples and oranges slows down food absorption after meals and, by itself, has been shown to regulate blood sugar fluctuations.

Last, since fat in the diet delays emptying of the stomach and the absorption of food in the small intestine, it also increases satiety. Also, remember it is important to focus on slowing down how long you take to eat. It takes your brain at least thirty minutes to recognize that you may be full. Therefore, hold off on second helpings until at least thirty to forty-five minutes from the start of your meal. Another strategy to avoid excess calories is to try a soup or salad, or both, at the start of the meal to lengthen the eating process and give your body time to tell you that you are full.

In recent years, several books touting new diets have surfaced, promising to help you increase energy and lose weight. These books share an appreciation of the health benefits of lowering insulin blood levels through diet. All four diet plans recommend attention to the glycemic index of foods or other measures of the carbohydrate content that can raise blood sugar and insulin. They also point to protein as a way to satisfy hunger, without influencing insulin levels as much as with the typical American high processed-carbohydrate diet. Detractors of this approach label them "high-protein diets," and point out the negative effects of too much protein on the kidneys.

In reviewing these books, what I find is not just an emphasis on increasing protein, but a clear recommendation to reduce processed foods—in particular, to avoid the processed grains. While most nutritional sources agree on the benefits of whole-grain products, most patients do not consume whole-grain foods.

In the study of nutrition there are many views of what is true, of which diet is more healthful. The consensus I derived from the above books was that one should eat a diet that does not cause high insulin levels. Avoiding high insulin levels is a priority for health and energy. High insulin levels after meals can be avoided by eating small meals that are low in sugar and processed starches but high in fiber, whole grains, and fruits and vegetables that are low-glycemic foods. Protein should be included in most meals. My approach is to individualize each diet according to low-glycemic-index guidelines and the preferences of the individual. Grains are discouraged unless they are whole-grain products, and even then in moderation.

Protein, fiber, and fat in food can delay the digestion and absorption process.

Last, since fat in the diet delays emptying of the stomach and the absorption of food in the small intestine, it also increases satiety.

Avoiding high insulin levels is a priority for health and energy.

Suggestions for Low-Glycemic/ High-Fiber Meals

Breakfast
- mix of a fruit, vegetable, and protein source
- smoothies with fruits, plus protein powder
- egg-white omelet with vegetables and low-fat cheese
- old-fashioned oatmeal, served with almond milk
- fruit salad with yogurt
- yogurt with sliced fruit and nuts
- protein leftovers from last night's dinner, plus fruit

Midmorning Snack
- apple quarter with a dab of peanut butter
- small cup of fruit salad with crushed walnuts
- hard-boiled egg
- protein shake
- carrots and celery sticks
- ¼ cup of nuts

Lunch
- Plan your lean protein source and add vegetables/salad and fruits.
- homemade chicken vegetable soup plus fruit salad
- chili plus fruit and spinach salad
- roasted skinless chicken breast plus steamed broccoli and fruit
- chicken fajitas with extra vegetables and a fruit or fruit salad
- Restaurants: Home-prepared foods are preferable, but if you must eat out, watch your portion size and try combinations of meat and vegetables. Skip the bread.
- With lunch, add a portion of fruit. *Also consider eating about two-thirds of your meal and saving the other third for a late-afternoon snack about three hours after finishing lunch.*

Midafternoon Snack
- leftovers from lunch (save a third of lunch)
- orange or similar-sized fruit
- protein shake

Dinner
- Plan your lean protein source and add vegetables/salad and fruits.
- Any lunch selection can be used for dinner.
- grilled chicken, and steamed or grilled vegetables
- grilled lean steak and side of vegetables, plus salad
- grilled or baked fish and side of vegetables and salad

Planning Portions

Many people skip breakfast or have a minimal breakfast and more than make up for it as the day goes on, including a dinner that is usually the biggest meal of the day. Contrary to custom, the amount of food consumed at dinner should be the same or less than at lunch. This is especially important if it is a late dinner and you will be going to bed within four hours. Remember, as far as calories go, what you don't use is stored by the body as fat.

An old saying regarding meal portions is *"Eat breakfast like a king, lunch like a queen, and dinner like a pauper."* This makes sense since you need more energy at the start of a long and busy day, but considerably less when your day is winding down. Research has shown that those who have a big, low-glycemic breakfast that includes protein (eggs, meat) tend to have fewer cravings, snack less, and overall tend to eat less the rest of the day.

Eat breakfast like a king, lunch like a queen, and dinner like a pauper.

Eating for Increased Personal Energy

Low-glycemic-index meals and snacks will increase your personal energy level, as well as help balance blood sugar and insulin levels. Combine as many of the approaches listed below into your present lifestyle as possible. The immediate objective is to reduce refined sugar and processed starches as much as possible. Here are several suggestions to help you reach that objective:

- Avoid sugar in all its forms.
- Avoid empty starches: wheat, corn, rice, and potatoes.
- Avoid soda pop and sugar/corn-syrup-sweetened beverages.
- Choose nonsugar drinks, diluted juices, and teas.
- Drink more water; your "weight divided by 2" equals the number of ounces per day.
- Choose fruits for snacks and desserts at work and at home.
- Limit eating out, especially at fast-food restaurants.

Low-glycemic-index meals and snacks will increase your personal energy level, as well as help balance blood sugar and insulin levels.

A large amount of food, even if it consists of fruits and vegetables, will still elevate blood sugar and insulin. Higher insulin can also mean more weight gain. Small amounts of whole foods mean small amounts of blood sugar elevations.

The guidelines and recommendations for increased energy also facilitate weight management. *With increased energy you are more likely to add exercise to your lifestyle—a must for weight management and weight loss.*

A large amount of food, even if it consists of fruits and vegetables, will still elevate blood sugar and insulin.

Nutrition for Weight Management

The word "diet" means what a person habitually eats. For many people, a diet has come to mean a limited range of foods that one is restricted to, for the purpose of losing weight. Though the nutritional emphasis in this program is on choosing a healthful diet for increased body energy and health, rather than for losing weight, most nutritionists would agree that such a diet as discussed earlier would make weight management easier as well. Still, it is a good idea to comment on healthful eating for weight loss as well, because weight management is so important for physical and mental health.

Interestingly enough, weight management is about energy management. Your current weight is a balance between the calories consumed and the calories burned for the energy that runs the body. If you consume more than you burn, you must necessarily store what you don't use as fat. Conversely, if you burn more than you consume, you must go into your fat stores for fuel and eventually lose fat and weight. This is why most successful weight loss programs combine decreased consumption of calories and increased burning of calories with increased physical activity. Over the years, I have found that most patients know how they should eat to lose weight, and they know, too, that they should exercise. They are just not able to follow through on the food choices and exercise that will ensure success.

The Balancing Act approach to weight management starts with the premise that *to successfully manage your weight, you must first manage your stress.* To see why we think this is true, return to your stress-calm continuum.

Stress <-----------------------------> Calm

The closer you are to the stress end of this continuum, the more you are on "survival" mode and less likely to take the time to plan more-healthful meals, portions, and schedules that support healthful nutrition. You are also more likely to choose fast foods or "comfort foods." Conversely, when your stress is adequately managed and you are closer to calm, it is easier to plan healthful meals and snacks and eat small meals. Regarding stressful issues interfering with healthful eating, stress may mean the usual, obvious life stressors or less obvious, deep-rooted emotional issues that need to be addressed before you can successfully manage your eating habits. If you suspect that personal emotional issues may be interfering with your healthful eating, please consult your physician for some guidance and possible referral to a mental health provider.

This relationship between stress and diet allows us to consider a poor-diet–healthful-diet continuum.

Poor Diet <----------------------------->Healthful Diet
Obesity <-----------------------------> Ideal Weight

The use of a poor-diet–healthful-ddiet continuum facilitates a change to more-healthful eating because, as discussed earlier, you have many choices that will move you away from a poor diet and toward a healthful diet. In addition, you know that weight management is possible because you are already on a continuum between obesity and normal weight. The actions that will move you toward a healthful diet and normal weight can be grouped into three related areas: (1) food choices, (2) portion control, and (3) stress management.

The first half of this chapter provides many recommendations for more-nutritious food choices by striving to increase high-fiber natural foods including fruits and vegetables and decrease high-sugar and high-fat processed foods and fast foods. Portion control is about moderation in general, with more freedom to increase portions of vegetables and salads. A good rule of thumb is to serve yourself and then put back one-third to one-half of the richer foods. If you are still hungry thirty minutes after eating, then go back for more. Also, limit meat portions to no larger than the size of your palm.

Personal experience has repeatedly shown me that the farther I am from the stress end of the above continuum, the easier it is for me to make time to exercise and to plan meals with more-healthful food choices and meal times. I find the portions are also easier to control when I'm more relaxed too. When personal stress increases or energy decreases, I tend to be more attracted to chips and sweets, foods that otherwise interest me much less. Likewise, making time to exercise is less likely to happen if I'm too stressed, even though that's when I need it most.

Although a healthful diet facilitates weight loss and weight management, if you are serious about weight loss, adding stress management and increased regular activity to your nutritional approach will greatly facilitate your success. Exercise reduces stress and increases your personal energy, both of which allow you to better follow your own good advice about healthful eating. If you review those magazine articles on people who have lost significant amounts of weight (and kept it off), you will find invariably it was done with healthful eating and increased physical activity. This reminds us not to rely on diet pills or special diets, but rather on a healthful diet that we can maintain for life, and on daily physical activity.

A 2005 medical research study compared weight loss using four popular diets, and found that at the end of one year the amount of weight lost was similar in all four groups. Participants lost the most weight in the first three months, but again with no significant difference between the four diets. The authors concluded that while the various diets that were tested all led to significant weight loss, the important thing was to pick a healthful diet that you will stick to. *It is perseverance that will ensure your success in managing your weight.*

You know that weight management is possible because you are already on a continuum between obesity and normal weight.

A healthful eating schedule means breakfast, lunch, and dinner with smaller midmorning and midafternoon snacks.

It is perseverance that will ensure your success in managing your weight.

Research, writings, and clinical experience in the last twenty years are revealing that much of what we accepted as healthful dietary guidelines has been misguided.

Foods that we thought were very healthful, such as whole wheat and brown rice, may be causing chronic inflammation and chronic diseases,

However you decide between the healthful and unhealthful diet, remember to use Balancing Act to get a handle on your stress so you can better plan your nutrition and weight management. For energy, health, and weight management, your "diet" should be made up of healthful choices and portions that you can eat for life, as well as daily activity and stress management. While there are many weight loss diets that will work, it is important to choose one you enjoy and are likely to stay with.

The Unhealthful Side of "Healthy" Foods

In the first part of this chapter we reviewed the basics of nutrition and long-held general recommendations about healthful foods and less healthful foods such as sugar. Much of this information is common knowledge. *Research, writings, and clinical experience in the last twenty years are revealing that much of what we accepted as healthful dietary guidelines has been misguided.* With the increase in chronic diseases over the last fifty years, *there has been more concern that the food in the standard American diet may be contributing to these chronic diseases.* As a medical practitioner for over thirty-five years, I have come to find a surprisingly powerful impact on health, both positive and negative, from the foods we eat. *Foods that we thought were very healthful, such as whole wheat and brown rice, may be causing chronic inflammation and chronic diseases, including autoimmune diseases, which are also on the rise.* Awareness of the power of food to influence health both positively and negatively is not something I learned in medical school or family medicine residency. I started to learn about healthful foods that could harm you after I had already been practicing medicine for twenty-five years. "*Let food be your medicine and medicine be your food,*" a quote ascribed to Hippocrates, generally regarded as the father of medicine, is more relevant to me than ever. I first heard this quote in 1999, at my first conference on medical nutrition with Dr. Jonathan Wright and Dr. Alan Gaby. For years I thought it was referring more to herbs and supplements that support health and healing rather than the actual food consumed daily. Now *it has become increasingly clear to me that food is medicine. Like medicines, food can heal as well as harm.*

About eight years ago I had the good fortune of meeting Dr. Stephen Gundry. My first encounter with Dr. Gundry was hearing him being interviewed by one of the greats of nutritional medicine, Dr. Jeff Bland. In that interview, Dr. Gundry, a world-renowned heart surgeon, was discussing his experience reversing heart disease with diet and supplements. As a family physician, reversing heart disease remains of great interest, since heart disease is still one of the top causes of death in our country. The more I listened to the interview, the more I was impressed that a heart surgeon would offer his patients an approach that could actually reverse the blockage of the coronary arteries, not just bypass it. I was fascinated and listened to that interview repeatedly.

After listening to that interview more than ten times, I called his office in

Palm Springs, California, and asked if Dr. Gundry would allow me to see patients with him for a day or two. What followed were six or seven visits to Palm Springs over the next six years. The first few years, I saw mostly older patients with chronic diseases, including heart disease, arthritis, and dementia. He would review numerous blood tests that included markers of inflammation beyond the usual blood test most doctors order. On the basis of the results, he would then recommend a specific diet that excluded grains and dairy, as well as some vegetables generally considered healthful, such as tomatoes. Dr. Gundry would also recommend different supplements that could be purchased at health food stores. When patients followed the diet and supplements as instructed, their symptoms improved and so did their blood tests. Usually he could tell if they were not following his recommendations from the symptoms reported, as well as the changes in the blood tests. I also had a chance to interview several of the patients myself after their appointment. I was very impressed with his approach and results. Once home, I began to give copies of his diet to all my patients, especially those with chronic or severe illnesses. *When my patients started to cut out sugar, grains, and dairy from their diet, we started to see positive results.* Most commonly my *patients would report more energy, fewer aches and pains, better sleep, and even weight loss.* Patients were happily surprised that they were improving without taking any new medications. I didn't understand yet how changing the diet could make such a difference.

Around this time, a patient recommended a book to me about a physician who had reversed her advanced multiple sclerosis (MS). Dr. Terry Wahls was a vegetarian and tae kwan do competitor who was diagnosed with MS around 2000. The way she tells it, she was a good patient and followed all the usual medical advice, but by 2005 she had to use a type of reclining wheelchair to do her medical rounds at her hospital. She came to the conclusion that despite their best efforts, her mainstream physicians may not be able to help her MS. She was actually getting worse. She began to go on the internet to review the research on MS, looking for a way to help her illness. There she began to learn about nutrition as an aid to her MS. *One of her early lessons was the realization that if one has an autoimmune disease, they should probably get off grains and dairy.* From there she went on to learn much about using food and supplements, as well as other modalities to design a program that helped her gain her health back. This is all discussed in her book *The Wahls Protocol*. Dr. Wahls and Dr. Gundry helped me understand that *one thing chronic diseases have in common is inflammation.* They were both promoting an anti-inflammatory diet as a way to restore health. Their diets, the food consumed as well as the foods avoided, were overall more alike than different. *Both Dr. Gundry and Dr. Wahls were using an anti-inflammatory diet to help patients improve or even cure their chronic diseases.*

It made sense that *an anti-inflammatory diet could help those with chronic inflammatory diseases, especially the autoimmune diseases like rheumatoid arthritis, psoriasis, and Crohn's disease.* In general, all the autoimmune

When my patients started to cut out sugar, grains, and dairy from their diet, we started to see positive results.

If one has an autoimmune disease, they should probably get off grains and dairy.

diseases are inflammatory, in that the immune system is an important part of the disease process. In autoimmune diseases, the immune system is contributing to the disease, as when the antibodies attack the joints in rheumatoid arthritis or the myelin covering the nerves in multiple sclerosis. In these more serious autoimmune diseases as well as milder ones like eczema and psoriasis, *mainstream medicine uses medications that reduce the inflammation by turning down the immune system response.* Little thought is given to what might be irritating or provoking the immune system to react the way it is reacting.

Reflecting on the Gundry and Wahls approaches to chronic disease, it became clear that both were reducing the inflammation causing the symptoms and changes consistent with the disease. That is, *when they removed foods that were somehow eliciting a response from the immune system and hurting the body, the body was able to begin to heal itself.* Besides taking out the bad foods, they also added foods that help the body heal, like bone broth and healthful fats. In addition, they used supplements that support healing, such as fish oils that reduce inflammation, as well as multivitamin and minerals.

This "new" approach to chronic diseases reminded me of a quote from Hippocrates. More than 2,000 years ago he said that *the role of the physician is to help the patient find the obstacles to health and help remove them, so the patient can heal himself.* Dr. Gundry and Dr. Wahls had found their way back to classical medicine, addressing root causes of chronic diseases. This is not the way we are trained in medicine. *My training in medicine suggested that chronic diseases needed pharmaceutical solutions.* Diet and lifestyle may be mentioned but generally ignored in favor of prescription drugs. This would explain why Dr. Gundry and Dr. Wahls were both getting such good results with their similar approaches. They were getting to a root cause, inflammation, and not just treating symptoms. Inflammation was more important in disease than I realized. Years ago I had heard one of my nutritional medicine mentors mention that inflammation is a part of about 80% to 90% of chronic diseases. The realization that most of the chronic diseases facing me in my busy medical practice had an inflammatory component suggested that *an anti-inflammatory diet might be a good starting point* in treating patients with chronic diseases. It also suggested that *if removing certain foods may support healing, then some foods were potentially harmful and could cause disease.* This is way beyond saying that too much sugar is bad for you.

Most of my patients were still getting a copy of Dr. Gundry's anti-inflammatory diet to follow if they had a chronic disease or just wanted to avoid chronic diseases of aging. I was still going to Palm Springs once or twice a year to learn more from Dr. Gundry. Interestingly, while his consultations with his patients did not seem to change much over the years from my perspective, what changed was the type of patients. Earlier, most patients were being treated for heart or cardiovascular issues. More recently, *patients were coming in with other chronic diseases, especially autoimmune diseases and less specific* diseases like *fibromyalgia and chronic fatigue. His anti-inflammatory approach was helping them too.* This observation affirmed that inflammation was a significant issue in most chronic diseases and that they might improve with an anti-inflammatory diet and lifestyle. I came to understand that the goal was to reduce inflammation. A big obstacle was the inflammation coming from our standard American diet. Another part of the inflammation was coming from our lifestyle. *Stress or worrying and sleep deprivation as well as toxins all could add to the inflammatory load on the body.* I still did not know why this was true, but it was too obvious to ignore. I was seeing good results in many of my patients with using this approach.

Avoiding certain foods to avoid illness and enhance healing was not new. Mainstream docs have sometimes advised patients to avoid gluten found in wheat and other grains if they were diagnosed with celiac disease. Generally, there was no significant recommendations about foods to avoid, except maybe sugar and fats. Over the last twenty years I had heard physicians I considered authorities in nutritional medicine, like Andrew Weil and Jonathan Wright, recommend the avoidance of certain "healthy" foods like wheat and dairy but not explain why. It was true that *many patients' symptoms and diseases improved when they limited or deleted certain foods such as wheat and dairy,* but I was not aware of a mechanism to explain it. Some used terms like "food allergy" or "food sensitivity" to explain why avoiding certain foods might help some patients. Interestingly, the answer to why an anti-inflammatory-diet approach was helping in numerous chronic conditions was already in front of me in Dr. Gundry's work.

When I started using Dr. Gundry's diet with my patients, I did so because I wanted to replicate the good results he was getting with his patients. I still had not learned why his approach worked, but it seemed that as in the case of Dr. Wahls, changing the diet was essential. He repeatedly mentioned lectins in foods like grains and dairy as something that should be avoided in the food we consumed. Gluten was a lectin, which some people with chronic diseases were avoiding or limiting. Dr. Wahls mentioned lectins in her book as well, but she did not seem to focus too much on the topic. Still, I did not appreciate how important lectins were in promoting inflammation till the spring of 2017, when Dr. Gundry's *The Plant Paradox* was published. There I found the answers to my questions and more. One very important answer was lectins.

To understand how "healthy" food can lead to chronic inflammation and disease, we must understand lectins. What makes these foods potentially harmful is that they contain lectins. *Lectins are proteins present in plants that can potentially harm us by damaging the lining of the small bowel.* The small bowel is where nutrients are absorbed after digestion. The lining of the small bowel is surprisingly only one cell thick and acts as a border between the outside world and the inside of your body. On top of that lining is the mucus and your microbiome, or probiotics protecting that lining. Outside this border is the immune system and blood vessels. If something

Once unwanted agents get in and the immune system reacts, you have the beginning of inflammation.

The #1 cause of inflammation is still stress, and the #2 cause is food. It may be easier to change your diet than to change your stress.

If you have a chronic disease, you probably have chronic inflammation.

is inside your intestine, it is not really inside your body until it crosses the border or lining of the small bowel. *Between the cells of the small bowel are tight junctions meant to keep unwanted materials from getting in between the cells. Anything that breaks down these tight junctions between cells will create a space through which unwanted proteins or infectious agents may pass through. This is called increased intestinal permeability or "leaky gut."* When these unwanted agents cross the barrier or "leak in," they are in the body. At this point the immune system, ever present at the border, reacts to defend you. *Once they get in and the immune system reacts, you have the beginning of inflammation.*

The immune system has two basic functions, to defend and to repair. In this case it is defending you from foreign proteins or substances that are not supposed to be there. This is *the essence of inflammation; the immune system is reacting to something that should not be there, whether it be bacteria or a foreign protein from wheat.* There are many things besides lectins that can disrupt these tight junctions and create a space through which lectins or other proteins or bacteria can pass through or leak in. Stress and certain drugs like ibuprofen and prednisone are able to break down these tight junctions. I believe that *the #1 cause of inflammation is still stress, and the #2 cause is food. It may be easier to change your diet than to change your stress.* If you could have changed your stress, you already would have left that stressful job or relationship. Again, *anything that causes leaky gut, whether it be stress, lectins, an infection, or too much ibuprofen, is going to set off an inflammatory response by an immune system that is only doing its job.* What starts as a protective response can become harmful and lead to chronic diseases when the inflammation stays turned on and becomes chronic inflammation.

The first half of this chapter reviewed the basics of nutrition to help you understand the different food groups and learn more about vitamins and minerals and why they are essential. The information was more about benefits from choosing these foods. When we think of unhealthful foods, we think of the many nonfoods in our diet, including sugar, sweets, and processed and packaged foods. *Reading a package label, it often becomes obvious there are numerous additives and chemicals besides the original* food, such as potato in a potato chip. What many of us are not aware of are *the lessons from Dr. Gundry and Dr. Wahls, that many foods generally considered healthful, such as whole grains and dairy products, can actually promote increased inflammation and chronic diseases.*

From both Dr. Gundry and Dr. Wahls, I learned concepts about food that have shaped the way I practice medicine today, with all patients, but more so those with chronic diseases. I take time to explain to all my patients the connection between food, inflammation, and chronic diseases. My approach to preventing and reversing chronic diseases is based on three basic ideas. First, *if you have a chronic disease, you probably have chronic inflammation.* Second, inflammation means that something is turning on the immune system. Third, *lectins in our food, especially grains, dairy, and legumes, turn on our inflammation by causing leaky gut, which allows foreign proteins to get in*. Perhaps this is why for reversing chronic diseases, Dr. Gundry likes to say, "First, stop making holes," by avoiding the lectins and other things that can cause the leaks. Then we need to repair the leaky gut with supplements and foods like bone broth and coconut milk. In addition, we support liver detoxification, since chronic inflammation has made more work for the liver to detoxify. Currently, all my patients get a copy of the lectin-free, anti-inflammatory diet as well as an information sheet to answer frequently asked questions. To learn more about lectins and the anti-inflammatory diet, patients are also referred to many of the YouTube videos where Dr. Gundry discusses lectins and other factors in our food and environment that also promote inflammation and chronic diseases.

I have come to appreciate that most chronic diseases have an inflammatory component. Lessons from Dr. Wahls and Dr. Gundry suggest that *if you have an inflammatory condition, an anti-inflammatory diet will be a good place to start*. Next would be an anti-inflammatory lifestyle, which means avoiding things that increase inflammation, such as stress, and *implementing more behaviors to reduce inflammation, such as good sleep, mild to moderate exercise, stress management, and activities like yoga, meditation, and mindfulness*. Also, avoiding negative thinking, negative people, and toxic relations as much as possible may reduce inflammation. Knowing the important role of stress in promoting inflammation and disease, the lessons in Balancing Act become more relevant in helping you with a mind, body, and spirit approach to developing your anti-inflammatory lifestyle.

☯ **Return to your breathing.**

Summary

The foods we choose, and how we combine them, can have an immediate and long-term effect on our optimal energy balance. The surprisingly high levels of sugar in our diet can lead to fatigue, irritability, and mood disorders and can increase the risk of common diseases like diabetes and heart disease. Eating high-fiber whole grains, fruits, and vegetables helps stabilize blood sugar and accompanying energy levels and lower cholesterol. Focusing on one nutrient—fiber—is a good start for decreasing the energy drain from eating high-glycemic-index foods, such as sugar and starches like processed wheat, rice, corn, and potatoes. High-glycemic foods will quickly increase blood sugar and insulin, as well as increase fat storage and triglycerides. Patients on a low-glycemic diet report an increase in energy and a decrease in sugar cravings. A low-glycemic diet helps keep the blood insulin levels lower by decreasing the sugar load presented to the body.

Eating strategies for higher energy: avoid sugar; cut out simple starches; add more fiber, vegetables and fruits, lean meats, and low-fat dairy; eat

Lectins in our food, especially grains, dairy, and legumes, turn on our inflammation by causing leaky gut, which allows foreign proteins to get in.

Implement more behaviors to reduce inflammation, such as good sleep, mild to moderate exercise, stress management, and activities like yoga, meditation, and mindfulness.

The foods we choose, and how we combine them, can have an immediate and long-term effect on our optimal energy balance.

Presence of mind is required to manage your stress, and remember the goal: optimal personal energy balance.

smaller portions more often. The size and timing of meals are important. Plan five smaller meals a day, about three to four hours apart. The benefits of following a low-glycemic diet include more energy and more-nutritious eating, which facilitates weight management. In keeping with the practical approach of Balancing Act, no special foods are required. You work with foods that are already available, and rearrange them. What is required is the presence of mind to manage your stress, and remember the goal: optimal personal energy balance. If you can follow the guidelines set forth in this chapter, you will begin to see the foods you eat have a positive effect on your personal energy and health.

With the increase in chronic diseases over the last fifty years, there has been more concern that the food in the standard American diet may be contributing to these chronic diseases. Foods that we thought were very healthful may be causing chronic inflammation and chronic diseases, including autoimmune diseases. When patients cut out sugar, grains, and dairy from their diet, we often see positive results, including improvement and reversal of chronic diseases and auto immune disorders. These lessons about using the anti-inflammatory diet to help patients are described in detail in Dr. Gundry's book, *The Plant Paradox*, and Dr. Wahls' book, *The Wahls Protocol*.

Exercise for Energy

7

Physical exercise is a sure way for basically healthy adults to immediately improve personal energy and to reduce long-term risk of numerous diseases. The benefits of regular physical activity make it an exceptional natural medicine that is available to all who are basically in good general health, and even for many who have chronic diseases or disabilities. Exercise is a superb antiaging medicine. The mind-body connection is clearly evident in the all-around benefits of physical activity on anxiety and depression. Aerobic exercises like walking and running increase endurance. Anaerobic exercises like weight training increase muscle mass and strength and strengthen bone mass. Walking is so beneficial and safe that it's one of the best ways to start building your own daily exercise program. Increasing a variety of activities in your daily routine can make a significant difference in your energy level too.

☯ **Bring your attention to your breathing.**

Spend Energy to Get Energy

Like diet, physical activity or exercise has been touted as a way to improve health in the young or the old, the sick or the healthy. Yet, as stated earlier, better health has not always been a sufficient incentive to get my patients to exercise more. A better incentive might be to reframe exercise as a prescription guaranteed to improve your personal energy level, immediately and in the long term.

For many Americans the idea of exercise conjures up images of sweat, pain, and boredom. The reality is that most people who engage in regular physical activity associate this exercise with increased energy, vitality, and pleasure. In *The Healthy Mind, Healthy Body Handbook*, David Sobel, MD, reminds us that the list of known benefits of proper exercise (see next page) makes it one of the best-known natural medicines, easily available, and free of harmful side effects. Those of us who exercise regularly will testify to the truth of Dr. Sobel's statement.

Exercise is beneficial for the body, mind, and spirit.

Exercise is beneficial for the body, mind, and spirit. Current medical research is studying and confirming many amazing health benefits of exercise. Some recent study results include the following:

- Men who walked a mile a day had a 30% reduction in risk of stroke. If they walked more than a mile a day, there was a 50% risk reduction.
- Subjects who rode stationary bicycles three times a week for nine months were able to improve short-term memory, concentration, and attention span.
- Adults who exercised regularly showed a significant reduction in the incidence of diabetes.
- Women who exercised at least four hours a week had a 37% lower breast cancer risk compared to women who did not exercise at all.
- Women who walked at a moderate pace for thirty to forty-five minutes twice a day had half the illness rate of those who remained sedentary.
- Nursing-home residents, trained to use exercise machines, doubled their muscle strength and increased their stair-climbing speed by 30%.
- Sleep-troubled adults aged fifty to seventy-six were found to experience improved sleep after following a four-month exercise program of moderate exercise, four times a week.

Some of the Ways That Regular Physical Activity Benefits Us

- increases personal energy
- reduces stress-related tension
- lowers blood pressure
- helps control weight
- reduces heart attacks
- reduces strokes
- increases stress resistance
- improves quality of sleep
- lowers risk of becoming diabetic
- decreases risk of osteoporosis
- helps protect against cancer
- reduces anxiety and depression
- increases strength and coordination
- reduces risk of falling in the elderly
- improves mental functioning and memory

Sedentary versus Active Lifestyle

The body can be described as a machine. Like many machines, it needs to "run" on a regular basis to maintain peak performance. Lack of physical activity, as in a sedentary lifestyle, is associated with many diseases. Heart disease, strokes, and cancer, the top three causes of death, are linked to a sedentary lifestyle. *A sedentary lifestyle is a risk factor for illness and death similar in degree to smoking, alcohol abuse, and a high-sugar, high-fat diet.*

During my high school years, I found a great deal on a used car with low mileage, due to its having been in storage for several years. Though it looked "like new," it turned out to be a bad investment, due to numerous unexpected problems that required repairs. The lesson learned is that long periods of inactivity can be harmful to the performance of a complicated machine like an automobile. The same is true about the human body. It runs better if subjected to regular physical activity. Recent research has underscored this point by describing a sedentary lifestyle as a risk factor for various diseases.

Regular physical activity is good natural medicine. An editorial in the September 2004 issue of the *Journal of the American Medical Association* summarized the current research: regular physical activity has health benefits for you regardless of your age or weight. In fact, regular physical activity is a proven remedy for both low fitness and excess body weight. For those who want to lose weight, regular exercise—along with caloric restriction—is a critical component of successful long-term weight management. Even without weight loss, regular physical activity increases fitness and reduces the risk of heart disease. Regular physical activity also increases insulin sensitivity and thus reduces the risk of adult-onset diabetes, even if a person remains overweight. In addition to these long-term benefits, there is the immediate benefit of increased personal energy level.

Medical Disorders Linked to a Sedentary Lifestyle:

- heart attacks
- cancer
- muscular injuries
- back pain
- osteoporosis
- strokes
- high blood pressure
- obesity

Regular physical activity increases personal energy.

A sedentary lifestyle is a risk factor for illness and death similar in degree to smoking, alcohol abuse, and a high sugar, high-fat diet.

Physical Activity and Increased Energy

Increasingly, over the past twenty years, numerous studies have confirmed that *regular physical activity can positively influence quality of life and longevity.* In the program presented in *Balancing Act*, regular physical activity is emphasized as a source of increased energy and vitality.

This increased energy becomes available both during and after the exercise. Along with increased energy, one can expect elevated mood, decreased anxiety, and increased resistance to stress. While there are numerous benefits to exercising, people who do so regularly often do so because it makes them feels good, both mentally and physically.

Since physical activity reduces the buildup of stress and tension, it reduces energy drain. *Regular physical activity increases energy gain and decreases energy drain.*

I exercise regularly to boost my energy level. One of my favorite energy-increasing exercises is bicycle riding. It is guaranteed to boost my energy and dispel whatever tension might have been building up inside me. Though I am quite appreciative of the positive effect of this exercise on weight management and reduction of heart disease and diabetes risk, I am most motivated by the immediate increase in energy and decrease in nervous tension that I experience after only twenty minutes or so of this activity. To that very satisfying end, I schedule regular physical activity daily.

When working intensely on projects such as writing this book or doing research, I usually set a timer for fifty to sixty minutes. At the end of that time, I engage in some brief physical activity like walking, biking, running in place, or stretching.

This activity energizes me, reduces nervous tension, and improves my mental state as well. As often as possible on regular workdays, I ride my bicycle to work, or, if I have to drive there, I park my car and ride a bicycle for thirty to forty minutes before I start my day. The long workdays preceded by this physical activity become more enjoyable and less stressful. It is easier to maintain continual attention to patients and to remain consistently observant, focused, and attentive.

Antiaging Effects

The increased energy, strength, and flexibility associated with increased physical activity are customarily associated with youth. A decrease in these markers as well as an increase in many diseases is usually associated with aging. Getting older is inevitable, but aging does not have to mean severe physical and mental deterioration. *Regular physical activity is an effective antiaging strategy because it can slow down the weakness and deterioration associated with the aging process.*

A recent study examined the relationship between exercise and age-related deterioration of health in senior citizens. The researchers found that people who walked an average of 2 miles per day were able to delay the infirmities of old age for an average of twelve years. This finding means that the infirmities that many consider to be a result of aging are really the side effects of sedentary and inactive lifestyles.

Many of the undesirable biological changes attributed to aging are the same changes associated with a sedentary lifestyle. The biological markers of aging listed in the first column below can often be delayed or improved, as indicated in the second column, with regular physical activity.

Aging can lead to

- decreased cardiovascular fitness
- decreased muscle mass
- increased body fat
- decreased strength and flexibility
- decreased bone mass
- decreased metabolic rate
- poor sleep habits
- decreased sexual performance
- decreased mental performance
- decreased energy

Exercise can lead to:

- increased cardiovascular fitness
- increased muscle mass
- decreased body fat
- increased strength and flexibility
- increased bone mass
- increased metabolic rate
- better sleep habits
- increased sexual performance
- increased mental performance
- increased energy

The multiple energizing and antiaging effects of exercise are related to how the human body utilizes oxygen for the production of energy. Some researchers suggest that the decrease in energy that is often experienced with aging may be due more to a *decrease in oxygen transport and utilization due to inactivity* rather than directly to growing older. Regular physical activity and, especially, physical training improve the body's ability to use oxygen more efficiently and create more energy. Exercise increases the flow of life-giving blood to the skin, tissues, and organs of the body.

This increase in life-giving blood flow might help explain why regular exercisers tend to look and feel better too. Beyond the age-defying benefits of exercise for the body are benefits for the mind.

Mind Benefits of Exercise: Stress, Anxiety, and Depression

Exercise is often helpful in healing three common energy-draining mental conditions: *stress, anxiety, and depression.* Research has confirmed that *regular exercise increases stress hardiness*; that is, the ability to experience

Many of the undesirable biological changes attributed to aging are the same changes associated with a sedentary lifestyle.

The multiple energizing and antiaging effects of exercise are related to how the human body utilizes oxygen for the production of energy.

stressful events with less psychological and physical impact. Researchers in Sweden found that factory managers who exercised regularly were more "stress-hardy"; more resistant to stress. Under stressful laboratory conditions, people who exercise regularly experience less muscle tension and anxiety. With the increased stress of college, students who exercise are less likely to experience medical problems that require visits to the doctor. This may be due to the positive effects of exercise on both mood and immune-system competence. Stress, as an integral part of modern urban life, is often unavoidable. Regular physical exercise increases personal energy and is readily available as an effective buffer against stress. *When your personal energy levels are high, you are less vulnerable to stress.*

Anxiety refers to the uneasiness and nervousness that accompanies worry and the perception of danger. When the threat is real, such as being in a crowded place when a fire breaks out, what you experience is fear. When you anticipate danger, or feel *as if* you are in a dangerous situation, but there is no real danger, what you feel is anxiety. Like stress, anxiety is another common, everyday example of the mind-body connection, because it has both mental and physical components that are clearly related. Research has shown that *as many as 75% of visits to a doctor's office are for symptoms related to anxiety*. These patients usually do not initially seek help with anxiety. Instead, they seek help for symptoms that are physical effects of anxiety. These often include increased heart rate, shortness of breath, insomnia, sweaty palms, nausea, and increased muscle tension.

In a state of anxiety, the body responds as if it were in danger of injury or death. In a real life-threatening situation, the body is programmed to turn on the Stress Response. In anxiety, or its more common form, worrying, there is often no immediate, real threat. However, the perception of danger in the mind is enough to turn on the Stress Response in the body. This inappropriate triggering can easily become a major energy drain, especially when it occurs frequently.

When the body is unable to discharge pent-up tension, much energy is drained in maintaining a state of alarm. This is sure to take its toll on the mind and body. In *Balancing Act*, worrying and anxiety are highlighted because they are common responses to daily living that can be major energy drainers. Reducing anxiety and worry is essential for conserving personal energy and increasing the quality of life. *Physical activity is very effective for reducing anxiety and worry.*

Research, as well as personal experience, has convinced me of the antianxiety effect of regular physical activity. Thirty minutes of aerobic exercise (walking, running) has been described as having a four-hour relaxing effect comparable to a low dose of a minor prescription tranquilizer. This makes aerobic activity a must for someone with generalized anxiety or panic attacks, as well as helpful for simpler anxiety and worrying.

When your personal energy levels are high, you are less vulnerable to stress.

Physical activity is very effective for reducing anxiety and worry.

Individuals who experience physical symptoms of anxiety, such as palpitations or gastrointestinal problems, are more likely to benefit from physical activity.

Those with predominantly mental symptoms, such as recurrent negative thoughts or difficulty concentrating, may also benefit from meditation or other types of relaxation exercises. Patients may need a combination of treatment and therapies, including medication, but, in my experience, patients with both mental and physical symptoms benefit from regular physical activity. It will probably be useful for you to experiment with different activities at varying levels of intensity to learn what is necessary for you to get the desired effects. Once you know what works for you, you will be able to use it regularly, or as needed, before and after those stressful, anxiety-producing situations that are sure to arise.

> *A patient in his thirties described himself as a "worrier." He had been able to successfully manage his anxiety symptoms with the use of prescription medication twice a day. After a while he grew tired of taking medication and agreed to try exercise to manage his anxiety. We worked on choosing an exercise program he could adhere to. By exercising twice a day—walking or swimming—he was able to successfully manage his anxiety without medication.*

Depression, like its cousin anxiety, offers another good example of how the mind and body are interconnected in health and illness. As such, one might expect that regular physical activity would have a positive impact on mood disorders like depression. The benefits of exercise on depression have been widely studied. *Researchers have found regular physical activity more helpful than psychotherapy for many people with the more common mild to moderate depression.*

> *At the University of Wisconsin, researchers assigned twenty-four patients with moderate depression either to an exercise program or to one of two forms of psychotherapy. The psychotherapy consisted either of one hour weekly for twelve weeks only, or of long-term psychotherapy for a year. Those in the exercise group ran with a trainer three times a week for forty-five to sixty minutes but had no psychotherapy. At the end of twelve weeks, three-quarters of those in each group had improved. However, at the end of a year, those in the exercise group were still running regularly on their own and were free of depression. Half of those in the other two groups had relapsed and were back in psychotherapy.*

Exactly how regular physical exercise influences mild to moderate depression is unclear. In his book *Mind Body Medicine*, Michael H. Sacks, MD, offers an integrative explanation to account for the beneficial effects of exercise on mood. He states, "The benefits may come from many factors; the decision to take up exercise; the symbolic meaning of the activity; the distraction from worries; the effects on self-image and the biochemical and physiological

Individuals who experience physical symptoms of anxiety, such as palpitations or gastrointestinal problems, are more likely to benefit from physical activity.

Researchers have found regular physical activity more helpful than psychotherapy for many people with the more common mild to moderate depression.

changes that accompany the activity."

Whatever the reason for the varied benefits to mental and physical health, exercise warrants a place in any personal wellness program. In general, people who exercise regularly as part of their daily routine feel better mentally and physically and positively influence the quality and length of their lives. *Exercising regularly can improve optimal energy balance by increasing energy and decreasing the draining effects of stress, insomnia, anxiety, and depression.*

Exercise Basics

Physical activity can be categorized as *aerobic* or *anaerobic*. The key differences between these two types of exercise are fuel source, intensity, and duration.

Aerobic activities such as walking, running, or biking are more active and involve the repetitive use of large muscle groups for a longer period of time. When large muscle groups are active, this increases the need for oxygen. In addition, the small muscle groups are also working to stabilize the larger ones. The body responds by increasing the heart rate and the respiratory rate to provide increased oxygen delivery to the appropriate tissues. Aerobic exercise is useful for weight management as well as to improve cardiovascular health.

Anaerobic exercise lasts only a short period of time or is of very high intensity, or both, as in weight training, sit-ups, or carrying a heavy suitcase. Anaerobic exercise burns mostly glucose stored in the muscles and liver. Since this type of exercise tends to be of shorter duration, it is not as helpful as aerobic for burning fat. However, since exercise such as weight training increases muscle mass, it can increase your metabolism and aid in weight management.

When exercise increases in duration and becomes moderate in intensity, aerobic metabolism dominates and a greater percentage of the fuel being used comes from fat. Some researchers say that it takes about thirty minutes of sustained aerobic activity before the body begins to burn fat for fuel. For weight loss, the activity may be mild to moderate, as in walking, but the longer it lasts, the better the results. The surgeon general and various groups such as the American College of Sports Medicine have come out in favor of *daily* exercise to combat the growing obesity epidemic in children and adults. *General guidelines recommend thirty minutes of daily activity to maintain weight and sixty minutes of daily activity to lose weight.*

For maximum cardiovascular benefit, you should participate in aerobic activity three times a week that is more demanding than that needed to lose weight. This means exercising at a moderate level, which raises your heart rate to a calculated level called the target heart rate zone (THRZ). *You gain the most cardiovascular benefit when you keep your heart rate in your target heart rate zone for about twenty minutes.* To calculate your THRZ, first

Exercising regularly can increase energy and decrease the draining effects of stress, insomnia, anxiety, and depression.

General guidelines recommend thirty minutes of daily activity to maintain weight and sixty minutes of daily activity to lose weight.

calculate the predicted maximal heart rate (PMHR). The PMHR is 220 minus your age. The THRZ, which is the desired heart rate for heart strengthening, is 60 to 80% of your PMHR. If you haven't been active for a while, you could start your zone at 50% of the PMHR.

Calculating Your Target Heart Rate Zone (THRZ)

First calculate your predicted maximal heart rate. Then calculate 60% and 80% of that rate. That is your target heart rate zone.

Example: For a fifty-year-old male, the PMHR is 220 – 50 = 170 beats per minute. The THRZ is 60 to 80% of 170, or 102 to 136 beats per minute.

Age	Predicted Max. Heart Rate	Target Heart Rate Zone
	220 – Age	(60–80%)
20	200	120–160
30	190	114–152
40	180	108–144
50	170	102–136
60	160	96–128
70	150	90–120

You gain the most cardiovascular benefit when you keep your heart rate in your target heart rate zone for about twenty minutes.

Check with your physician before starting your exercise program. Your physician can help you determine what kind of exercise is best for you, on the basis of your level of fitness and health, as well as advise you on your target heart rate zone. Once you know you have determined your THRZ, you gradually increase your aerobic exercise like walking, biking, or jogging to get into the zone. If you are below the zone, you can increase your resistance or pace. If you are above the zone, you should slow down to avoid strain or injury. *If you feel wiped out after your aerobic exercise, you are probably overdoing it.* If at any time the exercise feels too difficult, slow it down. We are more interested in developing the habit of exercising. You can always increase your activity later as you get stronger. While physical activity can be useful for weight management and to prevent heart disease, our main reason to exercise is to reduce stress and increase overall personal energy. You should feel invigorated and full of energy after you are done exercising.

A practical guideline for monitoring heart rate during moderate-intensity aerobic exercise is your ability to speak. With moderate-intensity exercise, you may not be able to sing, but you should be able to talk comfortably. If you cannot carry on a conversation while exercising, your heart rate is probably over target. To estimate your heart rate,

Check with your physician before starting your exercise program.

If you feel wiped out after your aerobic exercise, you are probably overdoing it.

take your pulse for fifteen seconds and multiply by four (or six seconds and multiply by ten).

Preparing to Start Your Exercise Program

To start a personal exercise program, you will need a change in your daily routine. In chapter 12, you will review the Six Stages of Change. The Action stage is the fourth stage and is preceded by the Preparation stage. Prepare to start your new exercise program with a change in your thinking. Use questions to begin the change process.

From where in your busy schedule will you steal the time to increase your physical activity? How can you fit it into your current schedule?

Another helpful step in preparing to change to a more physically active lifestyle is to create a positive motivation. First determine your primary motivation.

Why do you want to change now? What need causes you to be willing to exert the effort necessary to make this change? What will you do to be consistent in your effort?

Your motivating desire can be negative or positive. A negative motivation may help you get started, but its influence is usually short lived. A positive motivation gets stronger as you succeed. For example, when patients start exercising to avoid a heart attack, this negative motivation may help get them started. However, as the days go on and there is no heart attack, there seems less reason to stay with the exercise program. If one starts exercising to feel better and have more energy, the immediate and long-term increase in energy becomes a positive motivating and reinforcing factor over time. *When contemplating change, choose a positive motivation as soon as possible. It is more likely to lead to long-term compliance.*

My personal motivation for exercising regularly is not to manage weight or to strengthen my heart. I exercise to get more energy and to relieve my feelings of inner tension. Every time I exercise for more than twenty minutes, the payoff follows immediately. This helps reinforce the activity and increases the likelihood of doing it again, soon. The increased energy and decreased inner tension, which occur after only twenty minutes of continuous physical activity, make me feel better every time. The hard part is getting started.

Often I start to walk or to ride my bicycle thinking that it will be for only a few minutes. After ten or fifteen minutes I start to feel better and want to keep going longer. Once the resistance of inertia is overcome, it is easier to add a few more minutes. Now, as I plan each day, I decide where to fit exercise into my daily schedule. Though I plan to exercise

To start a personal exercise program, you will need a change in your daily routine.

When contemplating change, choose a positive motivation as soon as possible. It is more likely to lead to long-term compliance.

daily, I sometimes miss one or two days per week. This illustrates why I discourage patients from planning to exercise just three times a week, because if they miss one or two times, they will get only one or two periods of increased physical activity in that week. To increase energy and decrease stress, you need to exercise daily, if only because you have daily stressors and energy drainers.

Starting Your Exercise Program

Once you decide on your positive motivation and how you are going to fit it into your schedule, the next important step is to get started. Try to exercise daily, even if only for a few minutes. Initially, the important thing is to develop the habit of taking time from your full schedule to do something that is just for you. In some cases, I tell my patients who want to start using a health club that they should go there every day, even if they stay only for ten minutes, just to develop the habit. This is important, even if they just go in, change clothes, walk around a few minutes, change back, and leave. The immediate goal is to develop the habit of making time for the healthful activity. It is easier to get started if you make time in your daily schedule Start walking during your lunch break, after work, or after dinner. Effective aerobic activity does not mean exercising as hard as possible for as long as possible. While there are many forms of aerobic exercise, walking not only is the safest but is also very effective in achieving cardiovascular as well as other benefits.

Start by walking ten to fifteen minutes per day, then increase the time by five minutes each week, working up to thirty-five to forty minutes per day. This period of the day can become your personal time for reflection, planning, or prayer. If you must make some practical use of this time, consider returning calls on your cell phone or audio-taping messages to yourself.

If you feel any physical pain during or after your walk, you may be pushing too hard (and you should mention this to your doctor). It is better to slow down or decrease the intensity of your exercise than to push too hard, because if you get injured, you may have to stop exercising altogether. *Your goal is to develop the habit of healthful exercising.* Go for the habit. Once you have the habit, you will naturally increase the time and intensity. Interestingly, when you forgo exercise for a day or two, you will feel the difference. A reasonable goal, which provides most of the benefits associated with exercise, is to accumulate at least thirty minutes of moderately intense physical activity every day. It is not necessary to have a gym membership or fitness equipment to meet this goal. *Current research supports the belief that household physical activities and chores, such as climbing stairs, walking to errands, gardening, cleaning out the garage, or washing the car, count as exercise.* As you increase your level of activity, the immediate effects on personal energy and mood will support your continued effort. The long-term effects will add to your quality of life and vitality.

To increase energy and decrease stress, you need to exercise daily, if only because you have daily stressors and energy drainers.

Your goal is to develop the habit of healthful exercising.

Current research
supports the
belief that
household
physical activities
and chores
count as
exercise.

Current medical research is accumulating more and more evidence that exercise does not have to be strenuous to be health enhancing. Men who take part in light and moderate physical activity have fewer heart attacks than those with purely sedentary lives. Men who exercised moderately for just thirty minutes had the same protection from heart attacks as men who exercised three times as much.

Guidelines for Starting Your Exercise Program

1. Get your doctor's advice on the right diet and fitness routine for you.
2. Choose a positive motivation for increasing physical activity.
3. *Choose an activity that is enjoyable* (e.g., walking/dancing/ gardening).
4. Start a program that is realistic (i.e., fifteen to thirty minutes a day).
5. Make it a routine in your schedule.
6. Add increased physical activity into your everyday life pattern.
7. Exercise with a friend or group.
8. Do not work so hard that you feel pain.
9. If you get hurt, stop or slow down immediately, until you are healed.
10. Just get started!

Choose an
activity that is
enjoyable.

Aerobic exercise brings cardiovascular benefits, which decrease your risk of heart disease, such as lowering cholesterol and high blood pressure, losing fat, and increasing circulation to your heart and exercising muscles. Anaerobic exercise, such as weight lifting, improves and maintains strength, flexibility, and speed. Nevertheless, by itself, it cannot produce the desired cardiovascular benefits. Exercise specialists recommend, for a complete approach to fitness, that 70% to 80% of your total exercise time be devoted to aerobic activity, like walking. The remaining 20% to 30% should be spent on anaerobic exercise, like weight training.

The Basics of Weight Training

Weight training has the benefit of adding muscle mass and strength to your body. *More muscle means not only that you are stronger, but that you burn more calories, even when you are at rest.* Weight machines (especially with a pulley-and-cable system) or free weights are both useful for weight training. For healthful use, the weights should be used following a minimum of ten minutes of an aerobic workout like biking or running to warm up the muscles.

More muscle
means not only
that you are
stronger, but that
you burn more
calories, even
when you are
at rest.

In weight training for STRENGTH and ENDURANCE, you work with lower weights and higher repetitions (reps). This approach gives you strength and some increased muscle size while allowing your body to adapt in an easier and less painful way. Start with a weight that you can lift fifteen to twenty times. The ideal reps should be twenty for the first set, eighteen for the second set, and fifteen for the third set. The goal is to do a total of three sets, making sure to rest for thirty to sixty seconds between sets.

For increased STRENGTH and MUSCLE MASS, you use higher weights and fewer reps. This approach gives you strength and bigger muscles with less flexibility. Pick a weight that you can lift at least eight times with a moderate increase of effort by the eighth time. Do this eight to twelve times for one set, and then resting for thirty seconds and repeating the set of eight to twelve reps for a total of three sets.

An energizing and health-enhancing goal is to develop a lifetime habit of regular physical activity and weight training. Of the two types of weight training listed, the lighter weights with higher reps is preferred because of the decreased risk of injury and the increased endurance and flexibility. In both types of weight training, lift the weight to a count of two, and let it down again to a count of four, being careful not to rush through the motions. When you are able to do three sets as described, it is considered safe to increase the load gradually by 2.5 to 5 pounds, so that the three sets of reps can be done with moderate increase in effort, as before. If you are beginning weight training, be sure to take your time.

Weight training should usually be done every *other* day to allow the muscles time to repair and rebuild. Some people can do weight training daily if they work each group of muscles every other day, such as upper body on one day, and lower body the next day. It is normal to have a little soreness or discomfort the next day when you first begin working out, but this should not be extreme, and it should subside in one or two days. Stretching before and after lifting can aid in limiting soreness or discomfort. If you are not sure, wait a little longer before working out again, and work on a different group of muscles. If pain is severe, or it persists or increases, consult your physician.

You can get further information on weight training on the internet, by checking at your library, or, best of all, in a session with a personal trainer at your health club. Select a trainer who will pay close attention to your body's cues and teach you to do the same, rather than pushing you beyond realistic limits. By working on a reasonable program, in a few short weeks you will see and feel a positive difference.

Basic Weight-Training Guidelines

The guidelines below are for an average-sized, healthy adult and may differ for different people. *As always, you should check with your physician before beginning any new physical exercise program.*

- Warm up with aerobic activity for approximately ten to thirty minutes.

An energizing
and health-
enhancing goal is
to develop a
lifetime habit of
regular physical
activity and weight
training.

You should
check with your
physician before
beginning any new
physical exercise
program.

- For *strength and endurance,* pick a weight you can lift twenty times with some effort. Do three sets: twenty reps, then eighteen reps, then fifteen reps. When the three sets are easy, increase by 2.5 to 5 pounds.
- For *strength and muscle mass,* pick a weight you can lift eight times with some effort. Do three sets of eight to twelve reps. When the three sets of twelve reps become easy, increase by 2.5 to 5 pounds.
- Rest thirty to sixty seconds between sets.
- Always lift to a count of two, down to a count of four.
- Monitor your progress.

☯ **Bring your attention to your breathing.**

Summary

Increasing physical activity is a natural and effective way to increase personal energy and decrease stress. Any way that you can increase your physical activity will increase your energy level, whether you go to the health club, walk to work, walk during lunch break, or go out dancing. Research confirms that increasing activity around the house by such activity as washing windows, vacuuming floors, gardening, raking leaves, or painting all count as physical activity.

The hard part for many people is finding the time in an already busy schedule. You can strategize to include more physical activity in your everyday life. The benefit of the amount of physical activity in which you engage is cumulative. Adding weight training to your workout will add valuable muscle mass that burns more calories, even when your body is at rest. All of your physical activity adds up to more personal energy, resistance to stress, and better health.

Sleep for Energy

8

Restful sleep is the first, most basic, and most natural method we have of repairing the ordinary daily wear and tear sustained by our bodies, and of replenishing our personal energy. Often, people think that sleep is a completely inactive state, but sleep is actually an active state for both the mind and the body. In sleep, regular cycles of brainwave activity occur, each lasting about ninety minutes. Each of these cycles contains up to six stages, all of which are useful in the body's rhythm of rest and repair.

In our society today, numerous medical surveys have shown that most people do not get as much sleep as needed. Mild symptoms, such as daytime drowsiness, are more likely due to sleep deprivation than to an initially suspected boredom or eating heavy meals. Serious sleep deprivation also causes many stresses in the body's chemistry and can increase the risk of illness, accidents, and even death. Obviously, we all need to avoid sleep deprivation and make sure that we provide our bodies with adequate amounts and quality of sleep. Strategies for improved quantity and quality of sleep include keeping a regular sleep schedule, engaging in daily exercise, and managing stress. In addition, natural herbal remedies and prescription and nonprescription drugs can sometimes be used to help you establish a pattern of good sleep. The first steps to better sleep are to make it a priority, to gain a solid understanding of what sleep is and how it works in benefiting your body and, with your physician, to work on establishing the best healthful sleep pattern that you can.

☯ Bring your attention to your breathing.

Sleep for Personal Energy

Good sleep means more personal energy. The restorative power of sleep is well known. This healing aspect of sleep makes getting a good night's rest *essential* in any personal energy program. The body repeatedly confirms the importance of sleep. At the first sign of a cold or flu, a good night's rest may ward off an impending illness that might otherwise incapacitate you for a few days. If you do get sick, extra sleep time may speed recovery. In the midst of an overload of stress at home or at work, sleep supports healing and may even prevent the occurrence of stress-related symptoms.

To become more aware of the effects of sleep, you can prove its health-enhancing effects for yourself by keeping track of your personal energy levels and the number of hours you sleep. You can expect to notice an increase in your personal energy level on the days you sleep eight hours compared to the days when you sleep only six hours. Sleep is unique in that its benefits to personal energy, productivity, and well-being are universal, as part of the body's innate patterns for maintaining health. Sleep is natural to all of us; we are already programmed for sleep.

Good sleep, like calm, is your natural state; part of the human body's natural pattern. We know innately how to sleep, and our biological rhythm is set for a generally consistent amount of restorative sleep. Knowing this, we recognize the importance of removing any obstacles to getting good, restorative sleep. Getting enough good, sound sleep helps provide restoration and energy so that we can get through our daily activity. To claim your own natural gifts from good sleep, you can learn about sleep and how to get it and then commit to providing yourself with an adequate—and even generous—night's sleep as often as possible.

A commitment to good quality and quantity of sleep is necessary in planning for optimal energy. Unfortunately, when demands and responsibilities overload us, sleep time is often the first thing we cut back on. It's ironic, because when we are facing increased demands and overload of stress is the very time when we need to get *more* sleep. Yet, we often mistakenly choose to reduce our sleep time. Giving up sleep to try to achieve balance is like the archaic and misguided medical therapy of bleeding sick patients to try to make them stronger, or trying to improve your finances by earning less money. Good sleep is a strong personal energy gainer. Though most people can *get by* on fewer than eight hours of sleep, they do so at an actual *cost* to mind and body health.

Before we review strategies for optimal sleep, it will be helpful to review some of the current knowledge and research on the multilevel benefits of sleep, as well as signs and consequences of sleep deprivation. With a better understanding of these findings, you will be better able to appreciate sleep as an invaluable resource for daily replenishing your personal energy. In addition, you will have learned some new and different strategies to gain more optimal, natural, health-enhancing sleep.

Good sleep, like calm, is your natural state; part of the human body's natural pattern.

A commitment to good quality and quantity of sleep is necessary in planning for optimal energy.

Understanding the Nature of Sleep

Sleep is more than rest. We can "rest" without sleeping. We are also aware that sleep is not a state of complete mental and physical inactivity. Sleep studies show that the overall level of brain activity drops only about 10% during sleep and can increase dramatically during intense dreams.

While in deep sleep, some people have been known to eat, walk, talk, laugh, cry, kick, scream, or even attack another person. We can also understand sleep more by comparing it to other unconscious states, such as being in a coma or under anesthesia, which we recognize are not forms of sleep, because they are not easily reversible. Nor is hypnosis the same as sleep. The hypnotized person hears and responds to the suggestions of the hypnotizer.

Researchers have found that during sleep, significant changes regularly occur in brainwave activity, eye movements, body temperature, respiration, heart rate, and hormonal activity. In fact, while we sleep, the brain is often more active than when we are awake. *During sleep, the brain is very busy regulating multiple levels of brain and body functions.* Sleep enhances the mind's capability for learning new things and for recalling ideas from memory. Sleep is also important in influencing present moods. For the body, sleep helps regulate the functioning of the gastrointestinal, cardiovascular, and immune systems, as well as reenergizing the body to take on the activities of the next day. We can be certain that failure to get adequate sleep has inevitable impact on brain function, moods, and body functions.

Lack of adequate sleep poses costly and serious threats to both personal and community health. The problem of sleep deprivation has been increasing for years and is constantly being made worse by the faster and more-complicated schedules that many people feel forced to maintain. Today, there is a vast and growing body of knowledge about sleep, thanks to the many researchers who are studying this ubiquitous process, which is common to all humans and to all mammals in the animal kingdom.

The Active Side of Sleep

Until the 1930s, sleep was generally thought to be simply a passive, restful state. In 1935, scientists began studying brainwave patterns that occurred during sleep. Electrodes were attached to the scalps of volunteers to measure tiny electrical signals made by their brains.

Researchers discovered that sleep was characterized by separate and distinct brain wave patterns. During the course of a night's sleep, these brain wave patterns occurred in cycles that could be divided into six stages. This nighttime activity was distinguished from activity when the subjects were awake. Today we use the term "sleep architecture" to describe the cycles and stages of sleep and their interrelationships. There are two kinds of sleep: non-rapid-eye-movement (non-REM) sleep and rapid-eye-movement

During sleep, the brain is very busy regulating multiple levels of brain and body functions.

Lack of adequate sleep poses costly and serious threats to both personal and community health.

(REM) sleep. Non-REM sleep includes stage 1, stage 2 and delta sleep. REM sleep, also called fast sleep is associated with increased dreaming. Scientists have categorized sleep brainwave activity into several stages as follows:

- Calm wakefulness—slightly slower *alpha* waves, as person begins to fall asleep
- Stage 1 (about one-half to seven minutes in duration)—During this stage, reactivity to outside stimuli is diminished as senses turn off; heart rate decreases; breathing becomes more shallow and regular.
- Stage 2 (five to ten minutes)—Sleep, with specific brain waves with spindles; brain is asleep in non-REM sleep.
- Delta sleep (thirty to forty minutes)—slow, large, *delta* waves; deep sleep; difficult to arouse; breathing and heart rate slower; muscles relaxed
- REM sleep—fast *alpha* waves with *theta* waves; muscle tone absent; dreaming

Of the several sleep cycles that occur during a night's sleep, each one lasts about ninety minutes in adults (about two hours in children). The longer we sleep, the more cycles our bodies go through. *In each sleep cycle, we go from stage 1 to the deep delta sleep, then retrace back to stage 2 of almost awakening, before moving to REM or dreaming sleep.* Our eyes move rapidly from side to side, as if we are scanning our surroundings. After a few minutes of REM sleep and dreaming, we go back to the deeper delta sleep, then back again to almost awake, then another episode of REM sleep.

In the first cycle of the night, the REM or dreaming period lasts only a few minutes. With each successive sleep cycle, the REM period becomes longer. *Thus, the longer we sleep, the more cycles we complete and the longer time we spend in restorative REM sleep.* If we sleep fewer than six hours, we may get only three or four cycles, which include a shorter period of REM sleep. With eight or nine hours, we may have five or six cycles, with progressively longer REM dreaming periods. *During REM periods, the brain and nervous system are more active than during either wakefulness or deep sleep.* During the first REM period, lasting less than ten minutes, we are likely to experience our first dream of the night. During REM sleep the brain is active, but the body remains relatively motionless, providing rest for the body's structures and systems, and avoiding injury to self or others, which could occur should we act out our dreams.

The diagram below illustrates the various stages of the sleep cycle in a young adult.

In each sleep cycle, we go from stage 1 to the deep delta sleep, then retrace back to stage 2 of almost awaking, before moving to REM or dreaming sleep.

The longer we sleep, the more cycles we complete and the longer time we spend in restorative REM sleep.

REM sleep is restorative to the brain and to the mind.

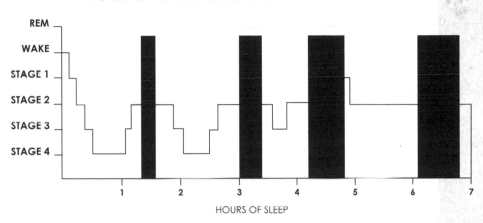

YOUNG-ADULT SLEEP HISTOGRAM

Healing REM Sleep

While the first part of the sleep cycles is restorative to the body by allowing for rest, the later REM sleep is restorative to the brain and to the mind. Researchers agree that the non-REM sleep of delta sleep is also essential for restoring and maintaining health. Increased blood flow to relaxed muscles during deep sleep helps the body recover and heal itself. Decreased body temperature during these periods helps conserve energy, which is necessary for repair and renewal of body tissues. During deep sleep, the immune system releases chemical mediators, which protect us from infections. Even a couple of hours of sleep deprivation can increase our susceptibility to viruses. *Getting the deep sleep your body needs will reward you with increased energy and alertness, and decreased susceptibility to diseases.*

REM sleep is restorative to the brain by allowing for the replenishment of neurotransmitters like norepinephrine and serotonin, and it improves learning, memory storage, and mental organization. The importance of REM sleep to learning can be observed in the increased activity in the brain areas that are associated with learning. For example, intense periods of learning and training in our lives are usually accompanied by an increase in REM sleep.

Just as memory retention and recall improve after sufficient REM sleep, a lack of REM sleep is associated with difficulty in learning and recalling previously learned information. *Those who get more REM sleep tend to do better on test taking and complicated mental tasks.* During REM sleep, things learned during the day are reorganized within previously stored memory. This may be why we are often able to see a solution to a perplexing problem in a dream, or after "sleeping on it." During this nightly memory reorganization, important memories are filed with similar or related memories, while less important information is forgotten.

Two important brain neurotransmitters, norepinephrine and serotonin, are involved with mood, and they also play a significant role in learning and

Getting the deep sleep your body needs will reward you with increased energy and alertness, and decreased susceptibility to diseases.

REM sleep allows for the replenishment of neurotransmitters and improves learning, memory storage, and mental organization.

Those who get more REM sleep tend to do better on test taking and complicated mental tasks.

remembering. Normally, the amount of these important neurotransmitters that is stored in the brain is used up during the day and then is replenished during REM sleep. Sleep deprivation, due either to decrease in quantity or quality of sleep, will interfere with replenishment of these substances, which may lead to difficulties in learning new information and remembering stored memories. Fewer neurotransmitters due to persistent sleep deprivation can contribute to serious mood disorders such as anxiety and depression. Increasing the amount of REM sleep by adding enough time in bed to ensure adequate sleep cycles can help refresh neurotransmitters, which in turn can help you improve performance, mood, and personal energy.

Note in the diagram above that with each successive sleep cycle, the duration of the health-enhancing REM period increases. In the first cycle, the REM stage may last only about ten minutes but, by the end of a fourth cycle, may last as long as sixty minutes. If, like many of my patients, you are sleeping less than six hours, that extra healing REM sleep of the later cycles may not be available for you.

With each successive sleep cycle, the duration of the health-enhancing REM period increases.

Basic Sleep Requirements

Though the exact amount of sleep needed for optimal energy and productivity varies with the individual, researchers have provided some guidelines. In general, if you wake up feeling rested and wide awake and retain energy *all* day long, you probably are getting the sleep your body needs for your age and activities. The younger you are, the more hours of sleep you need each day. Adolescents, especially during high school, tend to be chronically sleep deprived, though they often try "to make up for lost sleep" on weekends and during the summer. Most adults need the full eight hours of sleep per day that they have traditionally been advised to have. Many adults, however, are sleeping only six hours or less, per night. The table below lists sleep-requirement guidelines for the various age groups.

Sleep Requirements for Different Age Groups

The normal sleep cycles vary with age.

- Newborns: 16.5 hrs.; 6 mo: 14.25 hrs.; 1 yr: 13.75 hrs.; 18 mo: 13.5 hrs.
- Teens: Need 9.25 hrs. but get only 7.5 (more in summer). *The most sleep-deprived age group.*
- Adults: Age 29–64: need 8 hrs. but actually average only 6.7 hrs. during week, the least amount. Most are sleep deprived.
- New parents lose 1–2 hrs per night during baby's first year.
- Seniors: 65 and over: need 8 hours. This group is the most sensitive to noise and light. This group often has problems with sleep due to medications, and medical and emotional conditions.

The elderly have much less deep sleep, which makes them more likely to be easily awakened.

The normal sleep cycles vary with age. Children's cycles tend to last about two hours, while adults tend to have 1.5-hour cycles.

Children tend to have more deep sleep than adults, who have more deep sleep than the elderly. *While the elderly still need about eight hours of sleep, during their normal cycles they have much less deep sleep, which makes them more likely to be easily wakened by noise or light. These differences in sleep cycles with age are depicted below.*

NORMAL SLEEP CYCLES

CHILDREN

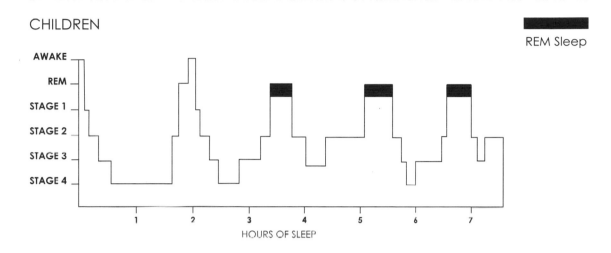

REM Sleep

YOUNG ADULTS

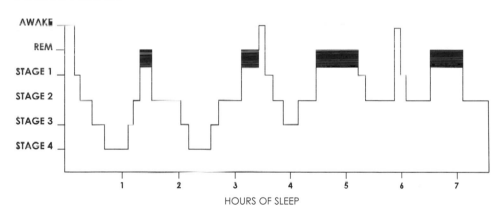

ELDERLY

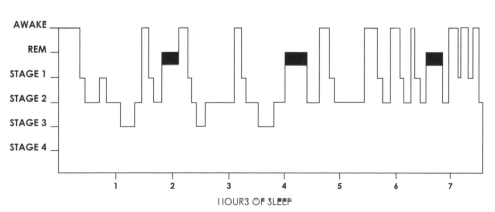

Sleep and Performance

What do researchers say is the recommended amount of sleep for optimal performance?

....

....

....

....

....

Ten hours of sleep is required per day for healthy adults, for optimal performance.

A surprisingly high percentage of adult patients in my practice tell me that they are getting only six hours or even less of sleep per night. When advised that eight hours is still necessary, they tend to dismiss it. Perhaps they're in denial, or perhaps they think that if they are able to get through the day, it must be okay. Unfortunately, although they may be managing to get through the day on six hours of sleep or less, it can cost their health and well-being much more than they realize (see "Personal Cost of Sleep Deprivation" below). They may be confusing the number of hours they can sleep and still get through the day with the number of hours the body needs for optimal performance.

The body needs eight hours or more of sleep each day.

Sleep researchers tell us that the body needs eight hours or more of sleep each day. Researchers at the Sleep Disorders Research Center of the Henry Ford Hospital in Detroit, Michigan, have demonstrated this with subjects who usually sleep eight hours but are given a chance to get two additional hours of sleep. They found that the subjects' performances improved in areas of energy, processing information, critical thinking, and creativity. Their conclusions further support the idea that *one of the best things you can do the night before a big test or presentation is to go to bed early.*

One of the best things you can do the night before a big test or presentation is to go to bed early.

For many adults, part of the price of living in modern cities is getting less sleep. *A hundred years ago, most people still slept about ten hours each night.* Since then, with the advent of electrical lighting everywhere and "cities that never sleep," the amount of sleep people get has steadily decreased. In the face of increased demands at home, work, and school, many people choose to cut back on sleep time as a way to balance their responsibilities. Unfortunately, this may lead to more imbalance rather than to the desired balance. Because many Americans have reduced their sleep time to eight hours and even less, and one-third sleep less than six hours a night, we need to examine the hidden costs.

The Personal Cost of Sleep Deprivation

Increased risk for moodiness, injury, or illness is the price extracted by sleep deprivation. Though you may be able to get through the day, it will be at the cost of a significantly reduced performance. Not only is your overall energy level decreased, but also you lose even more energy because you are more quickly angered or frustrated. Sleep deprivation makes it easier for you to feel overwhelmed with simple problems and moderate workloads. *If you give your body less sleep than it requires, your body responds as if you are under increased stress.* Your adrenal glands secrete more stress hormones, like cortisol and norepinephrine. Cortisol leads to an increase in blood sugar and suppresses the immune system, while norepinephrine leads to an increase in blood pressure. In addition, when sleep-deprived, you are more likely to consume high-sugar foods and caffeine drinks to help you stay awake, both of which put more demands on your adrenals. Because the immune system is revitalized during REM sleep, lack of sleep results in reduced immunity and increased susceptibility to whatever virus is in your surroundings. Productivity at work is likely to be reduced, due to the decreased ability to learn, to recall, and to solve problems.

Checklist of Personal Costs of Sleep Deprivation

- decreased energy
- increased sugar consumption
- reduced immunity to disease
- increased risk of premature death
- decreased learning and recall

- daytime drowsiness
- increased irritability
- increased stress
- increased forgetfulness
- reduced productivity

It is hoped that awareness of the costs of sleep deprivation will motivate you to give sleep the top priority that it deserves in your schedule, as a powerful tool for improving your energy, health, and productivity. A significant obstacle for some people in taking this step is that people who have become habitually sleep-deprived have often become completely accustomed to functioning at a reduced capacity. This reduced functioning feels normal. One way to find out how sleep deprivation may be affecting you is to experiment by increasing your sleep time by one or two hours per night for several nights. Then, monitor the effect of the extra sleep on your energy, mood, and productivity with your Behavior/Symptom Monitor Card (see appendix).

Signs of Sleep Deprivation

Even small amounts of sleep loss can have significant detrimental effects on how you think, feel, function, and make decisions. *Sleep deprivation reduces problem-solving ability, increases emotional irritability, and increases susceptibility to stress.* Lack of proper sleep can weaken the immune system

If you give your body less sleep than it requires, your body responds as if you are under increased stress.

and make you more vulnerable to infections. Sleep deprivation can also alter the functioning of your gastrointestinal and cardiovascular systems, aggravating irritable bowel syndrome, constipation, and hypertension. The longer the sleep deprivation goes on, the higher your risk of generalized fatigue and even depression. It may be helpful to review some of the common signs of sleep deprivation that many have learned to accept as a "normal" part of aging.

What are some of the ways that you can tell if you are not getting enough sleep?

....

....

....

....

....

Signs of sleep deprivation include waking up tired, and sleeping on the train to work, during meetings, and in front of the TV.

Morning grogginess is probably one of the most common signs of inadequate sleep. Dozing off on the commuter train on the way to work is another indicator. You may have experienced a heavy lunch that you thought made you sleepy, or a meeting that you thought was so boring that you couldn't keep your eyes open. These, too, can be common signs of sleep deprivation. A condition called narcolepsy can also cause a person to feel sleepy at more-than-usual times, but it is a specific disease condition that your doctor can diagnose, if that should be the case. Far more commonly, however, sleepiness after a heavy meal or a boring class or meeting is a symptom of an underlying physiological sleepiness that exists because of sleep deprivation to the body. People who suffer from insomnia will verify that heavy meals or boring situations do not have any sedative or sleep-inducing effects in and of themselves. If they did, people with insomnia would have the same meal at bedtime and expect to be able to get drowsy and fall asleep without any problem.

On any day that you have had eight hours of good sleep, you could have that same heavy meal and sit through the most boring of meetings and still not fall asleep. You might feel painfully stuffed or bored, but you would not get sleepy.

There are other physical signs that you might consider normal but that are actually signs of sleep deprivation. *If, when you go to bed, you go to sleep as soon as your head hits the pillow, you are probably sleep-deprived.* Normally, it takes ten to fifteen minutes to go to sleep. If you fall asleep while sitting

Sleep deprivation reduces problem- solving ability, increases emotional irritability, and increases susceptibility to stress.

Morning grogginess is probably one of the most common signs of inadequate sleep.

If you go to sleep as soon as your head hits the pillow, you are probably sleep-deprived.

in front of the TV, you are probably sleep-deprived. Those signs are not normal, and not a part of normal tiredness. Researchers in sleep deprivation advise that if you feel sleepy or drowsy in the daytime, there is a good chance you have a sizable sleep debt. The following table lists other signs of sleep deprivation, which you may have started to think of as "normal."

Checklist of Signs of Sleep Deprivation

- can't wake up without alarm clock
- wake up sleepy
- wake up tired
- doze on commuter train
- sleepy after small amount of alcohol
- get drowsy while driving
- need a nap to get through the day
- sleepy after a heavy meal
- too tired to play with kids
- sleepy during meetings
- trouble concentrating
- trouble remembering
- fall asleep in five minutes in bed
- fall asleep watching TV, concerts

Dr. Rosalind Cartwright, a sleep disorder specialist, reminded me that while most adults need eight hours of good sleep, it may not be true for everyone. She went on to say that "if you sleep only six or seven hours and still have energy all day with no signs of sleep deprivation, you're probably getting enough sleep."

Sleep Deprivation and Alcohol

One relatively common sign of sleep deprivation is worth special mention here because it can be potentially fatal. Sleep deprivation can augment the sedative effect of even small amounts of alcohol.

Research has shown that when an automobile crash is attributed to alcohol use, very often a less obvious factor or even the primary cause may be sleep deprivation. One recent study focused on the interaction of sleep deprivation and small amounts of alcohol use. Volunteers were given a small amount of alcohol or a placebo after completing three different sleep schedules: (1) a week of ten hours of sleep per night, (2) a week of eight hours of sleep per night, and (3) two nights of five hours of sleep per night. The subjects who were given the alcohol after eight hours of sleep experienced slightly more sleepiness than with the placebo. Those with two nights of five hours—or very little—sleep became very sleepy with the same dose of alcohol. However, those who had slept ten hours a night had little, if any, drowsiness from the alcohol.

If you sleep only six or seven hours and still have energy all day with no signs of sleep deprivation, you're probably getting enough sleep.

—Rosalind Cartwright

If you have gotten less than a full eight hours of sleep, even small amounts of alcohol may have a significant sedative effect on you.

The take-home lesson from this summary of the study is that *if you have gotten less than a full eight hours of sleep, even small amounts of alcohol may have a significant sedative effect on you and can interfere with your mental and physical functioning, especially in driving.*

Getting Restorative Sleep

In *Power Sleep*, Dr. James B. Maas provides four "Golden Rules of Sleep" that make sense:

1. Get an adequate amount of sleep every night.
2. Establish a regular sleep schedule.
3. Get continuous sleep.
4. Make up for lost sleep.

Having established that sleep enhances mind-body health, and having reviewed signs of sleep deprivation, I want to present ways to improve the quantity and quality of your sleep to increase your overall personal energy: the main goal of this program.

The benefits of increased sleep time for those deprived of sleep are often immediate and dramatic.

Attending to sleep is one of the most important positive health measures you can take for optimal energy and optimal health. *The benefits of increased sleep time for those deprived of sleep are often immediate and dramatic.* Older patients most often describe having increased energy and less of the fatigue that they thought was a part of getting older. Having more energy engenders a renewed interest in life activities and social interactions, which, in turn, increases the quality of life. Increased social support and interactions are associated with better health outcomes. Situations and people that may have seemed impossibly taxing before can become significantly more tolerable.

Many medical conditions will improve with more good-quality sleep.

Many medical conditions will improve with more good-quality sleep. Good sleep, like laughter, reduces some of the biochemical substances associated with inflammation. Reducing inflammation will help most chronic-pain conditions, including back pain, headaches, and arthritis. Chronic medical problems like hypertension and diabetes also respond favorably to improved quality of sleep. The increased secretion of stress hormones associated with sleep deprivation can cause a worsening of many chronic conditions. With adequate sleep, the levels of stress hormones are reduced, and there is less aggravation of many chronic medical problems.

Making something a priority usually means spending more energy on that topic or activity. Making sleep a priority means taking time to make plans to increase the quality and quantity of sleep. According to Dr. Maas, " Most people need to get sixty to ninety minutes more sleep than they presently get."

Your body has a natural biological "clock" that regulates early-morning secretion of several important hormones. As you change your schedule to allow you to get more sleep, *it is preferable to plan to continue to wake up at your usual time, and to get the added sleep at the beginning instead of at the end of your sleep time.*

When trying to catch up on sleep, go to bed an hour earlier but wake up at your usual time. *Cool-down activities are recommended for the thirty to sixty minutes preceding your expected sleep time.* It may be helpful to use some of the techniques you would use in getting younger children to go to bed. If 9:00 p.m. is your targeted bedtime, you would start toning down activity around 8 p.m., perhaps reading to the child while in bed, and then, "lights out" at 9:00 p.m.

Success is more likely if you establish a regular routine. This may mean having to go to bed without washing all the dishes, or without watching the often-scary and depressing nightly news. The hardest part for most "doers" and overachievers is "calling it a day." Sometimes, the second wind that comes in the evening makes it tempting to take on activities that will prolong your wake time. It may be useful to reframe ending the day's work as preparation for the next day. *That is, reinforce the idea that "tomorrow begins with good sleep tonight," so one of the best things to do for a better tomorrow is to prepare for a good night's sleep.* If you have signs and symptoms of sleep deprivation, look over the following guidelines for improving your sleep.

Finding Your Optimal Sleep Time

Presented here is a plan to determine the best amount of sleep time for you. If you have been very sleep deprived, you may want to start this plan on a weekend, or during a stay-at-home vacation when you have time to be flexible.

Plan to go to bed eight hours before you want to wake up. Stick to that bedtime for a week, while your body adjusts and resets its internal clock. If, after a week, you still show signs of sleep deprivation, go to bed thirty minutes earlier for the following week. To find your personal sleep quotient, keep adding fifteen to thirty minutes each week, until you can wake up without an alarm and have enough energy to get through the day alertly and comfortably.

Once you have a time that works for you, try to go to bed and wake up without an alarm clock at the same time every day, including weekends and days off. This is important for keeping your body clock regular. Waking up two hours later on weekends and then waking up at the old time on Monday morning will give you the same jet lag that occurs with waking up in a different time zone after traveling. The other problem with sleeping late on Saturday or Sunday morning is that it may make it hard to fall asleep that night, a condition sometimes referred to as "Sunday-night insomnia." The

> Cool-down activities are recommended for the thirty to sixty minutes preceding your expected sleep time.

> One of the best things to do for a better tomorrow is to prepare for a good night's sleep.

benefits of sleep are closely related to its duration and regularity. Some researchers believe that the time that you actually go to sleep is not as important as the duration and regularity of your sleep and wake times.

Reducing Sleep Interruptions

To take advantage of the energizing and health-enhancing benefits of sleep, you must develop a plan to optimize your sleep, in relationship to your unique schedule, responsibilities, and personality. If, as it is for most people, ten hours is simply out of the question for you, then try for eight. If that is still not possible, try to make what sleep you have continuous and without interruptions. *Six hours of uninterrupted sleep is more helpful than eight hours of fragmented sleep.* Ensuring that you sleep without interruptions may take a little planning, but it is well worth the effort. To reduce interruptions, consider turning off the phone at night, using earplugs and eye covers, and eliminating liquids three hours before bedtime, in order to avoid nightly trips to the bathroom. You can also purchase special shades and curtains, which will keep out the morning light a little longer. A cool, quiet, dark room is conducive to continuous sleep.

If sounds from within your home or outside activities like traffic are a potential problem, consider investing in a sound machine. Sound machines are available for approximately twenty-five dollars or less. They produce natural sounds like rain or ocean waves. These sounds can lull you to sleep or act to mask surrounding sounds that may be disrupting your sleep. These sound machines usually come with a shut-off timer, so you can leave it on while you fall asleep. If something awakens you, turn it on again.

Despite our best intentions, some occasional loss of our regular sleep is inevitable. Traveling, deadlines at work, a sick child, and numerous other situations and emergencies can set you up for short-term sleep deprivation. Once you understand the importance of sleep for almost all aspects of your life, you can work to safeguard your precious sleep time and keep the short-term problems as short as possible. Researchers have shown that sleeping one hour less a night over a period of a week can do as much damage as not sleeping for twenty-four hours. If you have a bad night of sleep, try to pay off your sleep debt by going to bed earlier the next night, rather than just waking later. While you might be tempted to sleep in longer on weekends to make up for those six-hour nights, it is best to follow the suggestions for a regular schedule, going to bed earlier and waking up at the same time every day. If this is not possible, then get the extra sleep hours whenever you can.

Naps for Restoring Energy

The thousands of Americans who are getting too little or poor-quality sleep can do something to regenerate themselves. *For most people, a short nap can restore one's personal energy level and return a sense of vitality and well-*

being. A well-placed nap can do all this in just a few minutes. Researchers recommend that the nap be around twenty minutes long, but definitely no more than thirty minutes long. A nap longer than thirty minutes may be counterproductive. With longer sleep time you slip into deeper stages of sleep and experience more grogginess and difficulty in waking up from your nap. The timing is also important. If you want more energy for extra work or a long drive in the evening, consider a short nap in the afternoon.

Studies of wakefulness during the day reveal that our lowest energy and wakefulness point during the day occurs about eight hours after waking up. For 6:00 a.m. risers, an ideal naptime would be between one and two in the afternoon. If you take your nap too late in the afternoon, it may delay your falling asleep at night. Sleeping on the job is not necessarily counterproductive. If you regularly get by on just six hours of sleep or less, you would do well to plan a fifteen-to-twenty-minute nap in the early afternoon. Find a quiet place where you will not be disturbed, to rest your eyes and body during the last part of your lunchtime.

Another option is to use your afternoon work break for a short nap, instead of a cup of coffee. A short nap will increase your energy, productivity, and sense of well-being. Napping is made easier if you actually lie down, rather than try to sleep at your desk, because a more comfortable position will facilitate falling asleep. Some large corporations are actually encouraging employees to take short afternoon naps because the results are ultimately good for the corporate bottom line. Some companies actually set aside quiet areas just for napping. Allowing for nap time cuts down on employee fatigue, boosts morale, and increases productivity, while reducing mistakes and accidents.

When I need the energy boost of some sleep while at work, I make time between patients for an energy-recharging nap. Usually, I know I need a nap when my personal energy level feels like a 5, out of 10, or less. I prefer to sleep on the floor, with my lower legs above me on the seat cushion of my office chair. I use a pillow normally tucked in a corner of my office, eye covers, and earplugs. After putting up a "Do Not Disturb" sign on my door, I set a timer for fifteen to twenty minutes and drift away, while practicing the Breath Awareness exercise. Often, I am not even sure if I fell asleep, but the time passed and I find that my energy is restored to a more favorable 7 or 8, out of 10. With the added energy, I can then provide renewed attention and better service to my patients.

Strategies for Optimal Sleep

Millions of working Americans, troubled by poor-quality sleep, are likely to benefit from the various strategies that have come out of the major research projects on sleep. As in changing any lifestyle behavior, the most important thing is to make your goal—in this case, getting life-enhancing,

A short nap can restore one's personal energy level and return a sense of vitality and well-being.

Our lowest energy and wakefulness point during the day occurs about eight hours after waking up.

energizing, and refreshing sleep—a top priority. If you want to improve the quality of your sleep, you will need to prepare for this positive change by practicing good sleep hygiene.

Preparation. Good sleep hygiene is all about preparing for sleep. *Start preparing for sleep at least an hour before you plan to be asleep.* Schedule a cool-down period, just as we do for kids when we want to get them ready for bed. Try a hot bath an hour before bedtime and allow time to soak for twenty to thirty minutes. The hot bath raises your core temperature, and as your body cools down after the bath, it is easier to fall asleep. Make sure your room is cool and quiet. A room temperature in the mid-t o low 60s is ideal. A fan can help create this cooler environment. After the bath, avoid mental and physical stimulation; consider light reading or watching mindless television programs. Materials that make you laugh are excellent tools. *Hearty laughter will relax your mind and body, making it easier to fall asleep.* Watching the news before bed may have an opposite effect and is not recommended. Limit drinking liquids at least three hours before bedtime, and empty your bladder before lying down, to reduce night trips to the bathroom. Avoid alcohol and caffeine after dinner, also, since they may interfere with sleep. Other stimulants to avoid especially near bedtime are smoking and vigorous exercise.

Milk products and turkey or tuna are high in the amino acid tryptophan, which triggers production of serotonin, a brain chemical that has sedating properties. If you are hungry, a light snack with these foods can promote the production of serotonin and favor sleepiness. A heavy meal may actually keep you up. A small serving of low-fat yogurt is a simple food to try as a snack before sleep.

Once you are in bed. Even if you are relaxed and ready to sleep, once you lie down and close your eyes, it will take a few minutes and may take from fifteen to twenty minutes to fall asleep. *Use the breathing awareness techniques that we have presented earlier in this program to keep you centered on the moment and to help you avoid replaying worries and preoccupations.* Another option is to use a sound recording or sound machine, with your choice of sound to lull you to sleep. Common favorites are pouring rain and ocean waves. Better yet, use either of these options from the moment you get in bed to help train yourself to go to sleep. If, after twenty minutes, you still can't fall asleep, it's best to get out of bed and read or watch mindless, nonexciting television. If worries or thoughts about today or tomorrow are keeping you awake, researchers recommend writing down the things that are on your mind and what you can do about them the next day. This exercise often works with my patients to let them put the day to rest.

Herbals, warm milk, and medications. Be sure to discuss your sleep needs with your doctor before beginning any kind of self-medication, even with common over-the-counter or herbal products. They may pose problems of interaction with other medications or may be involved with an allergy or

Start preparing for sleep at least an hour before you plan to be asleep.

Hearty laughter will relax your mind and body, making it easier to fall asleep.

Use the breathing awareness techniques to keep you centered on the moment and to help you avoid replaying worries and preoccupations.

other sensitivity. Natural sleep aids in the form of herbal teas and capsules, such as valerian root, may help you fall asleep. A simple cup of warm milk contains substances that are known sleep aids. Over-the-counter medications like antihistamines are often used to induce drowsiness. If these strategies are not successful, talk to your physician about prescription sleep medications. Let your physician know that you want help with sleep so he or she can help you find the best medication for you. A short course of sleep medication may be useful for temporary insomnia due to personal problems or a change in schedule and may help train you to sleep again. If necessary, your physician can also refer you to a sleep specialist to better determine the cause of your insomnia and the best way to treat it. What may be good for someone else may not be good for you individually, and you should, of course, never use medications of any kind that were prescribed for someone else.

Specialists. Sleep specialists use several behavior-based techniques such as sleep restriction, relaxation, and cognitive behavioral therapy (CBT). In sleep restriction, patients are initially allowed only five or six hours in bed each night to improve sleep efficiency. Sleep efficiency is the sleep time divided by the actual time in bed. The idea is to go to bed when very tired and associate the bed only with sleeping. As the sleep efficiency improves, more sleep time is added. Relaxation therapy uses techniques that turn on the Relaxation Response and reduce the arousal caused by stress and worries. Breath awareness and various meditation and relaxation techniques are used. CBT addresses behaviors and thought patterns that have been keeping your insomnia going. Behavioral approaches combine sleep hygiene activities such as those mentioned above, plus additional behavioral training to help you avoid worrying about sleep loss and its consequences. CBT has been found to be quite effective—as good if not better than sleeping pills.

Help is available. The take-home idea on sleep problems is that effective help is available for most cases. *Even sleeping an extra hour a day will positively impact your personal energy, well-being, and long-term health.*

Strategies for Optimal Sleep

- *Make good sleep a priority.*
- Plan a cool-down period.
- Take a twenty-minute hot bath.
- Use breathing-awareness exercises.
- Sleep in a cool room.
- Avoid stimulants.
- Limit liquids after dinner.
- Exercise during the day.
- Eat a light snack before bed.
- Wake up at the same time each day.

Be sure to discuss your sleep needs with your doctor before beginning any kind of self-medication, even with common over-the-counter or herbal products.

Even sleeping an extra hour a day will positively impact your personal energy, well-being, and long-term health.

Make good sleep a priority.

Advanced Strategies for Sleep

- Discuss sleep problem with physician.
- over-the-counter sleep aids
- Consider sleep medications and therapies.
- Consider evaluation by sleep specialist.

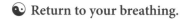 **Return to your breathing.**

Summary

Getting enough sleep is one of the things that is within your immediate reach to increase your personal energy level—it is something that you can change for the better right away. Understanding the importance of plenty of sleep will help you set a goal and stick to it. You must give top priority to your goal of getting a good night's rest, or it will not happen. Otherwise, you will be likely to give up sleep time when your schedule is overloaded. There is a significant price to pay in terms of mind and body health if you continue to function on less sleep than you need. *Adequate sleep, usually around eight hours per day for healthy adults, is restorative and energizing for both the mind and the body.*

Watch yourself for signs of sleep deprivation, such as getting drowsy in the afternoon during classes or meetings, after meals, or while watching television. *Strategies for better sleep include preparing for sleep by winding down during the hour before bedtime and using Breath Awareness and sound recordings or sound machines to ease falling asleep.* If you want to consider over-the-counter, herbal, or prescription medications to help you sleep, talk with your physician first and follow his or her recommendations. If you still experience difficulty getting enough good refreshing sleep, ask your physician to refer you to a sleep specialist for additional help.

Adequate sleep, usually around eight hours per day for healthy adults, is restorative and energizing for both the mind and the body.

Strategies for better sleep include preparing for sleep by winding down during the hour before bedtime.

PART

FOUR

THE
SPIRITUAL DOMAIN

The Basics of Spirituality

9

Spirituality clearly has an important role in increasing overall energy and positively influencing health, through support of the relationship between personal energy and health. A spiritual worldview influences a vast range of activities that impact your health, such as self-image, self-care, the quality of your relationships, and lifestyle risk factors such as overeating, smoking, use of illegal drugs, and abuse of alcohol.

The practice of modern medicine in the United States has been described as being based on models of illness rather than on models of health. That is, in training and practice, the practitioners of modern medicine are said to focus more on why people get sick rather than on why people get healthy.

It has become very important for me, after practicing as a physician for more than thirty years, to understand health and healing in a way that can be transmitted more fully to those in my care. I have found that spirituality, or a spiritual perspective on life, is a sure way to increase overall personal energy and to help move my patients further along the path toward their goal of health and well-being.

☯ Bring your attention to your breathing.

Spirituality and Health throughout History

From the beginning of recorded time, spirituality has played an important role in the healing process. In ancient Greece, the sick were sometimes left in the temple overnight to ponder the roots of their illness. The earliest doctors in Western history were usually the priests. In early American Indian culture, as in many older cultures, the shaman, or medicine man or woman, practiced medicine. In many cultures, shamans, *curanderas*, and *spiritistas* continue to practice spiritually based healing today. These healers traditionally blend spirituality with body and mind health. When faced with major or life-threatening illness, people in the past have turned to their spiritual beliefs for support and comfort, and as an aid in healing the body. Spiritual or religious beliefs can be profoundly effective and helpful in coping with the physical and emotional discomforts that often accompany the experience of illness. There is ample evidence that these same kinds of beliefs are helpful in coping with the more common discomforts of stress and everyday life as well. How fortunate it is for those who are able to draw upon these age-old support mechanisms for everyday *dis-ease,* and not just in the face of major illness. In *The Healing Journey,* Dr. O. Carl Simonton, one of the pioneers of mind-body medicine, writes, *"Our work with patients has demonstrated that health involves body, mind, and spirit. And while the mind can be used to influence the physical state, it is used most effectively when it is aware of the spirit."*

Examples and practical applications of mind-body medicine have been documented in medical literature for years, though for the past fifty years they have been upstaged by the more publicized pharmaceutical and technological advances of modern medicine. However, by the 1990s, renewed interest in the benefits of spiritual attitudes and beliefs on health was growing to the level that major conferences on "Spirituality and Health" were being sponsored by established institutions like Harvard University. At these conferences, presenters discussed significant research programs that applied the scientific method to measuring the benefits of spirituality on health. Well-documented medical research has provided plentiful examples of the benefits of spirituality on health in preventing disease, as well as in surviving catastrophic and life-threatening illnesses.

In an innovative 1988 study of spirituality and health, researchers examined the benefits of prayer on hospitalized patients. Almost four hundred patients in a coronary care unit in San Francisco were divided into two groups. Both groups received the standard medical care for patients in the intensive-care unit. In addition, a prayer group outside the hospital prayed for the experimental group. The participants in the study had no knowledge as to whether they were in the group receiving prayer or not, and there was no physical contact between the patients and the prayer group. The results were noteworthy. When compared to the control group that received only the standard care, the participants in the experimental group for whom the outside prayer group said their prayers experienced significantly fewer medical complications and required less use of medications.

Studies have shown various desirable benefits, such as improved pain control, less anxiety and depression, and more peace of mind, in those with strong spiritual beliefs. Researchers continue to look for evidence of health benefits from spirituality. The recognition of a link between spirituality and health is not new; what is new is its increased attention from researchers, as well as from the popular press.

Health involves body, mind, and spirit. And while the mind can be used to influence the physical state, it is used most effectively when it is aware of the spirit.

—O. Carl Simonton, MD

Studies have shown various desirable benefits in those with strong spiritual beliefs.

Communicating about the Basics of Spirituality

What does spirituality mean to you?

....

....

....

....

....

The term "spirituality" holds different meanings for different people, making it difficult to come up with a description of spirituality on which most people can agree. In *Why Religion Matters*, Huston Smith uses the terms "worldview" and "Big Picture" to describe the way we see things. He writes, "With us, life's problems press so heavily on us that we seldom take time to reflect on the way our unconscious attitudes and assumptions about the nature of things affect the way we perceive what is directly before us." In scholarly work, anthropologists, sociologists, theologians, linguists, and others also use the term "worldview," to describe the most-fundamental beliefs of a society about its universe and the group's physical and spiritual place within it. In this book I use both of the terms, spirituality and worldview, in related ways.

A spiritual worldview is one that holds, foremost, a perspective that there is more to life than the material world that we can recognize through our five physical senses. Spirituality acknowledges a world beyond the everyday activities and frustrations. It affirms some higher purpose and meaning to our lives and the workings of the universe and all that it contains. This higher purpose is generally an extension of a Higher Power that sustains, nurtures, and loves us unconditionally. In *The Path of Transformation*, Shakti Gawain writes, "Contact with our spiritual self gives us an expanded perspective on our lives, both as individuals and as part of humanity. It helps to make our daily problems seem not quite so huge and makes our lives feel more meaningful." *The need to find meaning and purpose in life has been described as a fundamental craving of human beings, which is deeper and more fundamental than the materialistic need for possessions.*

In his book Man's Search for Meaning, *first published in 1946, psychiatrist Viktor Frankl writes about his experience while imprisoned in a concentration camp for being Jewish during World War II. During his three years in one of the worst experiences anyone could live through, he made some observations of what influenced those who survived the*

The term "spirituality" holds different meanings for different people.

A spiritual worldview is one that holds, foremost, a perspective that there is more to life than the material world that we can recognize through our five physical senses.

concentration camp ordeal. He noted that the ones who survived best during this horrific experience were not the healthiest or the strongest ones, but those who had a purpose and meaning, such as to find a loved one or to tell the world what happened there. Frankl went on to start a school of psychology called "logotherapy." Logotherapy, or "meaning therapy," was based on his belief that the fundamental need for humans was meaning and purpose. As such, the cause of many psychological problems was due to lack of meaning and purpose in people's lives.

Huston Smith writes that **when there is a sense of meaning, life fits better**. He goes on, saying, "When the fit feels perfect, the energies of the cosmos pour into the believer and empower her to a startling degree." **He also describes signs of a poor fit as "a sense of meaninglessness, alienation and anxiety that the twentieth century knows so well."** The worldview that spirituality offers usually includes this much-needed, health-enhancing sense of purpose and meaning.

Signs of a poor fit: "a sense of meaninglessness, alienation and anxiety that the twentieth century knows so well."

—Huston Smith

Essential to most concepts of spirituality is the idea that we are closely related to a Higher Power. One way to envision this idea of being "made in God's image" is to imagine that the Higher Power is the ocean, and each one of us is a drop of water. The drop has many of the characteristics of the ocean, but the drop is not the ocean. If the Higher Power is called "God," then these characteristics can be called godlike, or divine. Different cultures give different names to the Higher Power, which may be called the "Great Spirit" or the "Life Force." No matter what it is called, the Higher Power is also the energy force behind the life process. To better understand what we mean by spirituality, we can try to list some general ideas about spirituality. Try listing some of the ideas about the spirituality we have discussed here that occur to you now, on the lines below. Jot down ideas from spiritual traditions that you know of, as well as original ideas of your own, or thoughts that come to you at random.

....

....

....

....

....

Drawing on lessons from older traditional religions as well as modern "New Age" and other modern forms of spirituality, one can come up with a list that could be called the "basics of spirituality." I have included some of these ideas in the paragraphs below. In reviewing this list I hope you will find several ideas that most people might agree describe what they mean when they say they are not religious, but that they are *spiritual*. It seems to me that each of the points in this list is the description of a spiritual worldview or a spiritual assessment of life.

From the earlier discussions we learned that your assessments create your response to life. ***At this point we can suggest that our spiritual assessments that make up the basics of our spirituality have the capacity for creating spiritual responses that foster an increasing personal energy and well-being.***

Some Basics of Spirituality

There is a Higher Power that creates and sustains life.
A description of the Higher Power's role as source and sustainer is found in words I heard on an audiotape of the life of St. Thomas More, which I paraphrase here: The force that took you from the union of your mother's egg and your father's sperm to birth as a newborn, nine months later, is the same force that has sustained you from birth to your present age. Having this concept in your worldview would go a long way to reducing everyday anxiety and worry. It suggests that you have never really been alone. This force has always been with you and is with you now.

Contact with your Higher Power is always available.
This idea implies that there is a potential relationship with the Higher Power at all times. Traditionally, religious prayer has been the means for accessing the Higher Power. In petitionary prayer, in which you ask for things, you reach out to the Higher Power for guidance and support. In meditative prayer, you are quiet and listen to your Higher Power. From a spiritual perspective, contact with the Higher Power does not require a specific religious wording or ritual in order to be heard. Gratitude to the Higher Power appears to create a two-way experience of the Higher Power.

Life has a purpose and meaning.
Spiritual purpose and meaning are usually oriented toward the care and well-being of others rather than the pursuit of material gain for the self. In his Spiritual Exercises, St. Ignatius Loyola writes that the purpose of life is to know and become one with God. You were meant to grow in consciousness and move toward a closer relationship with your Higher Power. St. John of the Cross points out that only your Higher Power can satisfy your yearning for wholeness. All other experiences can only fulfill you temporarily. Your life has a purpose and meaning that is part of a bigger plan, set in motion by the Higher Power. Even when you cannot see it, you are part of the plan. When you are able to see that you are part of the plan (consistent with your spiritual perspective), more joy and less suffering is available to you, no matter what the circumstances.

Your difficulties in life are the material you work with to develop yourself.
Difficulties in life are opportunities for growth. Your lesson begins with managing

Our spiritual assessments have the capacity for creating spiritual responses that foster an increasing personal energy and well-being.

your present life situation. If you are physically handicapped, your spirit can still soar. Being poor may actually be a blessing, if it gives you fewer distractions from growing in spiritual understanding. Material riches or physical beauty might similarly hinder your growth by keeping you focused on nonspiritual, material reality. It may be easier to learn lessons of love and forgiveness and self-acceptance, if you have a physically challenged body or other limitations. Your level of spiritual consciousness is a result of what you have gained from your lessons while in this body.

Fear comes from separation from your Higher Power.

Freud thought that all fear is essentially a fear of death. In the book A Course in Miracles *(Foundation for Inner Peace, Penguin Books), fear is described as the natural consequence of the separation from God. Since love is about oneness, and fear is about separation, they are opposites. As you bridge that separation and become closer to your Higher Power, fear loses its power over you. From a spiritual perspective, you realize that everything is okay, because you are always connected to the Higher Power and its higher purpose. Expressions echoing this concept are observed in the reports of near-death experiences by people who were clinically dead and were brought back to life. Many have described experiencing a relationship with a Higher Power that has left them more at peace, and without fear of death, when they have resumed their previous lives. Without fear of death, there is less fear of life. Death becomes a transition through which you are connected from one reality to another, all the while.*

Forgiveness is the key to love and peace of mind.

In his book Love Is Letting Go of Fear, *Gerald Jampolsky writes that forgiveness is the key to happiness. This is a powerful spiritual concept. As you grow in spiritual awareness, injuries to your ego and the fulfillment of your material desires become less important. Since your spirit is not affected by these frustrations, then no real injury has occurred. Forgiveness becomes easier, more reasonable, and flows freely, as a more natural response. Likewise, as you consciously practice forgiveness, you can begin to have more experiences of unconditional love and increased spirituality.*

Examining just a few ideas and descriptions about spirituality will help you get a sense of what we mean by spirituality. The topic of spirituality as a health enhancer has been well presented by Dr. Bernie Siegel, a Connecticut surgeon who wrote *Love, Miracles and Medicine* in the late 1980s, recounting his mind-body-spirit approach for his cancer patients. His message of love, spirituality, and healing spoke matter-of-factly about the use of love and spirituality to enhance healing. He went beyond conventional medicine in recommending unconditional love and forgiveness as important aids in the struggle to regain health. He admonished physicians to practice optimism and encourage positive spiritual values in patients with major illnesses, as in this quote: "Too often, I think, we are possessed by religion. Spirituality is a healing force. With spirituality there are no rules related to God's love and God's ability to sustain us."

Material riches or physical beauty might similarly hinder your growth by keeping you focused on nonspiritual, material **reality.**

As you grow in spiritual awareness, injuries to your ego and the fulfillment of your material desires become less important.

With his first book, Dr. Bernie Siegel inspired me to blend spiritual perspectives into the treatment of patients with life-threatening diseases. In time, it became easier to occasionally blend spiritual perspectives with my caring for patients with non-life-threatening diseases as well. To this day, three lessons remain firmly in mind—as important gifts from the teachings of Dr. Siegel. One is a quote, which I often use with patients, to bring levity to difficult situations and decrease their worry. "No one is getting out of here alive!"

The second lesson focuses on the difference between curing and healing. Curing is what happens to the body; healing is what happens to the person as they become more whole. I have taken care of HIV patients who became spiritually healed but who died of the physical results of their disease of AIDS. Conversely, I have had alcoholic patients who could be cured of their bleeding ulcers but who, sadly, remained far from healed as whole persons. As a physician, my role as "curer" is limited. In spite of all the powerful drugs and techniques at the disposal of modern medicine, it is still true that most cures, when they occur, happen through the body's own mechanisms. Healing, or helping patients to become more whole, is something that I have many more opportunities to do, daily.

The third way that Dr. Siegel influenced my role as a healer was in an epiphany, the day I said to myself: "I believe that Bernie Siegel's approach could help my patients, but I don't have to wait for them to get cancer." He helped me see the importance of fostering a spiritual worldview in helping my patients to heal, even if there was no medication or treatment available that could cure their physical ailments. He also helped me see the practical difference between spirituality and religion. As a physician, I could influence healing and sometimes also help cure my patients with positive, loving, and spiritual attitudes.

If spirituality is the road, religion is the map. The major world religions can be described as providing a map to their adherents, for traveling in the spiritual life, on the basis of each particular group's interpretation of what the "rules" are. While they may all agree on spiritual concepts like a Higher Power, and love of neighbor, the religions will disagree on rules, such as what women can wear in public, the correct position for prayer, or what can and cannot be eaten. I have often heard people say, "I believe in God," or "I am spiritual but don't practice any particular religion." For that reason, I prefer to use the term "spirituality" rather than religion, to reach more people when discussing the powerful health benefits of spirituality. If asked, most of my patients would say that they are spiritual or believe in God, even if they do not regularly practice any formal, organized religion. As such, many of these people, who have access to spirituality in their worldviews, also have access to the health benefits of spirituality, but many do not make use of them. They are like people who have a lot of money in the bank but have forgotten how to draw out money. They are like the man invited to the

No one is getting out of here alive!

—Bernie Siegel, MD

Curing is what happens to the body; healing is what happens to the person as they become more whole.

banquet who stands at the door and does not come in, though there is a seat with his name written on the seating card. They are like the woman who lives in a mansion but spends her time only in the basement.

Body–Spirit Continuum

The concept that human beings by their nature live in two worlds—body and spirit—was taught to me, as it may have been to you, as a child in my Sunday school lessons. It is a common idea in many of the world's major religions, and it is echoed in some of the other less known philosophies and religions as well. Later on in my own personal spiritual journey, this idea evolved into a spiritual construct that was useful in understanding my spirituality in everyday life. Influenced by traditional Christian teachings and, more recently, by New Age spirituality, I came to see myself living within a body-and-spirit dichotomy. This means that as a human I have one foot in the material world of the body/ego and one foot in the immaterial world of the spirit. I find it more useful to describe this ego/spirit dichotomy in terms of Light and Dark. Spirit is of Light and body/ego is of Dark.

Looking at common life experiences within this context provides helpful insights for managing life and personal energy. ***Love, faith, forgiveness, and compassion can be said to be positive, or of Light. Fear, hate, jealousy, and criticizing can be said to be negative, or of Darkness.*** This two-sided human experience can be shown as follows:

Light (positive)	Dark (negative)
▪ spirit	▪ ego
▪ immaterial	▪ materialistic
▪ love	▪ apathy
▪ acceptance	▪ jealousy
▪ compassion	▪ criticism
▪ forgiveness	▪ judging

One important point about this comparison is that ***when your consciousness is in Light, you cannot be in Darkness. Likewise, when your awareness is in Darkness, you cannot be in Light.*** Though our existence is made up of these two halves, ***at any given point in time you are either in Light or Darkness, often moving easily and quickly between these aspects of life.*** This Light-Dark construct can help elucidate common life situations, such as when someone says, "I love him/her so much, but I am so jealous." Since love is of Light, and jealousy is of Darkness, what this person calls *love* is probably not love but perhaps a form of possessiveness or a need to control, both of which are reflections of the ego, or Darkness related.

You may already have noticed that this Light-Dark construct lends itself to the concept of a life *continuum* as discussed earlier. ***You can see yourself on a continuum between Light and Darkness, or between Love and Apathy,***

Love, faith, forgiveness, and compassion can be said to be positive, or of Light.

Fear, hate, jealousy, and criticizing can be said to be negative, or of Darkness.

and practice actions and attitudes that will move you toward the desired end of the continuum. Referring to the earlier discussion on the life continuum, the spiritual responses listed under Light can be said to correlate with calm, health, and higher personal energy. As such, these can be described as spiritual energy gainers. The responses listed under Darkness correlate with stress, illness, and low personal energy and can be called spiritual energy drainers. In applying some of these insights to our daily lives, let us look for ways to choose from the attitudes and actions available to most of us, which will most enhance the experience of our spiritual nature and increase our personal energy and well-being.

☯ **Return to your breathing.**

Summary

Personal experience, anecdotal evidence, and medical research support the idea that spirituality is a powerful source of increased personal energy and healing. Spirituality accesses powerful energy, which can improve your quality of life and further your spiritual and emotional healing and, perhaps, your physical health as well. Since spirituality can mean different things to different people, it is important to arrive at a general appreciation of what spirituality means that most people would be able to agree with. Spirituality may include belief in the presence of a Higher Power that sustains us and is accessible to us all, at all times, and it may include the concept that we are all connected as one family, as well as the idea that there is a purpose and meaning to life. As a human being, you are part body and part spirit; what the New Age spiritualists describe as being of Darkness and of Light. Spiritual responses such as love, forgiveness, and compassion are identified with Light. Responses such as apathy, judging, and criticizing are identified with Darkness. The spiritual responses that are categorized with Light are those that support well-being and higher personal energy. Those that are categorized with Darkness as the ones that correlate with stress, illness, and lower energy. We can use this organization of positive and negative aspects to help us improve our own spiritual outlook and improve our personal energy and well-being.

At any given point in time you are either in Light or Darkness, often moving easily and quickly between these aspects of life.

See yourself on a continuum between Light and Darkness and practice actions and attitudes that will move you toward the desired end of the continuum.

Spiritual Energy Gainers

10

Just as your assessments of events create your responses to life, spiritual assessments create spiritual responses. Prayer, inspirational reading, love, forgiveness, and gratitude are responses to spiritual assessments. These activities, in turn, are conducive to more spiritual assessments. Prayer is an attempt to connect with a Higher Power. Inspirational reading positively shifts your worldview, lifting it to a higher level and away from pettiness and shallowness. Love can be an awareness of oneness with others. Forgiveness allows you to let go of the past and move on, letting go of old resentments and getting on with living your life more fully in the present.

Gratitude affirms your connection to and dependence on your Higher Power. All of these activities are potentially powerful energy gainers and may be used to positively influence your worldview and perspective on your life events, and to move you toward increased personal energy and health.

☯ Bring your attention to your breathing.

Spiritual Assessments

A spiritual worldview is fundamental for a richer, more meaningful life. If you already have a spiritual worldview, as a physician and fellow traveler I recommend that you draw upon it daily to improve your well-being and personal energy level. Any of the activities of Light listed in the last chapter, such as love and forgiveness, will enhance your spiritual worldview. If you don't have a spiritual worldview, I recommend reviewing Huston Smith's *Why Religion Matters*, as was mentioned in the last chapter.

Huston's book presents a sound intellectual argument for developing this life-saving, supportive, traditional perspective, rather than the materialistic view that dominates so much of our culture's thinking at present. How a spiritual worldview can create a richer, more meaningful life can be illustrated using the Life Formula. In the Life Formula, life is a series of events, each of which triggers an assessment. The *assessment creates* our experience of the life event.

Life Event—*triggers*---->Assessment—*creates*- --->Response

Where in the Life Formula does spirituality have its main effect: in the event, in the assessment, or in the response?

....

....

....

....

....

Spirituality is a form of assessment, which, in turn, creates a spiritual response.

Spirituality has a powerful impact on our experience of life because it operates in the "creative" part of the Life Formula, the assessment. **Spiritual assessments create spiritual responses.** Here we will use "worldview" and "assessment" synonymously.

Spiritual worldviews, like assessments, create spiritual responses. As your assessments of life become more spiritual, your B.E.S.T. Responses (Behaviors, Emotions, Sensations, and Thoughts) reflect the influence of spiritual perspectives. Each of the main points listed under "Basics of Spirituality" is a worldview or assessment about the mystery of Life.

For example, *if you believe in a Higher Power that loves and supports you, you experience more love and less fear and anxiety*. Thoughts become more positive. Your emotions are probably calmer. *Likewise, if you think your life has a meaning and purpose, you would probably worry less and learn to "let go and let God."* This would probably reduce a lot of the stress associated with worrying. If your Stress Response is turned on less frequently, you experience less stress.

Having more spiritually influenced behaviors, emotions, sensations, and thoughts may influence your lifestyle to be more healthful and to contain more personal energy. In the interest of harnessing the powerful energy that flows from a spiritual perspective, let's review some time-tested attitudes and activities, which will help you develop your personal spiritual worldview.

The following scenario, which came to me during a talk on spirituality, illustrates the creative power of spiritual assessments. On a hot, sunny

Spiritual assessments create spiritual responses.

If you think your life has a meaning and purpose, you would probably worry less and learn to "let go and let God."

Monday morning in Calcutta, India, a shopkeeper opens his front doors as he prepares for a big sale. Upon opening the doors, he is horrified to find a person lying in front of his store, either dead or dying. Alarmed, he gets on the phone, hoping to find someone to move this body from the front of his shop, maybe to the front of his nearest competitor.

While he is on the phone, he sees a thin, small-framed woman come with a helper and carry off his burden. His problem is solved. He is relieved and goes on with his plans for a big sale. Later, he hears that the strangers—the people who carried off the body—actually bathed and fed the near-death person to nurse him back to health. The shopkeeper cannot understand why anyone would go to all that trouble. "Are that little woman and her helper crazy?" he wonders.

Applying the Life Formula to this scenario, the event is a body lying on the sidewalk in front of the store. In the actions of the shopkeeper and the little woman we see two very different responses to the same event. Knowing that responses are created by assessments, we can speculate on what type of assessment each person was working from. The shopkeeper's assessment might be that this event is bad for business. With such an assessment, he would be expected to try to remove the source of his problem.

In this story the woman, of course, is Mother Theresa. Her assessment might be that the dying person was a child of God, her brother in spirit, and she responded appropriately to her spiritual assessment. Her spiritual assessment creates a spiritual response. From a nonspiritual or materialistic perspective, her response might appear to be nonsense.

Recalling the previous discussion of assessments, we can see that the assessment is what is inside the person. It is not that the shopkeeper is an evil person, but perhaps insensitive. In Life Formula language, what is inside the small woman is not what is inside the shopkeeper at this point in time. As discussed earlier, people will behave or respond to life in accordance to their assessments, or what is inside them. The creative nature of assessments applies here, too, though in a different qualitative sense. Spiritual assessments create spiritual responses. The practical power of spirituality is experienced through the spiritual assessments that we make in our everyday lives.

Spiritual Energy Gainers

What are some spiritual activities that can increase your personal energy?

....

....

People will behave or respond to life in accordance to their assessments, or what is inside them.

....

....

....

Prayer, spiritual reading, love, forgiveness, and gratitude
can increase your energy.

In this program, we recommend similar spiritual activities, such as prayer, spiritual reading, love, forgiveness, and gratitude, which can increase well-being and personal energy. Each of these easily accessible energy gainers will be discussed.

Prayer/Meditation

Relationships grow through communication. The more you communicate with the other person in the relationship, the better and more comfortable you will be in that relationship. This happens with prayer as well. Prayer is an attempt to communicate with your Higher Power. To communicate earnestly is to become one with the other, for the moment.

As such, communicating with your Higher Power has the capacity to be uplifting, inspiring, and energizing. Prayer should bring with it the comfort and strength that comes with being in communion for the time being with your greatest love. Praying leaves you with a rich, soothing fullness, which transforms your present reality, even while everything else in your life appears to remain the same. *Prayer transforms your perspectives of what is going on in your life.* Prayer still remains great medicine for the mind, body, and spirit and should be a part of everyone's healing tools. Most people experience more energy after prayer. This makes prayer an important part of a preventive medicine program, as well as a therapeutic plan in the face of illness.

People pray in different ways. Moreover, how they pray often changes over time. There are many books describing different styles of prayer.

Types of Prayer

Rote prayers are the ones you memorize, often as children, and can recite without much attention to what is being said.

Petitionary prayers are those in which you ask for something for your loved ones or for yourself.

Meditative prayer may be facilitated when you ponder a word, a phrase, another symbol, or a scene that has spiritual meaning.

Contemplative prayer emphasizes quieting the mind and experiencing the

Spiritual activities, such as prayer, spiritual reading, love, forgiveness, and gratitude can increase well- being and personal energy.

Communicating with your Higher Power has the capacity to be uplifting, inspiring, and energizing.

presence of the Higher Power; it is composed more of listening than of talking.

Although the Higher Power does not change, what will change is how the person praying conceives of the Higher Power, and how he or she communicates best with the Higher Power. For adults I recommend meditative or contemplative forms of prayer. Contemplative prayer is especially adaptable to brief moments during the day when you can stop to feel the presence of the Essence that sustains you.

Prayer transforms your perspectives of what is going on in your life.

Preparing for Prayer

- *Find a quiet place where you won't be disturbed.*
- *Decide on an amount of time to set aside solely for prayer.*
- *Sit in a chair that supports you, with your back straight.*
- *Close your eyes and practice Breath Awareness.*
- *Meditative prayer—choose a phrase that has meaning for you (e.g., "Lord have mercy; Fill my heart, Oh Lord;" or "Glory to you, Oh Lord"). Keep repeating your chosen phrase, staying centered on your breathing. Alternatively, choose a scene from the Bible or other spiritual literature, or imagine a spiritual scene and experience the scene as if you were there, again using your breath to stay in the present.*

Contemplative prayer—Centering on your breathing with your eyes closed, imagine feeling the presence of your Higher Power. Feel the Spirit come into you with every breath you take. Stay in this state of simply being, filled with the presence of your Higher Power, for as long as you have set aside.

For anyone who seeks to experience and develop their spiritual life, I recommend Father Mark Link's series Vision 2000. It presents an interactive format, which gives you daily inspirational passages, quotes, and anecdotes, and then asks questions for you to reflect upon.

Another good introduction is *Praying as the Saints*, which describes the life and spirituality of several well-known saints. Examples of how individual saints prayed will encourage you to emulate them and personalize your style of praying. For those seeking a deeper experience, the book *Open Mind, Open Heart*, by Thomas Keating, gives a good description of more contemplative, silent prayer. **Any time thus spent, opening yourself to the presence of your Higher Power, will, at a minimum, move you away from stress and toward calm and will increase your personal energy level.** Beyond that, it moves you to an awareness of the Mystery of Mysteries, which must necessarily support inner healing. When you find the right book on prayer for you, you will know it, because just reading about it will excite you and give you an immediate increase in your energy.

I admire those people, who, when they pray, speak to their Higher Power with the same respectful directness with which they speak to a loving parent. My grandmother prays like that. So does my mom. I have never done that very well. I learned to pray by repeating standard prayers memorized in the Catholic catechism. Later, during college, my prayers were petitionary, asking for material things or specific outcomes. Over time, these petitions evolved into requests for guidance and direction, such as "What would You have me do?" or "Where do You want me to go?" Mostly, I still did all the talking.

More recently, I find myself speaking less and listening more, practicing more silent prayer. In this contemplative form of prayer, I do a breathing awareness exercise, to let go of distractions. This helps me quiet my chatty mind. Then I imagine my heart opening up and receiving an influx of the Holy Spirit. Needless to say, the time spent in that receiving state is blissful. Life looks and feels different when my problems and conflicts are on hold. Still, all too often, my own tendency toward distractions and petty preoccupations makes prayer time a fragmented experience, with replays of my to-do list and the mundane activities that take up my daily energy. The experience of prayer is often a string of brief moments of peace and oneness with a Higher Power interspersed within the time allotted for prayer. It is a testament to the healing power of prayer that so little can do so much. It makes me wonder what would my life be like if I prayed twice as much, three times as much, as I do now? So, I go back and try again, as often as I can, to use prayer to move along the spiritual continuum, away from fear, toward peace of mind.

Fear <----------------------------------> Peace of Mind

Spiritual Reading

Reading is listening; spiritual reading is spiritual listening. There is a plethora of traditional and current literature to aid spiritual assessments at any level. During my college years and early twenties, I sought answers on the nature and meaning of life. I read from the scriptures of Judeo- Christian, Islamic, Buddhist, and Hindu religions. I came away with the understanding that each, in its own way, is trying to explain two mysteries, which, by definition, could not be known—God and the mystery of life. In its own way, each one had the truth. Truth is often hidden between the lines, in stories rich in symbolism. I came to realize that it would be easier for me to understand the symbolism if I studied the spiritual literature closer to my own cultural life experience. So, after years of looking for truth, I came back to study the Judeo-Christian version of the answers to my questions about life.

I recommend that you consider reading the spiritual literature you are most comfortable with, and let it show you the way. As you browse through the Psalms of David, or the book of Job in the Old Testament, you will feel the power of the written word. The Gospels in the New Testament are rich in stories and lessons. More intuitive or mystical-minded people may connect better with the Gospel according to John as a starting point. "In the beginning was the Word… " This is very rich stuff.

For some, a commentary on the Gospels of the New Testament may be more helpful as a starting point than the Gospels themselves. Kahlil Gibran's *The Prophet* is an inspiring short work on wisdom and spirituality. *Siddhartha*, a novel by Herman Hesse, depicting the early years of the Buddha, is informative and enlightening. New Age spiritual literature, such as *The Celestine Prophecy* and *A Course in Miracles*, provides a modern place to start your spiritual reading.

The more spiritual sources you review, the more you become aware of what they share in common, the basics of spirituality. It's been said that the areas in which religions agree (don't kill, don't lie) are probably close to the truth, and where they disagree (how to dress, what to eat) is probably further from the truth. Reading spiritual works is not about becoming a scholar, but about accessing the richness and power of spirituality as found in written form. You will feel an energy increase when you read spiritual literature the first time and, usually, every time. It can be a refreshing source of energy and enhanced well-being.

Love

"Real love is unconditional," wrote Rachel Naomi Remens in *Kitchen Table Wisdom*. The conditional love we usually give and receive is probably more correctly called "affirmation" or "approval," but not love. Real love, unconditional love, is hard to give. Unconditional love does not come easy to materialistic, ego-centered humans, which most of us are. Love is one of the great mysteries of life. My personal assessment of what love is comes from years of reflection and observation.

Love is not a feeling, though it can be experienced as a feeling. Love is not sexuality, though it may be felt through sexuality. Love does not mean you cannot say no, or that you must always agree. *Love is awareness that at some level, you and the object of your love are one.* When I feel empathy and connectedness with a stranger, that is love. To love my enemy is not to mean that I want him or her to win in the struggle of our opposition, but rather, that I know that he or she has dreams and wishes too. He or she has a family and loved ones who support her or him, similar to the loving support that I have. To love my neighbor, then, is to know that we are connected, part of a bigger family. I can love a relative and not like his or her actions. To love God means that I am aware that there is a connection between us. I am not God, but I am always an extension and a part of God. To know that God loves me is to know that even when I don't feel it, God still remains connected to me. *In a word, love is oneness.*

In trying to understand the nature of love, it is easier to say what love is not, rather than to say what love is. The idea that love is about oneness came to

Reading is listening; spiritual reading is spiritual listening.

The more spiritual sources you review, the more you become aware of the basics of spirituality.

Love is awareness that at some level, you and the object of your love are one.

In a word,
love is oneness.

me slowly over the years. This perspective has given me a practical understanding of love. While I recognize and accept that love remains one of the great mysteries of life, *the concept of love as oneness has been useful for remembering that, more than being just a passive feeling, love is an active awareness. In love, I remember that we are connected, even if I do not feel it.* In this concept of oneness, I understood what the saints and spiritual writers referred to when they said that *in love, when you give to others, you give to yourself.*

> *One day, when my son Marco was a toddler, he and I were both hungrily eyeing the last oatmeal cookie on the table. Those are my favorite cookies, and it was the last one. When I gave in and let him have the cookie, there was no sense of loss. In my love for Marco we are one, so in giving the last cookie to him, I was giving it to myself. I saw then that love is about oneness.*

Love as oneness became clearer when I felt an overpowering surge of emotions at the sight of my infant child; there was a yearning to take him into my body, to be one with him. In the passion of a couple in love, there is often a yearning to embrace and be as one, as if it were possible that they could share the same body. This sense of oneness would allow me to feel you being with me, though you may be thousands of miles away, or gone on to another plane.

Love is an awareness of the oneness between lovers.

In this way, I began to understand love as an awareness of the oneness between lovers. The one who is so aware loves. Though you love me, if I cannot see that we are one, I cannot love you, even though I may have fond feelings for you. I came to understand that God, by his nature, can love me, even in times that I don't feel the love or feel I deserve it. I learned to accept that God is love and, thus, one with all creation, which extends from Him. So, the ever-present love of God was always available for me. If I accepted that love, there was a connection to something higher and more meaningful.

I have come to understand that we are connected to each other, whether we feel it or not. The feelings are secondary.

To love God, it is necessary to feel one with the source of life. I sought to be one with God, through acknowledging the oneness between others and myself. The positive feelings followed. Since we are all a part of God, to truly love means feeling connected to all, not just your own family, or your own cultural group. *I have come to understand that we are connected to each other, whether we feel it or not. The feelings are secondary.* This is passed on to my children when I tell them that I love them. As they get past the toddler stage, they seem to think of love as conditional and dependent on their behavior, something they have to earn. So, to teach them, they must be told repeatedly, "Even if you get all As, I cannot love you more. I may feel pleased, thinking all As might help you have a better future, but I cannot love you more because you got all As, or any less because you didn't. I just love you." I think they understand, even if they forget at times. Once I felt I was loved, I became more lovable. Though often alone, I am rarely lonely. Maybe understanding this will be helpful for others too.

Forgiveness

In *Love Is Letting Go of Fear*, Gerald Jampolsky writes that "forgiveness is the key to happiness." *More than a key to happiness, forgiveness appears essential for healing and an effective way to improve your personal energy stores.* One of the main ideas of Jampolsky's book is that what most people want is peace of mind. People chase after power and financial success, so they can have peace of mind. The things they do to provide for their children's future are all done so they can have peace of mind. At the beginning of my classes, participants are asked, "What is it that you really, really want in life?" Surprisingly, almost all responded, "Peace of mind." A few said that what they wanted was happiness, or things, which could be connected to a feeling of peace of mind.

If your goal in life is really peace of mind, Jampolsky writes, you need to experience more unconditional love. The implication is that as you experience unconditional love for yourself and those around you, there will be no more fear, and peace of mind will prevail. Unfortunately, unconditional love is not easy for people to experience. Forgiveness is pivotal, because it opens the way to the experience of unconditional love. As stated above, what most people call love is more correctly called *approval*, which is based on performance. If you do it right, you are loved. If not, you are not loved. Since others are bound to disappoint you, this attitude is a setup for conflict, which creates separation from others if you do not remember your oneness with others. You don't have to like what people are doing, but you are still connected to them.

When you forgive someone (including yourself), you move toward accepting them as one with you. Forgiveness reestablishes the connection of oneness at some level. Oneness is the essence of love. *So, when you forgive someone, you move in the direction of love, even if the other person does not forgive you or still wishes you ill.* Forgiveness does not mean amnesia. People often ask if forgiving means to have to forget. No. To forgive means to let go of the emotional debt, so that you no longer experience the draining, negative emotions that were once a part of the painful response to the original event. You can still remember what occurred, but you are able to choose to not have it stir up any of the pain it once did. In forgiving, I also give up replaying the incident and the pain it caused me, and accept what happened as a part of life, which I can let go of, so I can go on with my life.

> *Years ago, an assassin tried to kill Pope John Paul II. The would-be assassin did not succeed in killing him, but he did manage to wound him. After the pope recovered from his wounds, he went to visit the man who had tried to kill him and was now in prison. During their face-to-face meeting, the pope forgave the would-be assassin. The act of forgiveness was not saying that the attempted assassination did not take place. In forgiving the man, the pope was not suggesting that he*

Forgiveness appears essential for healing and an effective way to improve your personal energy stores.

When you forgive someone, you move in the direction of love, even if the other person does not forgive you or still wishes you ill.

should be freed from jail. In forgiving the man, some would say the pope was freeing himself.

I have often heard people state they do not want to forgive another person, because they have been wronged and don't want to let the other person off as if nothing happened. I don't think that they understand that *forgiveness is meant to help the one carrying the hurt, to help the healing.* You do not forgive people only so that *they* will sleep better. You also forgive them so you can get your own life back.

Forgiveness is meant to help the one carrying the hurt, to help the healing.

Forgiveness is important for health in our Balancing Act model, because it saves *your* energy, which was being drained by living in the past through holding grudges, nursing old wounds, and judging others. Most people will readily admit that forgiveness increases their personal energy level in the short term and long term. From the writings of Caroline Myss, I learned that *we forgive so that we can "call our spirit back."* Forgiveness helps us let go of the past and move our energy into the present time. That may be why most religions and spiritual paths encourage living in the present as an aid in the spiritual journey. Forgiveness moves you toward the present. For this reason, you can expect forgiveness to be discussed and recommended in most programs that aim to reduce stress, or to enhance your healing from illness and disease.

For optimal personal energy, develop and excel in the skill of forgiveness.

During my third year of college, I had a steady girlfriend, who attended a different university. One day, while visiting me for the weekend, she made an unsolicited confession to me that she had recently had sex with someone from her school. I never figured out why she told me, but I remember it bothered me. A few days later, we attended a party with her crowd. After we had been there a while, the "other man" showed up. When I saw him, I began to experience feelings of pain and anger and thoughts of revenge. As I grew uncomfortable with these negative thoughts and feelings, I noted how comfortable he appeared to be as he walked in and was greeted warmly by others at the party. I remember thinking all those negative feelings were making me feel pretty bad, while he seemed calm and at ease. That's when I understood how much the grudge was affecting me. The person with the grudge has to carry the hurt and anger. I was carrying it, and I decided that I didn't want to carry it. So, I let it go. Forgiveness set me free.

If you need to make an effort to forgive, it may help to remember that when you forgive, it releases you from the past, to resume your life in the present. In *The Art of Happiness*, the Dalai Lama suggests that you think about the damage that not forgiving causes you, to help you resolve to forgive, for it is clearly in your best interest. From a practical perspective, forgiving allows you to increase your personal energy. In *Balancing Act*, forgiveness is one of the more powerful actions for increasing energy gain. *For optimal personal energy, develop and excel in the skill of forgiveness. Forgiveness is a tool both for getting you through the day and for moving you further along on your spiritual journey.*

During discussions on forgiveness, it is not unusual for participants to ask *how* to forgive. Yet, they probably already know how to forgive. There are so many times when you have forgiven, often without a second thought. *It may be easier to recall how you forgive if you call it "letting go."* Letting go of what? Perhaps it's letting go of an event, which caused you pain or disappointment. Letting go means releasing the pain or disappointment; letting it pass on like leaves passing by in a stream, or clouds passing by in the sky.

Personally, I find it easier to forgive by telling myself I do not want to carry the resentment or the grudge. I do not want to tie up my energy over that event. I'd rather let it go. Most of the time, that is all that is required. If I pull my emotional energy out of the event, it seems to evaporate. Those times when it keeps coming back, I resort to questions about why I am so invested in this event. Drawing on the Life Formula, I can remember that not forgiving is a response created by an assessment that I have made. Any attempts to challenge the assessment shift the awareness from what happened "out there" to what is going on in my heart and mind. General questions similar to the ones used for verifying assessments can help remove obstacles to forgiving.

Questions for Removing Obstacles to Forgiveness

What meaning am I giving to what happened?
What has to happen before I can let this go?
Is there something I want them to do before I can let go?
Is there something I must do before I can let go?

Any attempt to answer these questions moves awareness from emotions to intellect, where it is easier to use reason, for exploring personal issues tied to the emotional responses of begrudging and not forgiving. Most difficulties with forgiving are usually related to other people, friends, and family members, or people in your circle of acquaintances, such as at work or in the neighborhood. The idea I find very useful in dealing with all people is the pearl of wisdom that *at any given point in time, most people are doing the best they know how.* Once I realize this, the concern becomes not what they did (the event), but how I want to interpret it (my assessment).

In a typical day, the events or people that I forgive or let go may include the driver in front of me, who could have turned quickly enough so we both could have made the light. There was the assistant who did not stock my examination room properly, so I had to leave the patient to get the needed materials. Then there was forgiving a patient for arriving

Forgiveness is a tool both for getting you through the day and for moving you further along on your spiritual journey.

At any given point in time, most people are doing the best they know how.

thirty minutes late, and another one for trying to cover five old topics during an add-on, urgent appointment for a different condition. At home, it was forgiving my daughter, Nicole, for talking back to me in strong tones. It was forgiving my wife, Ann, for not mailing the letters she had agreed to mail for me.

After a while, we realize that the reason we need to forgive people is that we are repeatedly going to be hurt or disappointed, because others did not do things the way we wanted or that we thought they should be done. The problem is that if I remain angry at you, I'm the one who has to carry the anger. It is my energy that is used up, increasing my vulnerability to the energy-draining Stress Response. Often, in my inner dialogue, in the face of letting go or holding a grudge, I choose forgiveness because I sense that holding a grudge is just not worth it. I let go so I can live more fully, and more stress-free, in the present.

The realization that at a given point in time, people are doing the best they know how has done much to release me from the inclination to judge and hold grudges. This is not meant to excuse people's behavior. Still, at a given point in time, we are usually doing what we think is right. Even when we lie to be polite, we have decided that lying is what we need to do, at the time. Even when someone is rude to you, at that time, he thinks this is what he has to do. Usually, it isn't personal; he is acting out what is in him. If you were not there, he probably would have been rude to the next person to come along.

Even when someone is rude to you, usually it isn't personal; he is acting out what is in him.

Shifting my assessment allows me to create a response different from anger and pain. The new response may be to confront the person, directly or in writing. It may also mean breaking off relations, without bitterness. The new response created will be different from begrudging and will make it easier to forgive. For more-difficult cases, you may have to train yourself to act from a different assessment. Since your assessments are what are within you, this will mean changing the feelings inside you regarding the other person. *Reflecting on spiritual assessments may help shift your assessments about another person.* The Forgiveness Exercise below can be used to change the way you see the other person and help you with difficult cases.

Reflecting on spiritual assessments may help shift your assessments about another person.

The Forgiveness Exercise

Start this exercise as you would a short meditation. Sit in a quiet room, in a chair that supports you. Close your eyes and bring your attention to your breathing. Once you start to relax, bring your attention to the back of your closed eyelids as if you were looking into a dark room. In that room, down in front of you is a stage with an overhead light. Picture the person you would like to forgive in the center of that stage. Take notice of the feelings you experience as you see that person on the stage. Now, slowly imagine that person becoming younger and younger as you watch her or him on the stage. Continue to see that person becoming younger until what you see is a baby, among adult clothes. Imagine yourself going down to the stage and picking up the baby. Take notice of the feelings you experience when you hold that person as an innocent, harmless baby in your arms. While holding the baby, think about the issue you were having with this person as an adult. Become aware of any change in your feelings from when you first saw the person on the stage. After a short while, put the baby down and leave the stage to go back to where you were before.

Now, looking at the baby on the stage, slowly imagine that person growing up before your eyes. As the child is growing into adulthood, imagine what kind of life experiences were having an impact on that person as they grew up. You can use your imagination to make up some difficult experiences that you think that person may have experienced. Remember any actual experiences that you know of as well. These experiences would influence what kind of person this child would become. These experiences could also influence how you see the person now that they are grown up and standing before you on the stage. Once the person has returned to their current age, take note of how you feel now about that person. See if it is a little easier to understand that person and forgive them for what they have done to you.

Gratitude

The highest form of prayer is gratitude prayer.

In the book *Conversations with God*, by Neale Donald Walsch, during a discussion on prayer, God tells the author that *the highest form of prayer is gratitude prayer.* That caught my attention because it resonated with similar ideas I had run into before, about different levels of prayer.

I think of the passionate Psalms of David in the Old Testament, which so eloquently speak of gratitude to God. How different that form of prayer from the petitionary one in which we ask for a specific response, such as a victory, a winning lottery ticket, or a return to health. Though both forms of prayer seek to communicate with a higher power, the language is very different in gratitude prayer. Previous lessons on the role of language in creating your reality suggest that the language of your prayer may create different realities for you.

As long as we live in this physical body, life remains a mind and body experience.

As long as we live in this physical body, life remains a mind-and-body experience. Many of your mind-body experiences of life are created by the assessments you make in your mind. These assessments almost seem to follow mechanical laws with practical cause-and-effect properties.

As assessments are made in thoughts that are organized in language, *the words or language used in prayer can be expected to affect your experience of prayer.*

Upon examining the language used in different prayers, I found that when I pray, "God help me," I am asking for help. I am also saying that I am not receiving help at the moment. My body and mind are reacting to a reality in which I am not getting help, even as I hope to get it by asking. Of course, there would be no asking if there were not the belief that a Higher Power is listening and will respond. If I only add the letter "s," my prayer becomes "God helps me." This tiny change creates a body-mind state, acknowledging and affirming the ongoing help from a Higher Power.

My experience of this variation is a more empowering and more positive experience than with the first prayer. Your body-mind state will be influenced by this subtle change, even if you are not conscious of the change. Using language to create an expression of gratitude, my prayer becomes "Thank you, God, for helping me." In sincere gratitude, my body-mind is in a state of acknowledging the receiving of help and being connected to the source that gives to me in present time. This is much more inspiring and empowering. It is easy to see how your energy level responds to such a state of mind as gratitude. See for yourself.

Think of a situation in which you have experienced a feeling of gratitude toward someone. Maybe someone gave you a ride when you needed it, or loaned you some money, or brought you a gift of something you needed but wouldn't buy for yourself. Maybe a policeman let you off with just a warning. Reflect for a moment on how it feels to experience gratitude.

How does the experience of gratitude influence your feeling and your energy?

....

....

....

....

....

Gratitude feels good and comforting inside. It lifts the mood
and personal energy level.

The experience of gratitude is usually a positive one that can be very moving. People report that it makes them feel good and gives them a feeling of increased energy. Reflecting on recent experiences of gratitude, I find an underlying sense of connection with the one toward whom there is gratitude. This feeling of connecting with the other, who has given us something important, is reminiscent of the experience of love as oneness.

This may help explain some of the undeniably soothing and energizing effects of gratitude. Reflect on some of your own experiences with gratitude.

The words or language used in prayer can be expected to affect your experience of prayer.

The experience of gratitude is usually a positive one that can be very moving.

If you find the aforementioned benefits, then gratitude can help you too. In *Balancing Act, gratitude is a valuable tool for increasing energy and enhancing well-being. Gratitude does not require a religious or spiritual perspective to be effective.* I include gratitude under spiritual energy, because when applied in a spiritual context, it may result in more-profound spiritual responses. Many times, when I am feeling down, anxious, or sorry for myself, I can bring about a 180-degree turn in mood by doing the following Gratitude Exercise.

The Gratitude Exercise

I use this exercise more often on those mornings when I wake up feeling anxiety or dread about my "to do" list. This is a very uncomfortable feeling associated with negative thoughts and low energy—below 5, out of 10. I just start making a mental list of the things that I am grateful for and start saying to myself, "I thank God for my health, my car, my children," and on and on. Usually within five minutes my mood is lifted and my energy feels like an 8 or 9. With this striking shift in mood, I start the day amazed and grateful for the healing power of gratitude, itself.

This exercise can be done in a group or alone. The idea is to express to yourself mentally or verbally about something for which you are grateful. You try to pick things at random. Pick both from loved ones you are grateful for and material things you are grateful for. I also encourage you to pick things about yourself that you like, and express gratitude for them. Express your gratitude by naming the object you are grateful for after the phrase "I am grateful for... " If you find comfort with the word "God," then start each phrase with "I thank God for... "

Use the phrase that is meaningful for you. Here is how it might go:

I thank God for my children.	*I am grateful for my children.*
I thank God for my friends.	*I am grateful for my friends.*
I thank God for my health.	*I am grateful for my health.*
I thank God for my hair.	*I am grateful for my hair.*
I thank God for my work.	*I am grateful for my work*
I thank God for my spouse.	*I am grateful for my spouse.*
I thank God for sunny days.	*I am grateful for sunny days.*
I thank God for my eyes.	*I am grateful for my eyes.*

Gratitude is a valuable tool for increasing energy and enhancing well- being.

Gratitude does not require a religious or spiritual perspective to be effective.

I thank God for…   *I am grateful for…*

....

....

....

....

....

....

Spiritual activities have the potential to increase your personal energy.

Choose whatever things come to mind first. Don't think about it too deeply. You will find that there are many things you are grateful for when you think about it.

In a group, go around the room and have each person express one thing for which he or she is grateful. Go around the room as many times as you like. Alone or in a group, verbally or mentally, express gratitude for the material things (car, house, job), as well as the more important nonmaterial things (family, health, relationships). In just a few minutes, you will experience a shift in your emotional and energy level. When this is done in a group, each person takes a turn verbalizing something they are grateful for. In a group setting, the response is more powerful and energizing. It really works!

☯ **Return to your breathing.**

Summary

Spiritual activities have the potential to increase your personal energy. Spiritual activities that are guaranteed to increase your personal energy can be called spiritual energy gainers. Prayer, love, forgiveness, inspirational readings, and gratitude discussed here all serve to increase your personal energy and move you toward calm, your natural state. To the degree that you practice any of these energizing, health-enhancing activities, you will receive immediate and long-term benefits. This is one group of energy gainers where more is better. Yet, it is true that even a small amount of work in this area yields great riches beyond increased personal energy; that you may have life and have it abundantly.

Spiritual Energy Drainers

11

The positive impact of spiritual energy gainers on personal energy levels can be undone by spiritual energy drainers. Worrying, judging, holding grudges, blaming, and hopelessness are so much a part of everyday living that their harmful role as energy drainers is easily overlooked. In contrast to the spiritual energy gainers, these energy drainers embrace a more negative and pessimistic worldview. Worrying, which predicts a negative or threatening future, is so pervasive as to be considered normal and acceptable. Being judgmental is also negative and is too often based on incomplete information that leads to false assessments. Holding grudges is similar to judging and can tie up personal energy in the past. Blaming fosters the illusion that you are blameless. In hopelessness, there is the temptation to give up, to deny the inherent creative possibilities of the life force. The importance of recognizing and reducing the activity of these spiritual energy drainers is essential for optimal energy balance.

☯ Bring your attention to your breathing.

Spiritual Energy Drainers

In contrast to the spiritual energy gainers that are of Light—such as love, prayer, forgiveness, and gratitude—there are the spiritual energy drainers that are of Dark. Often, people work conscientiously on energy-gain activities but continue to experience lower optimal energy balance because they are not minding the ongoing energy drainers. Recall that your optimal energy level is the balance between the attitudes and behaviors that increase personal energy and those that decrease energy. It is important to be aware of and reduce your spiritual energy-drain activities because they undermine your personal energy balance and spirituality.

What are some spirit-related activities that can be personal energy-drainers?

....

....

....

....

....

Worrying, judging others, holding grudges, blaming others, and hopelessness
are spirit-related activities that can cause energy drain.

While spiritual energy gainers come from and support a spiritual worldview, spiritual energy drainers are energy-draining responses to life events that are created by a nonspiritual, ego-centered worldview. Worrying, judging, holding grudges, blaming, and hopelessness are spirit energy drainers.

In the spirit-ego dichotomy described in chapter 9, spirit and spiritual energy gainers such as love and forgiveness are of Light. Conversely, ego and the spiritual energy drainers are of Darkness. Spirituality, like love, is related to the "oneness" of everyone and everything at some level. *Ego and spiritual energy drainers are related to a worldview of the separateness of everyone and everything; that there is no oneness.* Awareness that we are a part of that "all" is reassuring, feels good, and is health enhancing. Love is an assessment of oneness, which creates a positive B.E.S.T. Response, reflecting that attitude of oneness. Attitudes and activities that contribute to separation and division of the Whole foster spirit energy drainers, as discussed here, and lead to loss of well-being and personal energy. We all take part in these energy-draining activities at one time or another. If we recall the stress-calm continuum, we can imagine a spirit energy gain–energy drain continuum, where stress correlates with spirit energy drain and calm with spirit energy gain.

Stress <---> Calm
Spirit Energy Drain <----------------------> Spirit Energy Gain

In times of high stress we are more likely to fall into habitual blaming, or habitual worry, for example, and may have difficulty putting a stop to it. The practice of these activities does not make us bad people—but spiritual energy drainers can certainly increase our stress, can make us feel bad, and can negatively influence the quality of our lives and our relationships.

Spiritual energy drainers are related to a worldview of the separateness of everyone and everything; that there is no oneness.

Worrying

Worrying is probably the most commonly practiced spiritual energy drainer and is a great source of negative thoughts and energy loss. We all have passing negative thoughts, when we happen to be in the frame of mind that says, "What if something goes wrong?" Serious concern over the outcome of something is valid, and we all need to weigh outcomes and analyze them realistically. Habitual worry, however, is something else. It is when we begin to dwell on doubts and fears and negative thoughts and replay them over and over again that a passing thought becomes worrying.

Recall that whatever you replay again and again will become a stronger attitude or behavior. Just as being *startled* is not the same as dwelling in fear, a brief moment of worrisome thinking is not the same as dwelling in worries. The former is generally harmless, while the latter is potentially harmful. Worry is an expensive energy drain and potentially harmful because it uses up so much of your life energy, replaying negative-outcome scenarios, and mind-body responses. It's when we actively maintain the negative projections that we are vulnerable to the negative effects of worrying.

While most people worry on and off some of the time, chronic worriers spend a more significant part of their everyday life worrying. Earlier, we defined stress as the body's response to a perception of threat or overload. *Worrying triggers a fear response because it is related to a perception of threat.* This perception of fear readily turns on the Stress Response and leads to the negative mind-and-body effects discussed earlier.

Many of the patients who visit the doctor with stress-related symptoms have no physical basis for their symptoms. Patients with medical complaints for which there is no organic basis will often present the doctor with common stress-related symptoms, such as fatigue, headaches, back pain, abdominal pains, and insomnia. Medical workups, including blood tests and advanced diagnostic tests, yield no explanation for the patient's symptoms. This can be frustrating for both patient and doctor, and a good doctor will help the patient become aware of the nonphysical causes that may be playing a part in the physical ailments. In many of these people, the mind-body connection converts their increased mental and emotional worries into physical complaints.

Worrying can be described as the opposite of optimism. In optimism, or hope, the future is viewed with positive expectations, with a tendency to hope for the best or to "look on the bright side" of things. It is about foreseeing a positive future. Worrying is about foreseeing a negative future that you experience in the present. In many cases, worrying is like living a lie. *The pain and anguish that follow worrying may simply be based on a lie, because most of the things we worry about do not happen.*

Worrying is a great source of negative thoughts and energy loss.

Worrying triggers a fear response because it is related to a perception of threat.

The pain and anguish that follow worrying may simply be based on a lie, because most of the things we worry about do not happen.

Take a simple test. Think of the last five big fears that you faced in the past few years that caused you much worry when you were going through them. Ask yourself how things turned out. Did things turn out as bad as you expected? Looking at my own life and having asked this question in our workshops, I have had to recognize that, again and again, things turned out OK or, at the very least, turned out much better than expected. A quote often used in our workshops states, "Let us be of good cheer, for the things we suffer most never happen." From a spiritual perspective, worrying can be seen as a lack of trust in God.

During my college years, when I was home for the summer, I often went out with friends and stayed out late. When I arrived home, my mother was always up waiting for me. She stated matter-of-factly, without criticizing, that she could not sleep till I got home because she worried for my safety. Like most people, who are used to worrying, she was ready to defend her readiness to worry. "When you have children, you will worry too." I would remind her that she was the one who taught me to trust in God, and that worrying that something could happen to me was denying that trust. As with most people, nothing worth worrying about ever happened to me during those years that I was living with Mom. At that time, I didn't know what I know today, how most things usually turn out well in time. Yet, even then, thanks to my mom, it seemed clear to me that worrying was something to be avoided. To this day, Mom is a worrier, though she worries less and doesn't lose sleep over her worries. Thanks to her, I worry less.

The temptation to worry can be strong and persuasive.

There are times when I am tempted to worry. The temptation to worry can be strong and persuasive. Yet, I know that worrying only drains my energy and weakens me further. I know well how strong the temptation to worry can be. Recently, on a rainy Friday evening, I was at home relaxing. Ann, my wife, had gone out to dinner with her work friends. Around 10 p.m., she called to say she would be home in about fifteen minutes. After thirty minutes, she had not arrived home, and the negative questions began. Where is she? Why isn't she home yet? Did something happen on the way home, in the rain? Rather than keep replaying these questions, the obvious next step was to call her cell phone. No answer. The questions suggesting a negative assessment started up again. Now, my mind was suggesting answers to these questions. Maybe she had an accident. Maybe she is in a hospital. All these "maybes" were negative assessments of the event: spouse late in arriving.

This kind of event happens to all of us, very frequently. Fortunately, over time I have developed a built-in alarm that goes off when I am tempted to worry. This alarm reminds me that worrying is a negative energy drainer. The alarm tells me: "Don't worry; it won't help. Focus on your breathing and figure out what you can do." To avoid the temptation to worry about Ann, I reminded myself that I didn't

Worrying drains a lot of energy, but undermining your spiritual optimism that things will work out.

know what happened, but I had no reason to assume it was an accident or injury. It also helped to think about the perspective that to start worrying was not trusting in God. The use of reason to remind me that I had no basis for making a negative assessment also helped. Focusing on the breathing helped make the experience something to observe, and a further way to learn how people worry, rather than it being just a worry that was sure to turn on my Stress Response. At 10:45 the phone rang, and Ann explained that she had stopped at the grocery store to pick up a few things. She had forgotten her phone in the car. And of course, she had no negative experience of the event I had struggled with. It was over, and everything turned out well, as happens far more often than not.

If worrying is bad for you, then there is harm in the act of worrying, even when you worry for a loved one or a sick child. *Worrying drains a lot of energy by undermining your spiritual optimism that things will work out, creating instead a threatening future outcome that must place your mind and body on vigilant mode.* Worrying also furthers the illusion that you can predict the future.

Learning that something as common as worrying is harmful yet is usually ignored as a "normal part of life" reminds me of the period of time when medicine was learning about the threat of germs. The famous scientific research of Louis Pasteur in France during the early 1800s was showing that disease was actually transmitted by unseen organisms, which were later to be called bacteria. The established institutions of medicine were very slow to accept that the microscopic germs, or bacteria, could be agents that transmitted deadly diseases.

It was not uncommon for patients to survive a surgery, only to become ill and die of bacterial infections days later. Decades later, after the British surgeon Joseph Lister was drastically reducing the death rate following abdominal surgeries by using simple sterilization techniques, many learned physicians held on to the old ways. They continued to do surgeries with bare hands and with no respect for sterilization techniques. Countless people continued to die from infections, often brought about by physicians who did not accept the seriousness of the unseen germs. We are advanced enough in medicine today to treat worrying as respectfully as we treat germs. Today, most people use simple hand-washing to prevent the threat of germs. *We would all do well, too, to practice simple techniques to get rid of the ubiquitous "worry germ."*

Antiworry Strategies

Once you realize the potential harm to mind-body-spirit from worrying, you may be motivated to work to avoid it, whenever it pops up. At least, you can stop minimizing or defending it as natural and, instead, choose more constructive, alternative ways to respond to difficult situations.

We would do well to practice simple techniques to get rid of the ubiquitous "worry germ."

Worrying is
a response
created by an
assessment of
threat that is
usually false.

You can remember to use the Life Formula:

Event --------> Assessment ---------> Response

By employing the Life Formula, you can influence your amount of worrying by actively, intentionally, changing your behaviors, emotions, sensations, or thoughts (B.E.S.T. Response) that make up the worry response. Better yet, try changing your negative assessments to positive ones and turning them into affirmations, such as "Things usually turn out well," to create positive thoughts and feelings.

Using the Life Formula, try the perspective that *worrying is a response created by an assessment of threat that is usually false.* Practice the Breath Awareness exercise and utilize meditation and physical activity such as running in place. *Instead of worrying, you can strategize, create a plan, or make a list.*

Instead of
worrying, you
can strategize,
create a plan, or
make a list.

Do the things you know how to do to distract your mind. Try a spiritual assessment, "I trust that God will see me through this difficult situation," to create a spiritual response. Try prayer to move you toward calm and a more spiritual perspective. Turn the worry situation into an opportunity to develop your spiritual self by consciously turning over the problem to God. Use your fear at the moment as a reason to ask for spiritual strength to trust and accept, rather than to continually replay the worry in your mind.

Practicing a "Let go and let God" attitude doesn't mean you give up. It means that you do the best you can in a situation and then give up the emotional attachment to the outcome. Instead, you can teach yourself to focus on trusting that God will provide. This approach helps you develop your spiritual self while you reduce worrying time.

Antiworry Strategies

Since you usually
don't know the
whole story, most
judgments you
make are based
on limited
information.

- Label worrying as toxic and energy draining.
- Recall the concept that worrying is of Darkness; trust is of Light.
- Stop defending worrying as natural.
- Strategize, create a plan, and make a list of options.
- Change your worry response as you would the B.E.S.T. Response.
- Remember that you do not know how things will turn out.
- Practice positive assessments and affirmations.
- Practice Breath Awareness to observe your worry-self.
- "Let go and let God."

It is reassuring to remember that during the times that you practice any of these strategies, you cannot be worrying at the same time.

Judging

Judging is an expensive energy drain. The dictionary defines *to judge* as "to form an opinion about something through careful weighing of evidence and testing of premises." Without that careful weighing of evidence and testing of premises, judging is merely an unverified assessment, or opinion. *Since you usually don't know the whole story, most judgments you make are based on limited information.* This is not to say you should not have opinions. However, it is important to remember that they are just opinions, and probably not the whole truth.

The energy draining of judging occurs when we carelessly elevate simple opinions about others to the level of truth. We get into trouble when we make opinionated or condescending pronouncements about others, which are, more accurately, a reflection of our intolerance than of their inadequacies. In situations where it is your responsibility to judge someone else's actions or behaviors, it is best to do so in careful accordance with the rules, guidelines, or laws that come with that recognized and accepted role of judge or evaluator. A teacher, for example, must judge students in strictest fairness, and in keeping with the rules of their profession, the school, and society's laws and expectations. Straying outside the domain of that responsibility and judging others in regard to their looks, or social or political standing, or because of their affiliation with some group, is a negative energy-draining action in every way.

Inasmuch as judging of others is usually based on partial or unverified assessments, it shares many of the negative consequences of lying to ourselves. Just as lying is negative, energy draining, and of Darkness, so is unwarranted judging. The responses created by unfounded assessments lead to more separations and divisions, which undermine the oneness of love and the Higher Power. Judging others is also likely to lead to misunderstandings and conflict, consequences that increase energy expenditure, as long as they exist. Spiritual literature is emphatic on the importance of not judging others, for several reasons. *Judging others hinders our spiritual growth.* When we judge others, we assume that we know the whole story, which is usually not true. *Judging fosters separation and conflict.*

In judging others, you reinforce an illusion in yourself that you know what is right and wrong for others, a realm best left to the gods. Rather than judge, you can remind yourself that you don't know the whole story. This may lead you to better ground your assessments by asking questions about what you are judging, such as "What other reason could there be for this person's action or words?" Better yet, just decide that you don't have to judge, and practice letting go of the temptation to do so. Otherwise, your judging can further lead you to even more energy-draining grudges.

Judging occurs when we carelessly elevate simple opinions about others to the level of truth.

Judging others hinders our spiritual growth.

Judging fosters separation and conflict.

The consequences of judging can be summarized as follows:

- Keeps you in Darkness.
- Causes you to live a lie.
- Creates separation.
- Creates conflict.
- Undermines your experience of love.
- Supports illusions about the nature of reality.

From Gerald Jampolsky's Love Is Letting Go of Fear, *I learned the concept that judging is the antithesis of love. I couldn't understand it until I saw the situation in terms of the dichotomy of Light and Dark, spirit and ego, from* The Course in Miracles. *Judging is of Darkness, while forgiveness and love are of Light. I realized that when I judged, I had to carry the emotional weight and energy drain of my judging.*

When I gave up judging, it had a positive effect on me. I was more comfortable around people whom I would normally judge. In time, the experience gave me developmental skills for practicing unconditional love, which could be given to others as well as to myself. As with forgiveness, I found it easier to learn how to love by giving up the temptation to judge, rather than by trying to love unconditionally. To this day, I find it easier to avoid judging someone than to experience unconditional love for them. When I give up judging, I feel more of the oneness so important in the experience of love. In this way, giving up judging is like forgiveness; it facilitates the way to the experience of unconditional love. Over the years, it has become easier to not judge people.

Nowadays, rather than trying to not judge or to love unconditionally, I simply remind myself that at a given point in time, people are generally doing the best they know how. When I remember this idea, though I may not like something that a person has done, I find it easier to let it go and not judge. A sense of oneness with them, as fellow travelers just trying to get through life, seems to follow, even if ever so briefly.

Antijudging Strategies

- Label judging as an energy drainer.
- Remember that when you judge, you have to carry it.
- Recall that judging is of Darkness, forgiveness is of Light.
- Use Breath Awareness to get past the urge to judge.
- Realize that you don't know the whole story.
- See "not judging" as practicing forgiveness.

Grudges

A grudge is making a negative judgment against someone and then deciding to keep this negativity alive. Holding grudges is an extension in time of judging, so that the original injury cannot be released or forgiven. If the injury cannot be forgiven, then you remain locked in the past. It is an energy drain, because of the amount of energy necessary to maintain those attitudes.

When you hold a grudge against someone, who carries it? Who is losing energy?

The person holding the grudge has to carry it. Her or his energy is being used up to finance the grudge.

When you hold a grudge against someone, you are the one who carries it, using your energy to finance the grudge. Like pouring good money after bad, this gets very energy-expensive, fast. Worse, it leaves you living in the illusion that you have lost something, when from the spiritual point of view, the spirit is alive and well, unharmed by the events that hurt you. All too often, the event might have disappeared into the past, were it not for the grudge keeping it alive in the present. Grudges keep you separated from others and block the experience of love, which wants to bring all together. Grudges also keep your life energy in the past and away from the eternal Now.

My class participants unanimously agree that there are few, if any, real benefits to holding a grudge, yet many also acknowledge that they are still doing so. They also agree that there are important personal benefits to letting go of grudges. It allows you to let go of the past, to start over. It frees up a lot of energy.

In *Why People Don't Heal*, Caroline Myss reminds us that *for healing to take place, you need as much of your energy in present time as possible.* One reason why people don't heal, she suggests, is because too much of the energy of their life force is tied up or "plugged into" grudges from past hurts and disappointments. The antidote to "grudging," like judging, is forgiveness. With forgiveness comes all the life- and energy-enhancing benefits described earlier. If nothing else, think of the energy economics involved here, and release any grudge for improved personal energy.

When you hold a grudge against someone, you are the one who carries it, using your energy to finance the grudge.

For healing to take place, you need as much of your energy in present time as possible.

Antigrudge Strategies

- Label grudges as energy drainers.
- Recall that grudges are of Darkness.
- Remember that grudges chain you to the past.
- Practice forgiveness.
- Label grudges as obstacles to spiritual growth.

Blaming

Blaming others is an extension of judging and related to grudge holding. Likewise, because it supports division and conflict, it is of Darkness. It supports the illusion in your mind that you are a victim and without blame.

Blaming can be a costly energy drainer because it keeps you focused on a past event and makes others responsible for the quality of your life experience. This is seen readily when you listen to your friends talk about the breakup of a personal relationship or a marriage. More often than not, the speaker will tell you all about what the other person did that led to the breakup. It is no wonder that for many divorces, the judicial system had to come up with the term "irreconcilable differences."

You can readily see how, in Life Formula terms, blaming keeps you focused on the event, or what the other person did, as the cause of your response. As discussed earlier, *personal healing begins when you focus on your assessments of the event as the true cause of your responses to life events.* People who speak of "creating their own reality," and then blame others for what is not working out in their lives, are not able to see how they have contributed to their present situations. Blaming places all the responsibility on "life" or on the other person.

During my training in family therapy, I came to see blaming as extremely hurtful to relationships, and something to be avoided for the sake of harmony in relationships. Usually in the first session with a new couple, it is important to explain the rules of engagement that apply during the therapy sessions. One of the most important guidelines is to avoid blaming. Clients are advised that if one is blamed, the other must be blamed as well. Instead of using blame, the task at hand is to see how each side is contributing to the problems at hand. This approach can help you learn how, all too often, you share responsibility for what you are experiencing in a relationship and thus, frequently, also in the other areas of your life. In most cases, agreeing to eliminate blaming had the immediate effect of reducing the amount of hostility between the husband and wife. In all areas of life, not blaming quickly reduces the level of hostility between you and whomever you are tempted to blame. Sharing responsibility for the conflict at hand affirmed that it was a couple's problem, and allowed for dialogue to continue for improving the situation.

Blaming keeps you focused on a past event and makes others responsible for the quality of your life experience.

Personal healing begins when you focus on your assessments of the event as the true cause of your responses to life events.

In family therapy sessions, stopping the blame game allows the therapist to guide the clients into describing their feelings about what is going on. Later, they could seek to understand where their feelings were coming from. In Life Formula terms, when you stop blaming, you stop focusing on the event and begin to discuss your response to the event. Later, you can decipher what kinds of assessments (what is in you) contributed to or created the response to the event. *The cause of conflict is usually going to be in the different expectations and ways of looking at things (assessments) of those in conflict.* It is not fair to blame others because they have different assessments about life. Remember that others are responding from their assessments just as you are responding from yours.

I used to experience a lot of frustration with my support staff when they were not putting my patients in the exam rooms fast enough. Then one day I realized that I was getting myself all worked up about it and blaming them for how I was feeling. I realized that they were juggling other jobs besides putting my patients in the rooms. Also, there were always other things I could attend to while I waited for my patients. I saw how I was contributing to my discomfort. In situations like this where I can remember that people are usually doing the best they know at a given time, it is harder for me to blame and easier to accept, and to relax and go with the flow.

Traditional wisdom gives us the admonition against blame that "people who live in glass houses should not throw rocks." *The spiritual perspective is that we are all living in glass houses.* Haven't you noticed?

Antiblaming Strategies

- Recall that blaming is of Darkness.
- Label blaming as making you a victim.
- Label blaming as energy draining.
- If you must blame, blame both sides.
- Ask how you contributed to problem.
- Practice forgiveness.

Hopelessness

Hope is an acknowledgment of the creative possibility inherent in life. Hope, like faith, is believing in things not seen; that things will turn out all right. Hope activates assessments about what is possible, what can be achieved. *Hope is the basis of optimism.* The opposite of hope and optimism is hopelessness. Hopelessness is a major energy drain. It brings the dynamic, creative motion of life to a dead stop. *The mind-body connection translates hopelessness into attitudes and behaviors, which tell the mind and body to stop trying, to give up.* As hope is of Light, hopelessness is dark. It negates your spirituality, which sees meaning and purpose, no matter the situation.

The cause of conflict is usually going to be in the different expectations and ways of looking at things.

The spiritual perspective is that we are all living in glass houses.

Hopelessness is not the same as helplessness. Helplessness is what one feels when there is nothing one can do to help oneself, as when a patient is on a ventilator or in a body cast. However, even in a helpless situation, there can be hope that good things may still come. Personally, I have been inspired by Christopher Reeve, the actor best known for his movie role as Superman. In spite of a neck injury, which left him paralyzed from the neck down, he exhibited hope that good things would still come. Even after his accident, his work did much to increase public awareness of the human side of those living with paralysis and encourage scientific research toward helping them walk again. Despite his bleak situation, he remained socially active and was an inspiration to many people.

As hope can have a profound positive influence on body, mind, and spirit health, so can hopelessness have a negative effect. Feeling hopeless about a specific event, like not getting a specific job or losing a relationship, can be energy draining but not dangerous. More than energy draining, hopelessness can be life threatening if it persists or escalates.

Hopelessness is most dangerous when it pervades most or all of one's view of life. When one can no longer see the light at the end of the tunnel, there may be no reason for going on. This state of Darkness can snuff out the experience of the Light of the Spirit and put an individual at risk for injury or suicide. It may be caused by depression, or certain medical illnesses. This level of hopelessness is an emergency and should be acknowledged as a severe level of illness requiring immediate attention. If you or a loved one is in a state of persistent hopelessness, this should be treated as an emergency equal to active bleeding.

I have come to see that *worrying is to anxiety as hopelessness is to depression.* Just as prolonged anxiety may lead to depression, persistent worrying may lead to hopelessness. Consider a hopelessness-hope continuum to screen yourself for this potentially dangerous spirit energy drainer. If you are able to move in the direction of hope with any of the mind-body-spirit activities discussed previously, you are probably in little danger and would benefit from practicing more-energizing activities. If you are not able to move away from the hopelessness-colored worldview, get help from a professional counselor or your physician. Do not wait. Remember that when hopelessness persists, you are at increased risk of injury or death.

In my early twenties, during the spiritual phase of my journeys of discovery, I experienced the "dark night of the soul" as described by the fifteenth-century mystic and writer St. John of the Cross. During those times when "the salt loses its flavor," when I could not find a sense of satisfaction and well-being, I remember a Darkness of mood and feeling of hopelessness. I wondered if I was experiencing clinical depression. In his writing, instructing those seeking spiritual guidance, St. John of the Cross noted a difference between depression and depressed feelings due to a spiritual longing for union with God. If you feel depressed and can find no comfort anywhere, not even in spiritual activities, you may be clinically depressed. If you feel depressed but can find comfort and joy in prayer, inspirational reading, or other spiritual activities, what you are experiencing may not be depression but, rather, a spiritual longing for union with God. Fortunately, for me it was the latter, and I have sometimes used this distinction to help patients consider the basis of their feelings of depression and hopelessness. (Note: This anecdote is not meant to encourage self-diagnosis. If you are experiencing symptoms of depression, be sure to consult a physician and get a comprehensive examination and professional diagnosis.)

Antihopelessness Strategies

- Recall that hopelessness is of Darkness.
- Try a spiritual perspective on your situation.
- Practice spiritual energy gainers.
- Treat hopelessness as an emergency.
- Seek counseling from a physician or therapist.
- Speak with a spiritual counselor.

⚫ **Return to your breathing.**

Summary

Spiritual energy drainers are most harmful because we often do not realize the harm they do. Just as activities such as love and forgiveness can be described as being of Light and having a positive effect on our personal energy and our lives, the negative activities of worrying, judging, holding grudges, blaming, and hopelessness are all of Darkness and are very energy draining. These energy drainers limit the boundless, creative, and generous Life Force. Instead, they support unhealthful illusions that we should worry, judge, begrudge, and give up hope. These actions also undermine love, by creating separation from others and by creating a spiritual environment for living that is based on fear rather than one that is based on love. *At the least, these spirit energy drainers tie up much of our personal energy, and at most they support a nonspiritual, pessimistic worldview.*

There are many ways that we can create positive, generous, and forgiving habits of thinking that help us forestall these energy-draining negative habits. Some of these more healthful habits provide avenues for us to return to the energy-gaining moods, actions, and attitudes that help us improve our relationships, and to foster a more creative lifestyle. Every time that we are successful in rejecting a negative action, we help weaken that habit and strengthen a new, more spiritual lifestyle of positive habits instead.

If you feel depressed but can find comfort in prayer and spiritual activities, what you are experiencing may be a spiritual longing for union with God.

At the least, spirit energy drainers tie up much of our personal energy, and at most they support a nonspiritual, pessimistic worldview.

PART

FIVE

BALANCING
YOUR ACT

Balancing Your Act

12

Balancing Act is a wellness program originally developed from conclusions derived from an extensive study of human responses and interactions with stress. The study of stress is a rich source of understanding how life works, and, as such, has provided the basis for a program of self-awareness, analysis, and development that can be used to further personal health and well-being.

This Balancing Act program presents a practical model of health in which your personal energy level is used as a measure of health and is combined with a mind-body-spirit approach to maintaining higher personal energy. This two-part model can be applied to creating your Personal Energy Program (PEP). The PEP incorporates five interrelated, ongoing activities for the improvement of personal energy:

1. practicing Breath Awareness
2. monitoring your personal energy
3. using mind-body-spirit actions for higher energy
4. modifying your responses to life by changing your BEST response
5. using words to modify perceptions of stress and other life events

It is important to recognize that obstacles to positive change will always be likely to occur. One very important way to support positive change is to redefine learning and change, in your personal perceptions and conceptions, as processes that will grow stronger with repetition. Remember: Persistence makes change probable.

       Bring your attention to your breathing.

This last chapter reviews the main ideas and actions presented in *Balancing Act* that you can use for more-effective management of everyday personal energy and mastery of life. This chapter is also suited for a quick review of the entire program.

The origins of the Balancing Act program came from the study of stress. Stress is easy to recognize, and within the range of experience of all adults. Stress is so much a part of our lives that *the lessons we can learn from stress are really lessons about how life works.* Though life itself remains a mystery for all of us, in the previous pages you have learned to observe how stress works, and, as a result, you have learned quite a bit about how life works as well.

Knowledge of how life works and skill in applying that knowledge can increase your ability to make positive changes. Yet, even with knowledge and skill, change may be elusive, or perhaps downright difficult. Before summarizing the main points of *Balancing Act,* it will be useful to review how change works and how to facilitate change. *Taking change from* possible *to* **probable** *will help you* **balance your act** *toward optimal personal energy.*

Facilitating Change: From Possible to Probable

Life by its very nature is made up of perpetual change. Whether slowly or rapidly, our lives are always changing. We experience many changes, small and large, over the years, in many areas of our lives: where we live and work, our major and minor relationships, our wanted and unwanted habits. Yet, when we decide we want to change to a more healthful lifestyle, one of the certainties of life is that we will encounter obstacles to our intended change.

If you are having trouble actively moving in the direction of your plans for positive change and optimal personal energy, you may be stuck in the inertia of your usual accustomed and ingrained habits. This section reviews several important ideas that are useful for removing and persevering through obstacles to arrive at a more healthful lifestyle. When it comes to successfully making a change for the better, it is not enough to know what you need to do. To change for the better, you also need to act. To change effectively will require learning, preparation, action, and repetition.

Knowing and Learning

Teaching adults to manage their stress more effectively brought me to the conclusion that most people were not successful in their attempts to manage their stress, not because they didn't want to—but because they did not know how. In this instance, I am using the definition of "know" that I learned from Matthew Budd, MD, at a workshop he gave in the early 1990s. At that time, Dr. Budd was a practicing internal-medicine physician who presented mind-body medicine workshops called Ways to Wellness to patients in the Boston area.

Functionally speaking, to know something means that you can actually do it. Just understanding a description of how to do something does not mean you know how to do it.

For our purposes, *you know something when your body has learned to do it.* If you know how to drive, you could probably sit in almost any car and, even blindfolded, start the car and get it moving. The same thing could be said for typing. If you know how to type, you can probably do so with your eyes closed. That is because your body has learned to do these functions. The point is that *knowing the definition of a particular behavior in your mind is not really knowing the behavior itself unless your body can actually carry it out.* When you consider what this statement means, you can readily extend the idea to see that many, many people—although they may recognize and desire it—do not *know how* to relax.

Understanding this is important because it explains why most people are not able to maintain a healthful, energizing lifestyle: they do not know how to do it. Often, people are apologetic and say that they can't do it or that they are just too lazy. Neither of these reasons are correct. Very often these are hardworking people who do too much for others and not enough for themselves. It is probably closer to the truth to say that they are not prioritizing the desired behavior or that they do not know how to fit it into their schedule. They do not know how to effectively handle increased stress. They do not know how to eat a healthful balanced diet. They do not know how to include regular exercise in their daily schedules. If they are able to recognize and admit that they don't know how to do it, then we can focus on learning how to do it.

To learn means to acquire different ways of doing something. From Dr. Budd I also learned that *learning creates possibilities for change. (Conversely, change creates possibilities for learning.)* If you learn Spanish, your experience of a vacation in Mexico will change. When taking a test, if you have thoroughly learned the material it will change how you experience the test.

Learning is about repetition. You need to hear and heed "the call to change" again and again. If you want to quit smoking, you need to hear yourself say you want to quit again and again, not as a criticism but as a reminder. Learning usually requires repeating a behavior until it becomes automatic. Compare how you drove the first week that you were on your own with how you drove after six months of driving. At six months, the repetition had made the driving movements automatic, requiring less concentration and conscious thought. *Repetition is necessary for most learning.* Most behaviors can be learned, if you make the time to practice them. You can learn to speak Chinese, use a computer, sail a boat, fly a plane, or almost anything else, if you practice repeating specific actions. Usually it is just a matter of time and number of repetitions. Learning to increase energy-gain behaviors and decrease energy-drain behaviors will be facilitated by repetition or practice.

Most people seem to have practiced energy-draining attitudes and behaviors much more than the energy-gaining ones. It all comes down to what you practice. *Remember: In life, what you practice is what you get to keep.* To unlearn behaviors, you practice a different behavior. Most of you have learned good and bad behaviors by repetition. Many of your responses to stressors in your life are the thoughts, feelings, and behaviors that you have learned and reinforced through long-standing repetition—many of these you may have been practicing for decades.

Synonyms for the word "learn" include action verbs such as *acquire, practice,* and *change.* These words remind us that learning is a form of action. *Learning is a form of action made easier and stronger through repetition.* Most of what you "know," whether desirable or undesirable, has been learned through repetition. Understanding *knowing* and *learning* as presented here facilitates coaching for change and improving personal energy. Though you have some mental knowledge about improving personal energy, you don't yet know how to do it automatically. With practice and repetition you will soon know how to maintain optimal personal energy automatically.

> In life, what you practice is what you get to keep.

> Learning is a form of action made easier and stronger through repetition.

Change as a Process

Learning about change creates possibilities for change. One very important point for those who are working toward change is that change usually takes place over time. *Change is a process.* A process is defined as "a series of actions directed to some end." For example, driving a car is a process that has a specific sequence. You must start the engine before you put the transmission into drive. If you put the transmission into drive first, the engine will not start. Changing an attitude or behavior can be quite difficult. Ask anyone trying to change a lifestyle behavior, such as quitting smoking, giving up alcohol, or losing weight. *Approaching change as a process allows for planning, which can be supported by repetition.*

> Change is a process.

The concept of change as a process has been researched and established. In the book *Changing for Good*, the authors, James O. Prochaska, PhD; John C. Norcross, PhD; and Carlo C. DiClemente, write about their research on the process of change. They worked with more than one thousand people who were able to permanently change high-risk behaviors such as smoking, gambling, alcohol abuse, high-fat diets, and sedentary lifestyles. Studying the people who had succeeded in changing their behaviors revealed change as a process made up of six well-defined stages, which are listed in the table below.

Six Stages of the Process of Change

1. noncontemplation (not interested in changing)
2. contemplation (thinking about changing)
3. preparation (getting ready to make a change)
4. action (making the change)

5. maintenance (supporting the change made)
6. termination (the behavior is no longer a temptation)

These stages are easy to describe in people who are trying to quit smoking. In the noncontemplative stage, they are not even thinking about quitting. In the contemplative stage, they occasionally think about quitting and may talk to a doctor about wanting to quit but are not ready to do much about it. In the preparation phase, they are trying behaviors to cut down, such as experimenting with nicotine patches or prescription medication, and maybe setting a quit date. In the action phase, they stop smoking and struggle with the psychological and physical withdrawal symptoms. During the maintenance phase, they practice the behaviors and perhaps use medications that may help them stay off the cigarettes. In the last stage, termination, they complete the process, and smoking is no longer an issue for them; even if an opportunity occurs, they still will not smoke.

Approaching change as a process allows for planning, which can be supported by repetition.

An important key to success in the change process is recognition of the stage you are in, because different strategies are useful at each stage to promote your being able to move on to the next stage. For example, the authors of *Changing for Good* point out that at a given point in time, only 20% of the people in a behavior-changing workshop will be in the action stage. That means that the other 80% are probably not ready to make a change. Many fail at change, the authors state, because they have not prepared for the action stage. When working with patients on lifestyle change, I find it helpful to review the six stages of change and help patients determine what phase each one is in. Then we can choose the most focused and useful strategies to support the change process.

Contrary to popular belief, the process of change is usually not just movement in a single direction. *Often during the change process, you may regress and go back to the undesired behavior. This does not mean you have failed.*

It seems that change frequently also includes moving back to a previous stage before advancing. One of my favorite medical school teachers told me something that helped me during a difficult time in my life and that I often share with patients: "Sometimes you have to take one step backward before you can take two steps forward." It is interesting to note that most people who successfully quit smoking do so after five or six attempts, not the first time.

Preparing for change includes visualizing yourself in the new role, planning ahead for inevitable setbacks, and practicing the desired change.

Sometimes you have to take one step backward before you can take two steps forward.

Your perception of your ability to change is crucial. Because your perception creates your response, if you have the perception that you can change, you will be able to keep trying and persist, despite setbacks. Persistence makes sense if you remember that *change is possible because you are on a continuum between the undesired and the desired behavior.*

Continuum—Change Is Possible

The concept of continuum, first discussed in chapter 1, reinforces the idea that change is not only possible—it is also likely if you make the effort. The continuity between stress at one end and calm on the other revealed that these two seemingly opposite life conditions are intrinsically connected. Applying the concept of a stress-calm continuum reassures you that no matter how stressed out you are, you are still connected to calm. In life, we are never completely static but are always moving back and forth between the two ends of this continuum. The important point for mastering life is that *there is always something you can do that will move you away from more stress and toward more calm.* This concept of continuum—connecting what seem like opposites—can also be applied to other such related variables as health–illness or low energy–high energy.

Stress <--> Calm

Illness <---> Health

Low Energy <--> High Energy

The same principle applies to other seemingly opposite forces in our lives and makes the concept of *continuum* a useful tool for managing stress and life. The concept of continuum reminds us that we are always moving back and forth over time, between the extremes of any of the life forces we are observing. Whatever continuum you choose to work with, the idea of a continuum reassures you that change for the better is possible because there are actions you can take that will move you toward your desired goal.

Envisioning life challenges in continuums is helpful for planning strategies for change.

If the problem is poor eating habits, it is helpful to envision a poor-eating–healthful-eating continuum:
Poor Eating <---> Healthful Eating

For anger problems, consider an anger-peace continuum:
Anger <--> Peace

For sleep problems, consider an insomnia–good-sleep continuum:
Insomnia <--> Good Sleep

For each continuum, you can make a list of actions, easy or difficult, small or large, that will move you in the direction of your desired goal. In life, change is inevitable. Recognizing this simple truth and symbolizing it with a continuum, we are better able to observe and recognize our ability to change. Observing how we are always on a continuum encourages us to persevere because we are able to see how we are always connected—on the path, in other words, between where we are and where we want to go—and that even the smallest or most-subtle actions can move us in the direction of positive change.

With continuums, the way is clear for positive change. Numerous actions that can move you toward the desired end are revealed. What is still required is persistence in the actions that move you.

Persistence: Making Change Probable

Persistence is the key to success in change. According to accepted studies, it takes about six to eight weeks to change your ways. During that time, practice facilitates change, but you must persist. Persistence means to continue trying to move forward in the face of difficulties and setbacks.

Another word for persistence is repetition.

Another word for persistence is repetition. The desired attitude or behavior must be practiced repeatedly to give the desired change more presence in the mind, and thus in the body. The importance of the role of persistence can be seen in students who are learning such easily observed disciplines as playing the piano or practicing martial arts. They practice the same movements again and again and again. Over time, the repetitive moves become automatic. Eventually, in a recital or competitive combat the actions practiced are automatic and the change in the students' behaviors is complete. Change, then, is a process facilitated by knowledge, skill, and repetition. You must have knowledge of what to do, skill to do it correctly, and persistence to keep practicing. The knowledge of what to do is presented in the sections that follow. *The persistence to make the change complete is within you.*

The persistence to make the change complete is within you.

The importance of persistence was obvious when I was watching my daughter Nicole, then my son Marco, and later my younger son, Brendon, learn to ride a bicycle. When frustrated by the difficulties of making progress, each of them resisted practicing riding the bicycle. Each one wanted to give up. I kept encouraging and reassuring them, saying, "It is all about practice. If you continue to practice, you will get better." Eventually overcoming their initial resistance, each one was able to persist. Now they all ride bicycles and enjoy the new skills they developed. I hope they also learned more than just how to ride a bicycle.

Lessons from Stress: How Life Works

In summarizing the material presented here, you will want to remember stress as a teacher about life. One of the early lessons from the study of stress was the existence of a mind-body connection, in which the mind influences the body and the body influences the mind. This mind-body connection is an integral part of the life experience. *If stress in a word is perception, life in a word is perception.* Just as perception turns on the Stress Response, perception in a sense creates your responses to life, your experiences.

The observed association between increased stress and low personal energy suggests personal energy as a marker of health and quality of life. From an energy point of view, stress occurs due to an imbalance in your personal energy. Just as financial stress is due to more money going out than coming in, *stress is more energy going out than energy coming in.* When you have more energy coming in than going out, you will be calmer, and less vulnerable to stress. Less stress means more energy and well-being. This inverse relation between stress and personal energy can be described as a continuum between low energy and high energy. Within this continuity between apparent opposites, life experiences move us back and forth between low energy and high energy. Knowing this, we can choose mind, body, and spirit experiences to move toward high energy and calm. The following lessons from the study of stress can be applied for increased personal energy and well-being.

Lessons from Stress: How Life Works

1. Life is a mind-body experience.
2. Your perceptions create your reality.
3. Your personal energy level is a reflection of your health.
4. You live on a continuum between low and high personal energy.
5. You can use mind, body, and spirit actions for higher personal energy.

1. *Life, like stress, is a mind-body experience.* Life, like stress, is a mixture of mental and physical experiences. Likewise, disease is a mind-and-body experience; physical disease has mental components, and mental *dis-ease* has physical components. *Personal experience and scientific research affirm the role of the mind in influencing illness and wellness.* An important lesson from studying this mind-body connection is the role of perception in creating stress and coloring life experiences.

2. *Your perceptions create your reality.* Perceptions of danger turn on the Stress Response. Similarly, how you perceive life events influences your experience of them. *Moreover, life is influencing your perceptions while your perceptions are influencing your life and your personal energy.* This creative power of perceptions to influence your life and personal energy makes it essential that you learn to manage your perceptions in order to successfully manage your life.

3. *Your personal energy level is a reflection of your health.* Stress is associated with low personal energy. High energy is associated with successful management of stress and better health. The ability to measure personal energy as a marker of health facilitates the ability for self-health. It is easier to work on developing a higher personal energy level than to work on "being healthy." In this energy-based paradigm, you can use various activities to increase your energy and enhance health.

4. *You live on a continuum between low and high personal energy.* You are always on a continuity or continuum between stress and calm. This continuum correlates with other continuums such as illness and health, and low energy and high energy. The low-energy–high-energy continuum facilitates health when you practice activities that move you toward high energy and health.

5. *You can use mind, body, and spirit actions for higher personal energy.* The concept of continuums affirms that change for the better is possible if we practice the right actions. We are beings with mind, body, and spirit domains. Taking a mind, body, and spirit approach to increasing personal energy increases the number of ways that you can move yourself toward higher personal energy and health.

These ideas come together to form a simple and practical model of health: *health is personal energy, and you can use mind, body, and spirit actions to maintain higher personal energy and health.* This program provides hope to those seeking better health and balance because it is founded on ideas accessible to all and within the range of experience for everyone. A practical strategy to transform these ideas into a Personal Energy Program is presented in the next section on "Self-Health Actions."

Self-Health Actions

Converting the lessons that you have learned about stress into your Personal Energy Program (PEP) uses five interrelated actions called the self-health actions. This section will review each step and how they all fit together into your personal energy program. The model is simple and easy to remember: health is about energy, and the goal is optimal personal energy, using any of the numerous mind, body, and spirit activities discussed in the previous chapters and reviewed here.

So, let Breath Awareness lead the way, monitor and maintain your energy in the desired range, and manage your perceptions.

Self-Health Actions

1. Practice Breath Awareness.
2. Monitor your personal energy.
3. Energize using mind-body-spirit actions.
4. Change your life by changing your B.E.S.T. Response.
5. Word your perceptions to change your life.

Changing your life for the better is not easy. It is a lifelong process. *You don't fix life, you manage life.* You manage life by managing your personal energy moment to moment.

Life is influencing your perceptions while your perceptions are influencing your life and your personal energy.

Health is personal energy, and you can use mind, body, and spirit actions to maintain higher personal energy and health.

When I was growing up, my elders would often say that health was one of the most important things in life. Like most healthy young people, I dismissed that as old-people's talk. Now that I am older, I better understand what they were saying. It is wisdom. I often admonish my patients that in the second half of life there are few things as important as developing wisdom and awareness about how life works. This awareness can lead you to seek health of mind, body, and spirit, by using your personal energy level as a measure of health. With more personal energy and persistence, you are better able to develop the attitudes and behaviors that will support you in leading a better life.

STEP 1: Practice Breath Awareness for Presence of Mind, Awareness, and Personal Energy

If you have been practicing Breath Awareness (BA), you are already experiencing some of the immediate and long-term benefits on mood and personal energy. Breath awareness by itself changes your life, because with it, you can move your attention to the present. In the present you can better see how life works. In the present you release yourself from the energy-draining worry of the future and the regrets of the past. More important, you have access in the present to the creative power of life. As you practice BA and develop it to the level where it is ongoing and second nature to you, you cannot help but grow in the awareness that sets you free from the energy-draining mental suffering so prevalent today.

Breath
awareness
also will change
your life for
the better.

Another immediate benefit of BA is that you move in a positive direction along your various continuums. While you practice BA, you move toward calm and higher personal energy. At the very least, you stop moving toward more stress and lower energy. Breath awareness also helps by slowing down your automatic perceptions, which, more often than not, are nonvalidated energy drainers. This gives you the option of choosing a validated perception or, better yet, not choosing a perception at all. For these reasons, I like to emphasize that *Breath Awareness alone will change your life for the better.*

STEP 2: Monitor Your Personal Energy

Just as you do well to know your checking-account balance when you are paying bills, you do well to know your personal energy balance during your daily activities. When you pay attention to your personal energy levels, you will notice that your energy level fluctuates as you go through your day.

In between
morning and
bedtime, there
are numerous
fluctuations of
your energy that
you accept as
normal.

To monitor your personal energy level, simply take note of how much energy you feel at the moment, and rate it on a scale of 1 to 10 (10 being the best). In a few seconds you can quantify your personal energy level as easily as you would glance at your watch to check the time. For most people, energy level is higher after rising in the morning and lower at the end of the day. *In between morning and bedtime, there are numerous fluctuations of your energy that you accept as normal.* You may notice that time spent with certain people leaves you with less energy, while time spent with a more positive few leaves you feeling energized. Situations associated with stress are more likely to lower your energy, while pleasurable experiences increase your personal energy level.

Monitoring your personal energy level at various times of the day allows you to respond to drops in personal energy. Otherwise, you may not notice until your energy is too low for your level of activity, and you become weighed down with stress-related symptoms (e.g., increased irritability, headache, or a cascade of negative thoughts).

Once your energy level is low, you are more vulnerable to stress, and everyday situations may become more difficult. For example, it is easier to generously handle a complaining person if your energy is at a level of 7 than at a level of 3 out of a high of 10. Moreover, maintaining a higher personal energy level is important because it is more difficult to motivate yourself for self-care when your energy is low. For example, you are more likely to choose a fast food or avoid exercise when your energy is lower. Conversely, with higher energy you may take time to choose better food and exercise. You can use the Behavior/Symptom Monitor Card in the appendix to record your energy level, as well as the effect of specific mind, body, or spirit interventions on your personal energy. Taking early notice of a decreasing energy level will allow you to respond with mind-body-spirit actions that can increase your energy level.

> There is always something you can do to move you toward increased personal energy.

STEP 3: Energize Using Mind-Body-Spirit Actions

There are numerous mind, body, and spirit actions that you can use to improve your personal energy. *This fact gives hope because there is always something you can do to move you toward increased personal energy.* Now you can move through life with the certainty that if you persist in your efforts to maintain higher personal energy levels, you will be rewarded because that's the way life works. By accepting life as a mind-body-spirit experience, you increase your number of options that positively influence your personal energy level. If you don't want to do something physical to improve your energy, you can do something mental. If you don't feel like doing something mental, you can do something physical or spiritual instead. While each of the three domains is self-sufficient for increasing energy, together they make optimal energy probable. The Personal Energy Program Worksheet presented at the end of this chapter will help you plan your Personal Energy Program. Use the Behavior/Symptom Monitor Card found in the appendix to keep track of the improvement in your personal energy.

> A mental approach for more personal energy begins with choosing mental actions, such as Breath Awareness, positive self-talk, and affirmations to move toward higher personal energy.

A mental approach for more personal energy begins with choosing mental actions, such as Breath Awareness, positive self-talk, and affirmations to move toward higher personal energy (chapter 4). You can use positive self-talk to support and reassure you because the mind-body connection can be used to influence your body with positive thoughts and words. Try affirmations that say something positive to yourself, so your body can respond in a positive manner. An affirmation such as "Things will work out" can have a calming effect that moves you away from stress toward calm. The pivotal point of using the mind in this program is managing your perceptions of life events to create more-desirable responses to life. This technique is reviewed in step 5.

The body approach to increasing personal energy means eating better foods, exercising more, and sleeping better. Avoiding sugar and processed foods and eating a low-glycemic-index diet in five small meals will lead to increased personal energy (chapter 6). Regular aerobic exercise such as walking will give you more energy (chapter 7). Improving the quantity or quality of your sleep will lead to more energy (chapter 8). Since the body is the most limiting factor of the three domains, it is essential that you improve your performance in the areas of nutrition, exercise, and sleep. You can begin improving your performance in these essential areas of body energy by implementing small changes as part of a larger plan for improvement in body-related energy.

The spirit approach to increasing personal energy includes energy-gain activities that are powerful energizers, both for those who have developed spiritual beliefs and those who have not (chapter 10). For those comfortable with a Higher Power, prayer or spiritually inspirational reading often provides a boost in physical energy, as well as being spiritually uplifting. Other spiritual actions, such as forgiveness and loving care, may require more reflection and practice, but they bring ample rewards in peace of mind and personal energy to all who practice them. Gratitude, as described in the Gratitude Exercise (in chapter 10), is guaranteed to move you toward awareness and peace of mind, with increased energy as well. Spirit- and mind-based actions generally require less effort than body actions.

STEP 4: Change Your Life by Changing Your B.E.S.T. Response (Chapter 4)

Recall from the Life Formula (Event --> Perception --> Response) that your everyday responses to life events can be described as a four-part B.E.S.T. Response: Behaviors, Emotions, Sensations, and Thoughts. These four parts are interrelated, so that if you change one of them you can change the others as well. This is helpful because in the face of a negative, energy-draining response, you can change your responses with a little effort, thus increasing personal energy levels and reducing your level of discomfort. Using thoughts to change your responses is easier than using physical behaviors but may be less effective. Physical behaviors take more effort, but they have a stronger influence on changing the other parts of your response. Here are examples of ways to change your response to life events by changing one of the B.E.S.T. Responses.

The body approach to increasing personal energy means eating better foods, exercising more, and sleeping better.

The spirit approach to increasing personal energy includes energy-gain activities that are powerful energizers, both for those who have developed spiritual beliefs and those who have not.

TO CHANGE YOUR	YOU CAN
Thoughts	Use: Emotions—to create humor by exaggerating Sensations—to distract yourself with a shower Behaviors—to balance on one foot
Emotions	Use: Thoughts—to question your feelings Sensations—to change how you feel with stretching Behaviors—to run in place for ten minutes
Sensations	Use: Thoughts—to reassure yourself Emotions—to create humor Behavior—to go for a brisk walk
Behaviors	Use: Thoughts—to contemplate desired behavior Emotions—to feel your happiness with change Sensations—to take note of your energy level

Another effective way to change your B.E.S.T. Response is to use one of many mind-body interventions discussed in chapter 4 that can have an immediate effect on how you think and feel.

Mind-Body Interventions

Mind-body interventions work because the mind-body connection is a two-way street. If you practice a positive mental act, it will have a positive effect on the body. If you practice a positive physical act, that will have a positive effect on your mind. David S. Sobel, MD, whose writings on the mind-body connection have influenced me, taught an easy way to remember these interventions by grouping them under the five senses and movement. Any of these interventions can be used to produce a positive, therapeutic response. Using mind-body interventions to modify your B.E.S.T. Response improves your mastery of life. These easily accessed interventions rekindle the hope that solutions are available; that there is something you can do to improve your present situation.

The mind-body interventions described here are examples of applying the mind-body connection for health enhancement. You are probably already using some of these interventions but would benefit from using them more often as part of a relaxing and energizing program. Grouping them under the headings of the five senses plus movement makes them accessible and easy to remember. *The effectiveness of these mind-body interventions is seen*

Mind-body interventions work because the mind body connection is a two-way street.

The effectiveness of these mind-body interventions is seen in how they move you toward calm and higher energy.

in how they move you toward calm and higher energy.
Here they are briefly summarized to give you more behavioral options for planning your Personal Energy Program.

Sight: nature, pictures of loved ones, inspiring movies, art
Using sight as a positive intervention includes cloud watching, walking in the woods, favorite movies, watching children, and looking at pictures of loved ones.

Sound: music, voices of loved ones, humor, inspirational speakers and positive self-talk
The mind-body connection is probably most readily put to the aid of good mental and physical health when we practice supportive, encouraging self-talk, whether in affirmations or plain talk, to ourselves.

Taste: food
The taste of home-cooked meals may also evoke a conditioned response that may be comforting, as well as tasty.

Smell: natural fragrances, perfumes, essential oils
Scents can trigger powerful, vivid memories, both pleasant and unpleasant. This author uses oils, scented with cinnamon and other spices, as a refresher and mood elevator.

Touch: massage, hugs
Touch is an important factor in health of the mind-body. Encourage hugs within your family and circle of friends.

Movement/activity: physical activity, dancing, yoga, stretching
Physical activity has a very positive effect on the mind and body. The body enjoys movement, and this enjoyment is readily transmitted to the mind.

STEP 5: Word Your Perceptions to Change Your Life

Your perception of the events in your life, not the events themselves, is what creates your response to everyday life.

The concept that you create your own reality, that you have the ability to change for the better, has much appeal to those seeking a better life. How you create your reality is described by the Life Formula, which states that life is a series of events that turn on the assessments (perceptions) that create your response. *That is, your perception of the events in your life, not the events themselves, is what creates your response to everyday life.* To use this knowledge as a beam of light to guide you through everyday life as you choose more-truthful perceptions is one of the keys to mastering life. It is sad, but true, that much of our pain and suffering in life are created by false perceptions or assessments. Once you choose an assessment of an event, your mind will create a response consistent with your interpretation, whether the assessment is true or false.

Since most of the things we worry about never happen, the worrying and the accompanying stress are needless. Since negative assessments quickly turn on the Stress Response, if you take action to verify your perceptions, you will prevent many energy-draining false alarms. Practice verifying assessments, especially negative ones. Verify your assessments by asking simple, direct questions such as "How do I know this is true?" and "What other reason could there be?" The answers to these questions can reveal whether your perception is true or is just an opinion. If not true, you may choose to dismiss the perception or at least hold off on a final assessment. If your perception is true, more questions, such as "What are my options?," will direct you in which way to go.

Going one step further, it is important to remember that because perceptions create your response to life and perceptions are made in language, the *words* that you use also contribute to creating your response to life events. *The words you use on yourself and on others have the power to influence your personal energy level and how you think and feel.* So, use positive words freely and negative words sparingly to create a more positive, energizing life experience. In the words of William James, "Wisdom is knowing what to overlook." Practice "overlooking" negative assessments that often color your world negatively. Choose your "I don't really know" option to release you from everyday energy drainers.

> *Once I understood the creative power of words and perceptions, I realized that too often I was making judgments where none was needed. Because the words that I use in my thinking make a difference, I try to avoid negative wording of my perceptions. Sometimes it is best to just not say anything to myself; to resist the temptation to make a hastily negative assessment or judgment. Knowing the creative power of assessments, I often choose not to make a definite assessment if one is not necessary. This may mean saying, "I don't know why such and such happened," instead of making an assessment that may be incorrect and lock me into an unnecessary mind and body response.*

Together, these five self-health actions will improve your personal energy and quality of life. Though, for the sake of instruction, these steps are discussed separately, they are to be practiced together. These self-health actions are what you *do*, what you practice, for creating and maintaining your ongoing PEP. The last section of this book is an exercise that will help you set up a visual model of your PEP. It is not absolutely necessary for creating and maintaining your PEP, but you may find it useful to have a pattern to follow at the beginning.

☯ **Return to your breathing.**

The words you use on yourself and on others have the power to influence your personal energy level and how you think and feel.

The End of the Beginning

In summary, optimal health is related to optimal personal energy. *Balancing Act* presents a path to wellness; a way to influence your health and well-being by influencing your personal energy level day by day, moment by moment. You already have a personal energy program with which you currently manage your personal energy. *Balancing Act* provides you tools to create a Personal Energy Program (PEP) for optimal personal energy and health. Create your PEP by using Breath Awareness, maintaining higher personal energy with mind-body-spirit actions, modifying your B.E.S.T. Response, and choosing more-positive perceptions.

This is only the end of the beginning.

The Breath Awareness exercise is essential to help maintain the presence of mind to remember to apply the other four self-health actions. In keeping with the philosophy of the lessons about knowing and learning, you will see that this is not the end of the program. *This is only the end of the beginning.* It is a prologue to the new and more-fulfilling patterns that you will be able to develop in your life, as you practice the techniques you have learned.

Persistence is the key to success in changing.

After you finish here, put the book down for a while, for a few days or a few weeks. Then go back and read it again. If stress in a word is perception, change in a word is persistence. *Persistence is the key to success in changing.* It won't always be easy, but it works. As living beings, we are wired for change. If you follow the guidelines presented here, life itself will help you. I will leave you with a quote by President Calvin Coolidge on persistence and how life works, which inspired me when I first read it and inspires me still, after many years.

- *Nothing in this world can take the place of persistence.*
- *Talent will not; nothing is more common than unsuccessful men with talent.*
- *Genius will not; unrewarded genius is almost a proverb.*
- *Education will not; the world is full of educated failures.*
- *Persistence and determination alone are omnipotent.*

Exercise: Putting It All Together: Your Personal Energy Program

Earlier chapters presented information and techniques from medical, nutritional, psychological, and spiritual disciplines that could be used as specific actions to positively influence your personal energy level. Now, using the self-health actions listed above and your preferences for particular actions, you can design your Personal Energy Program (PEP).

For your PEP, you will choose actions to practice from the mind, body, and spirit domains that will influence your personal energy. For overall increased personal energy level, you practice energy-gain activities and attitudes that positively influence your energy balance. In addition, you acknowledge and practice avoiding energy-drain activities and attitudes. That is, do more "energy-good things" and do fewer "energy-bad things." The difference between your energy gain and energy drain is your optimal personal energy balance. This concept of energy balance is combined with body, mind, and spirit domains, as shown below.

Table 1 presents some of the general mind, body, and spirit variables discussed earlier, which influence energy balance positively and negatively. Table 2 presents examples of more-specific variables for creating your personal optimal energy program. Table 3 is blank, so that you can fill in the specific actions or attitudes you want to choose for your personal program. In designing your personal program, list specific activities that apply to your current situation and personal preferences. Use the blank table to design your Personal Energy Program Action Plan—your personal, comprehensive, and holistic approach to health.

In choosing the mind, body, and spirit energy action, you will first want to choose Breath Awareness as an energy gain action that is useful in all three domains. Take the time to write down all of the actions you would like to take to increase your energy gain and decrease your energy drain. Using tables 1 and 2 as guides, fill in the blank table 3 with your preferences.

After reviewing the general categories of activities and attitudes listed in the sample tables, write down specific attitudes and activities that you want to do more of in the Gain column, and those you want to do less of in the Drain column. Do this for each of the mind, body, and spirit domains. In the Drain column, list activities that you know cause you to lose energy, even if you are not ready to stop them. The act of acknowledging them as energy drainers begins to increase your awareness and helps prepare you for action at a later date.

For the Gain column, list your preferences to the best of your knowledge, at a level that you are likely to perform. To reinforce positive change, it is important to pick a level you can successfully accomplish. Even if the goal is a daily thirty-minute walk, start with ten minutes, if you know you can do that for sure. Write down specific actions. For example, for body energy gain, instead of the general term "exercise more," you might write "twenty-minute walk during lunch hour." For mind energy gain, instead of "meditation," you might write "use relaxation audiotape for ten minutes upon rising."

Improve energy balance and move toward optimal health by working on both the Gain and Drain sides of your plan simultaneously. Keep a copy of your plan where you can see it at home and at work. After two to four weeks of following your plan and experiencing an improved energy balance, you may want to rewrite your personal plan on the *basis of your results to date. Repeat the process as often as you wish. While following your plan, thereaare times when, for whatever reason, you may not meet your daily goal. Remember—you are on a continuum, and you have not completely failed by any means—your attention to your plan has, of itself, moved you at least a small amount closer to your goal—tomorrow, more physical, mental, or spiritual action may move you even closer. Have faith in yourself and in your new awareness and just keep trying—with persistence, you are sure to make real and life-changing progress.*

	Increase Energy GAIN (+)	Decrease Energy DRAIN (−)
BODY	Breath awareness Natural diet Sleep/rest Mind-body activities Exercise	Smoking Fast/processed food Insomnia Alcohol/drugs Pessimism
	....	....
	....	....
	....	....
	....	....
MIND	Breath awareness Go with flow Inspirational reading Verify assessments Meditation	Worry Distorted perceptions Self-criticism
	....	....
	....	....
	....	....
	....	....
SPIRIT	Prayer Forgiveness Gratitude	Grudges Hate Hopelessness
	....	....
	....	....
	....	....
	....	....

	Increase Energy GAIN (+)	Decrease Energy DRAIN (−)
BODY	Breath awareness Almonds at work In bed by 10:30 p.m. Small meals every 3–4 hours Salad at least once a day Walk 20 minutes during lunch	Cut out sugar/pop Coffee half decaf Quit smoking
MIND	Breath awareness Classical music at work Read novel in bed Book on tape for commute	Resist worrying
SPIRIT	Morning prayers Schedule retreat Gratitude exercise at bedtime	

PERSONAL ENERGY PROGRAM WORKSHEET

	Increase Energy GAIN (+)	Decrease Energy DRAIN (−)
BODY		
	....	....
	....	....
	....	....
	....	....
	....	....
	....	....
	....	....
MIND		
	....	....
	....	....
	....	....
	....	....
	....	....
	....	....
	....	....
SPIRIT		
	....	....
	....	....
	....	....
	....	....
	....	....
	....	....

PART

SIX

APPENDIXES

Appendix I

SELF-HEALTH CONCEPTS

1. Your optimal health correlates with your optimal personal energy.

2. Stress impacts your energy and reveals an ever-present mind-body connection.

3. You live on a continuum between stress and calm, between low energy and high energy.

4. Mind-body-spirit actions can move you to calm, health, and high energy.

5. Perceptions are mind actions for influencing your personal energy and life experience.

6. Eating, walking, and sleeping are body actions for personal energy.

7. Love, forgiveness, and gratitude are spirit actions for personal energy.

BEHAVIOR/SYMPTOM MONITOR CARD

Name: .... Wt: .... BP: ....

WEEK 1

Date							

	S	M	T	W	T	F	S
a.m.							
12 N							
6 p.m.							

WEEK 2

Date							

	S	M	T	W	T	F	S
a.m.							
12 N							
6 p.m.							

WEEK 3

Date							

	S	M	T	W	T	F	S
a.m.							
12 N							
6 p.m.							

WEEK 4

Date							

	S	M	T	W	T	F	S
a.m.							
12 N							
6 p.m.							

X= physical exercise
R= relaxation exercise
RATE SYMPTOM: 1–10
P= prayer

STRESS (10= high)
TENSION/MOOD (10= good)
DIET (10= healthy)
PAIN (10= high)

PURPOSE:

To increase awareness of the behaviors/symptoms that you want to change. The more Rs (relaxation exercises) and Xs (physical exercise) you have, most likely, the lower your symptoms will be—and you will FEEL BETTER!

INSTRUCTIONS:

1. Date your chart ahead of time (this will give you more incentive to fill it in each day).

2. Determine which behavior/symptom you are going to monitor: stress, diet, tension/mood, pain, etc.

3. You are going to rate your overall behavior/symptom level three times per day:
    - Morning (a.m.):   From the moment you get up until noon
    - Afternoon (12N):   From noon to 6 p.m.
    - Evening (6 p.m.):   From 6 p.m. until you go to bed

    Use a number between 1 and 10 that represents your overall behavior/symptom level for each time period (box), with 10 being the highest.

4. Make note of positive healthy activities by using an "X" for physical activity (exercise), an "R" for relaxation exercise, a "P" for prayer. Smokers can keep track of the number of cigarettes smoked in each period as "III," etc.

5. It is helpful to draw a diagonal line in each box; this way you can track bothersome behaviors/symptoms on the bottom of the square and track positive activities (X), (R), or (P) on the top.

6. Keep your chart in a place where you will see it several times a day (e.g., on your refrigerator). Keeping it visible will
    - help you become aware of and chart the behavior or symptom you want to change (e.g., stress level).
    - remind you to engage in daily positive activities that may support the desired change.

GLYCEMIC INDEX CHART

(lower glycemic index is preferable)

This chart is provided only as a general introduction to the glycemic index. You can learn more by searching the internet for "International Table of Glycemic Index."

GRAINS

Extremely High More than 100	High 80–100	Moderately High 60–80	Moderately Low 40–60
Puffed rice Cornflakes Rice, instant Bread, French Bagel, white Kaiser roll Bread stuffing Graham crackers Waffles	Bread, wheat, whole meal Tortilla, corn Shredded wheat Muesli Bread, rye, crispbread Bread, rye, whole meal Rice, brown Porridge oats Corn, sweet Rice, white Croissant Wheat crackers Taco shells	Buckwheat All bran cereal Bread, rye, pumpernickel Macaroni, white Spaghetti, white Spaghetti, brown Linguine	Buckwheat All bran cereal Bread, rye, pumpernickel Macaroni, white Spaghetti, white Spaghetti, brown Linguine

VEGETABLES

Extremely High	High	Moderately High	Moderately Low
Potato, instant Parsnips, cooked Potato, baked Carrots, cooked French fries	Potato, mashed Potato, new, boiled	Yam Potato, sweet Green peas Baked beans (canned) Kidney beans (canned)	White beans Brown beans Lima beans Green peas, dried Chickpeas (garbanzo) Black-eyed peas Kidney beans Black beans Red lentils Soybeans, canned Soybeans, dried

FRUITS

Extremely High More than 100	High 80–100	Moderately High 60–80	Moderately Low 40–60
Watermelon	Apricots Raisins Banana Papaya Mango	Fruit cocktail Grapefruit juice Orange juice Pineapple juice Pears, canned Grapes	Apricots, dried Orange Apple juice Pea-s Apples Peaches Plums Cherries Grapefruil

SNACKS

Hard sugar candy Donut Vanilla wafers Rice cakes Tapioca Pretzels	Corn chips Chocolate bar Crackers Cookies Pastry Ice cream, low fat Angel food cake	Cookies, oatmeal Potato chips Sponge cake Caramel cookie bar	Candy coated peanuts Peanul candy bar Peanuts

DAIRY

	Ice cream, low fat		Yogurl Ice cream, high fat Whole milk 2 percent milk Skim milk Yogurt, low fat, artificial sweetener

Appendix IV

RECOMMENDED READING

Mind-Body Medicine / Stress Management

Benson, Herbert. *Relaxation Response.* New York: Avon Books, 1975.

Cousins, Norman. *Anatomy of an Illness as Perceived by the Patient: Reflections on Healing and Regeneration.* Toronto: Bantam, 1981.

Frankl, Viktor. *Man's Search for Meaning.* New York: Washington Square, 1984.

Goleman, Daniel. *Mind Body Medicine.* New York: Consumer Book, 1993.

Jampolsky, Gerald. *Love Is Letting Go of Fear.* Berkeley, CA: Celestial Arts, 1979.

Myss, Caroline. *Why People Don't Heal.* New York: Three Rivers, 1997.

Remen, Rachel Naomi. *Kitchen Table Wisdom.* New York: Riverhead Books, 1996.

Siegel, Bernie. *Love, Miracles and Medicine.* New York: Harper & Row, 1986.

Simonton, O. Carl. *The Healing Journey.* New York: Bantam, 2002.

Simonton, O. Carl. *Getting Well Again.* New York: Bantam, 1978.

Sobel, David. *The Healthy Mind, Healthy Body Handbook.* Los Altos, CA: DRX, 1996.

Weil, Andrew. *Eight Weeks to Optimal Health.* New York: Ballantine, 1997.

Nutrition

Balch, Phyllis, and James F. Balch. *Prescription for Dietary Wellness.* New York: Avery, 1992.

Eades, Michael R., and Mary Dan Eades. *The Protein Power Life Plan.* New York: Warner Books, 2000.

Gundry, Steven R. *The Plant Paradox.* New York: Harper Collins, 2016.

Sears, Barry. *Enter the Zone.* New York: Harper Collins, 1998.

Sears, Barry. *A Week in the Zone.* New York: Harper Collins, 2000.

Sugar Busters. *Sugar Busters.* New York: Ballantine, 1999.

Wahls, Terry. *The Wahls Protocol.* New York: Avery, 2014.

Spirituality

Foundation for Inner Peace. *A Course in Miracles.* New York: Viking, 1996.

Link, Mark. *Vision 2000.* Allen, TX: Tabor, 1992.

Gibran, Kahlil. *The Prophet.* New York: Alfred A. Knopf, 2003.

Hesse, Herman. *Siddhartha.* Boston: Shambhala, 2000.

Lama, Dalai. *The Art of Happiness.* New York: Riverhead Books, 1998.

Hutchinson, Gloria. *Six Ways to Pray from Six Great Saints.* Cincinnati: St. Anthony's Messenger, 1982.

Keating, Thomas. *Open Mind, Open Heart.* New York: Continuum, 1992.

Smith, Huston. *Why Religion Matters.* New York: Harper Collins, 2001.

Gawain, Shakti. *The Path of Transformation*. Novato, CA: New World Library, 2000.

Walsch, Neale Donald. *Conversations with God*. New York: G. P. Putnam's Son, 1996.

General Readings

Benson, Herbert, and Eileen M. Stuart. *The Wellness Book: The Comprehensive Guide to Maintaining Health and Treating Stress-Related Illness*. Secaucus, NJ: Birch Lane, 1992.

Golan, Ralph. *Optimal Wellness*. New York: Ballantine Books, 1995.

James, H. *Power Sleep*. New York: Villard, 1998.

Hafen, Brent Q., Keith J. Karren, Kathryn J. Frandsen, and N. Lee Smith. *Mind/Body Health*. Boston: Allyn and Bacon, 1996.

Levey, Joel, and Michelle Levey. *Living in Balance*. Berkeley, CA: Conari, 1998.

Prochaska, James O., John C. Norcross, and Carlo C. Di Clemente. *Changing for Good*. New York: Avon Books, 1994.

Appendix V

Lessons from Stress: How Life Works

1. Life is a mind-body experience.
2. Your perceptions create your reality.
3. Your personal energy level is a reflection of your health.
4. You live on a continuum between low and high personal energy.
5. You can use mind, body, and spirit actions for higher personal energy.

Self-Health Actions

1. Practice Breath Awareness.
2. Monitor your personal energy.
3. Energize using mind-body-spirit actions.
4. Change your life by changing your B.E.S.T. Response.
5. Word your perceptions to change your life.

Appendix VI

QUICK PERSONAL ENERGY PROGRAM (PEP) BREATHING TECHNIQUES

Breath awareness remains the focal point of various relaxation techniques guaranteed to reduce your stress and increase your personal energy level. As described in chapter 1, simple Breath Awareness can be used to increase your personal energy any time. Here are a few variations of Breath Awareness that may be useful in situations where the usual Breath Awareness is not enough.

Counting Breaths I

Bring your attention to the rhythm of your breathing. Count your breaths so that in and out is "one," in and out is "two," and so on. Do this to the count of five or ten and start over. Do this for as long as needed.

Use this in situations where the basic Breath Awareness technique is not enough to keep you centered.

Counting Breaths II

Bring your attention to the rhythm of your breathing. This time, count your breaths so that out and in is "one," out and in is "two," and so on. Do this to the count of five or ten and start over. Do this for as long as needed.

Since this technique requires a little more effort at Breath Awareness, it helps you stay centered in situations where Counting Breaths I is not enough

4-7-8 Breath Awareness

Breathe in through your nose to the count of "4." Hold your breath to the count of "7." With the tip of your tongue behind the upper back of your front teeth or using pursed lips (like blowing out a small candle), breathe out to the count of "8." Practice this to get the timing right, and use it as many times as you need for immediate stress/tension release.

This technique is surprisingly effective in reducing the sensation of stress when you are feeling "stressed out." Use this technique often throughout the day to prevent the buildup of tension.

Rapid Nasal Breathing

With your mouth closed, breathe through your nose in short and rapid cycles for ten to twenty seconds, ending with a long, deep inhalation and a long, slow exhalation through pursed lips. Repeat this if needed; one or two times is usually enough to bring instant calm.

This technique is very effective for destressing and may also be used throughout the day to prevent the accumulation of tension.

Meditation/Relaxation Exercise Using Breath Awareness as a Focus Point

Start by finding a quiet place where you won't be disturbed. Sit in a comfortable chair and close your eyes. Bring your attention to your breathing. Stay with your breathing and let go of outside thoughts. When you find yourself distracted by outside thoughts, acknowledge them and let them go, as you bring your attention back to your breathing. Let go of any outside thoughts and return to your Breath Awareness. Stay with your breathing. Let go of all outside thoughts as if they were passing clouds, as though they were like leaves in a stream.

Continue this cycle of staying with your breathing and letting go of outside thoughts for the time allotted for this relaxation exercise. Start with five or ten minutes. Over time, build up to twenty to thirty minutes. A soft timer/alarm can be helpful so you can relax and avoid having to keep checking the clock. After finishing your relaxation exercise, notice the difference in your personal energy level.

NOTES

NOTES

NOTES